Psychoanalysis and Family Therapy

Psychoanalysis and Family Therapy

Selected Papers

Helm Stierlin, M.D., Ph.D.

Jason Aronson, Inc.
New York, N.Y.

Includes bibliographies and index.
1. Family   psychotherapy.   2. Group   psychoanalysis.
3. Schizophrenia. I. Title.
RC488.5.S74   616.8'915

ISBN: 0-87668-257-3

Library of Congress Catalog Number: 77-2275

Typeset by: Jeanne Lombardi
            New York, N.Y.

Manufactured in the United States of America

ACKNOWLEDGMENTS

Chapter 1: Existentialism meets psychotherapy. *Philosophical and Phenomenological Research* 24: 215-239, 1963.1

Chapter 2: Bleuler's concept of schizophrenia: a confusing heritage. *American Journal of Psychiatry* 123: 998-1001, 1967. Copyright 1967, the American Psychiatric Association.

Chapter 3: The adaptation to the "stronger" person's reality. *Psychiatry* 22: 143-152, 1959. Copyright 1959, the William Alanson White Psychiatric Foundation.

Chapter 4: Lyrical creativity and schizophrenic psychosis as reflected in Friedrich Hölderlin's fate. In *Friedrich Hölderlin, An Early Modern*, E. E. George, ed. Ann Arbor: University of Michigan Press, 1972, pp. 192-215. Here reprinted with the permission of the University of Michigan Press and of the editor.

Chapter 5: Relational dynamics in the life course of one schizophrenic quadruplet. In *Genetic Factors in "Schizophrenia"*, A. R. Kaplan, ed. Springfield, Ill.: Charles C Thomas, 1972, pp. 451-463.

Chapter 6: The functions of inner objects. *International Journal of Psycho-Analysis* 51: 321-329, 1970.

Chapter 7: The transmission and elaboration of delusions in families. *Studium Generale* 20: 693-700, 1967.

Chapter 8: Parental perceptions of separating children. *Family Process* 10: 411-427, 1971.

Chapter 9: Group fantasies and family myths—some theoretical and practical aspects. *Family Process* 12: 111-125, 1973.

Chapter 10: Psychoanalytic approaches to schizophrenia in the light of a family model. *International Review of Psycho-Analysis* 1: 169-179, 1974.

Chapter 11: Shame and guilt in family relations: theoretical and clinical aspects. *Archives of General Psychiatry* 30: 381-389, 1974.

Chapter 12: Roles and missions in family theory and therapy (Rolle und Auftrag in der Familientheorie und -therapie). *Familiendynamik* 1: 36-59, 1976.

Chapter 13: Family therapy with adolescents and the process of intergenerational reconciliation. In *The Adolescent in Group and Family Therapy*. New York: Brunner/Mazel, 1975.

Chapter 14: Countertransference in family therapy with adolescents. In *The Adolescent in Group and Family Therapy*. New York: Brunner/Mazel, 1975.

Chapter 15: Toward a multigenerational therapy. Shortened and revised from: Family Theory: An Introduction. In *Operational Theories of Personality*. New York: Brunner/Mazel, 1974.

CONTENTS

Part II
Family Dynamics
and the Separation Process

Part III
The Theory and Practice
of Psychoanalytic Family Therapy

INTRODUCTION

Psychoanalytically oriented family therapy is as yet a concept rather than a discipline. The following essays show how this concept took shape for me. They trace a journey that led from psychoanalysis to family therapy. The individual chapters represent way stations in a process of learning and thinking which spans my professional career. Let me mention a few of the most important way stations.

A first station was Heidelberg, where I studied philosophy and medicine from 1946 to 1953. There Karl Jaspers, Alfred Weber, Alexander Mitscherlich and Viktor von Weizsäcker were my most influential teachers. Their names stake out an intellectual field replete with tensions and contradictions. For example, in the evenings, I would study Freud's works in Mitscherlich's newly founded Psychosomatic Clinic, only to hear the next morning in Jaspers' seminar that Freud was (besides Marx) the evil genius of our times. What Nietzsche and Kierkegaard had originally conceived, Freud—according to Jaspers—trivialized and made palatable to a sensation-hungry public. Increasingly for me, though, Freud's thoughts, scientific candor, and humanity grew stronger, while Jaspers' star faded. Nonetheless, my critical preoccupation with Jaspers and other existentialist authors continued for some time and pervades the first chapter, Existentialism Meets Psychotherapy. Finally, I came to see Jaspers as the prototype of the "distant observer"—a psychiatrist-philosopher who prevented psychoanalytic and psychodynamic approaches from taking hold in German academic psychiatry.

Another way station was Munich, where, after my graduation from medical school, I stayed from 1953 to 1955. There, too, the fields of psychiatry and medical psychology were racked by tensions. As an intern at the outpatient department of the university clinic for internal medicine, I had a chance to familiarize myself with psychoanalytic approaches to psychosomatic problems and started my first training analysis. However, when I subsequently entered the University Hospital for Nervous and Mental Diseases as a first-year resident, my psychiatric experiences were mostly negative. Schizophrenic patients were treated with numerous electroshocks, hysterical ones with painful electrical currents. Young psychiatrists were trained to become distant rather than participant observers, and psychoanalytic points of view were not welcome.

I knew from my reading that there existed in the United States a kind of psychiatry different from the one practiced in Munich. One American author, above others, had come to represent in my mind a more dynamic and humane psychiatry: Harry Stack Sullivan. Therefore, I did not hesitate when I got a chance to work at the psychiatric hospital where Sullivan, more than thirty years before, had revolutionized the treatment of psychotic patients— the Sheppard and Enoch Pratt Hospital in Towson near Baltimore, Maryland.

Thus, Towson became the next way station. I was fortunate to find there a person who conveyed to me Sullivan's ideas, yet was an original teacher and therapist in his own right: Lewis B. Hill. I subsequently translated his *Therapeutic Intervention in Schizophrenia* into German. Still today I hold it to be one of the most important texts for psychiatrists and psychotherapists. At Sheppard Pratt a resident was usually in charge of up to twelve patients. Individual psychotherapy had priority, but tranquilizing drugs in moderate doses were also given. Electroshock and insulin treatments were used only rarely and soon fell out of fashion. It was a different world than the one I was used to in Munich. At Sheppard Pratt I got to know intensely many relatives of my psychiatric patients and began to realize the importance of the family in the origin and course of their troubles.

The next way station was Chestnut Lodge, a small, private sanatorium on the outskirts of Washington, D.C., where most patients were schizophrenics under intensive, psychoanalytically oriented psychotherapy. I worked at the Lodge from 1957 to 1962. There, too, I was on Sullivan's tracks. For it was there that he had given some of his most famous seminars and lectures (which were later published by his disciples). Frieda Fromm-Reichmann (who unfortunately died only a year after my arrival), Otto Will, Edith Weigert, Hilde Bruch, Clarence Schulz and others in these years further familiarized me with Sullivan's concepts.

A therapist at Chestnut Lodge saw as a rule no more than six patients, each in four or more hourly sessions per week. During my stay I wrote the paper which forms the third chapter in this volume, The Adaptation to the "Stronger" Person's Reality. It deals with the role of the mother-child relationship in the origins and treatment of schizophrenics. My book *Conflict and Reconciliation*, reflecting my Chestnut Lodge experience and published in 1968, also centers on this theme. At that time not only the mother but the whole family began to take on importance for my work with the schizophrenic patient. For example, I remember how I reacted with pain and dismay when a young schizophrenic girl who had seemed to be progressing well in her psychotherapy with me suddenly left the hospital under pressure from her parents. Otto Will, my supervisor, consoled me with a dictum by Sullivan:

"Frequently it is the first sign of progress with schizophrenics, that their relatives want to take them out of treatment." I have found much to ponder in this statement over the years.

While I worked on the staff of Chestnut Lodge, I received psychoanalytic training at the Washington Psychoanalytic Institute. Schizophrenia persisted as a focus for the application of newly won psychoanalytic insights and principles, as well as for my growing interest in family dynamics.

The study and therapy of families was then still in an exciting, pioneer phase. Unlike psychoanalysis, which had one seminal founder, modern family theory and therapy did not clearly originate with one or two authors. Rather, it burst forth as a stream to which a group of pioneers, working simultaneously at different places, contributed and still contribute. Their names comprise more or less the roll of past and present editors and editorial advisers of the journal *Family Process*. These pioneers shared their insights and enthusiasm, but they used concepts and approaches which, while often similar, bore their author's distinctive imprint. From this group, it was mainly Gregory Bateson, Don Jackson (who had also worked as a psychotherapist at Chestnut Lodge), Theodore Lidz, Murray Bowen, Nathan Ackermann, Lyman Wynne and Ivan Boszormenyi-Nagy (and their associates) who influenced me. Most of them I got to know during my Chestnut Lodge years. For these authors too the problems of schizophrenia provided the main stimulus for pioneer work in family therapy and theory.

My own definite turn to a psychoanalytically oriented family therapy began in 1965, after a two years' stay at the Sanatorium Bellevue in Kreuzlingen, Switzerland, and two trips to New Zealand and Australia. I then returned to the United States to work at the National Institute of Mental Health in Bethesda, Maryland on a team headed by Lyman Wynne, Chief of the Adult Psychiatry Branch, which was intensely engaged in the research and therapy of families. From that point on, I have struggled with the task—which I find today as urgent as ever—of reconciling the paradigms of psychoanalysis and family therapy.

Regarding this task, which pervades most of this book, a few more words: Thomas Kuhn, a philosopher of science, has called a paradigm a scientific concept which reorders available data, creates new meaning, and opens up major new perspectives. By this definition, I consider family therapy and theory to be a paradigm. Jay Haley has perhaps best captured its essence:

> One cannot call family therapy simply a new method of treatment; it is a new way of conceptualizing the cause and cure of psychiatric problems. Family therapists are distinct as a group largely because of a common assumption. If the individual is to change, the context in which he lives must change. The unit of treatment is no longer the person, even if only a single person is interviewed; it is a set of relationships in which the person is embedded.

However, the reconciliation of the paradigms of psychoanalysis with those of family therapy cannot produce a conflictless synthesis. Before we can truly reconcile the two, we have to recognize what separates them. For example, we have to take into account that family theory implies a system rather than an individual (or at best a dyadic) approach, that observable transactions often have primacy over inferable intrapsychic processes, and that therapeutic activism may be more effective than a passive furtherance of insight. Also, we must accept the fact that family theorists and therapists needed to create a new language that befitted their subject and, in some respects, was scientifically more up to date than that of psychoanalysis. To a large extent, this was the language of modern cybernetics. But once such demarcation is achieved, we need to consider how the two approaches complement and require each other. Here the

focus is on those mostly unconscious and/or unnoticed mechanisms which in psychoanalysis show up in intrapsychic conflicts
and defenses, and which in family theory recur in family myths,
processes of delegation, "invisible loyalties," the trading of
dissociations, mutual enslavements through shame and guilt, and
many more. To me, these dynamics imply yet also transcend a
psychoanalytic point of view. They open up a perspective which I
have tried to explicate in this book, one that owes much to the
work of Lyman Wynne, Margaret Singer, Ivan Boszormenyi-
Nagy, Gregory Bateson, Theodore Lidz and their respective
associates.

Whether and how the above task of reconciliation succeeds
depends then not least on the language and concepts that reflect as
well as shape our clinical experiences. But here much needs to be
done. For neither the language of classical psychoanalysis
grounded in 19th-century physics and neurology nor that of most
contemporary family researchers and therapists shaped by
modern information theory seems capable of expressing what is
essential. The formulations offered in this book can, at best, be
only a first attempt at the new language required.

Part I

At the Beginning of Family Therapy: The Problem of Schizophrenia

Chapter I

Existentialism Meets Psychotherapy

Since the first decades of the century existentialist ideas have increasingly influenced the theory and practice of psychotherapy. These ideas were accepted or rejected with equal intensity by practicing analysts and psychotherapists. Yet even as the ideas were being adapted to the needs of psychotherapy, the ideas themselves were changing.

What is the contribution of existentialist thinking to psychotherapy? With this question in mind I will present first an exposition of those existentialist ideas which, in my opinion, had the greatest impact on psychiatric thinking. I will try to show how these ideas were transformed while being adapted to psychiatric needs. Second, I will attempt a critique of these ideas, focusing on their value in psychiatric theory and practice. In order to sustain this critique, I will introduce some insights which recently have emerged from the study of schizophrenia—still the most taxing and puzzling therapeutic problem.

What is Man and what should Man be like? Man chained to a perishable animal nature, its needs, enjoyments, tensions; but also Man endowed with imagination and consciousness, driving him to find meaning in his existence and to perfect himself in the light of such self-found meaning? Can we, in answering this question, hope to know what to aim for in psychotherapy? Will not this answer supply the guiding principle for our work with patients?

In a way, we raise this question not because we know too little, but because we know too much. Increasingly, we know of the man-madeness of our norms and institutions—the family structure, religious beliefs, the many intangible aspects of a given culture—but we know also of the norm-madeness of Man. Norms and institutions, we have learned, in a fantastically complex and variable interplay of forces, shape the inner-most modes in which we feel, express, and conceive right and wrong. But norms and institutions, we also find, change when our awareness of their relativity and man-madeness makes us challenge them. They lose their unquestioned grip on us and become eroded. The matrix of this orientation to change is modern science. The sciences of comparative anthropology, sociology, child-psychology, the analytic study of ego functions (and especially of ego-development) all contribute from different angles to our knowledge of the interplay of forces through which Man's existence is constantly threatened and precariously maintained. The modern analytic science of Man, in other words, both reveals and accentuates Man's existence as an unstable equilibrium.

Much the same can be said of existentialism. Existentialism also denotes a body of ideas about Man. These ideas, developed in the last century by writers such as Kierkegaard, Nietzsche, and Dostoevski, in this century were revived, systematized, and further developed by Heidegger, Jaspers, Camus, and others (see References I). Although varying greatly in their points of departure and in their manner of elucidating problems, these writers emphasize the precariousness of Man's existence due to the erosion of all traditional, outside-imposed values. But also, they point to a new dignity, a deepened humanity, which may result from staunchly facing the precariousness of human existence.

The instability of human existence, in other words, as revealed in the ever-questioning and relativizing process of modern science, is also the theme of many existentialist writers. But while natural science—and again I mean mainly the psychoanalytical study of Man—assesses this fact rather indirectly in conveying to us a sense of the open-endedness of all our endeavors, existentialist writers often do so relentlessly and bluntly: "God is dead" (Nietzsche), "Being is being toward death" (Heidegger), "Man on earth has his existence and nothing more" (Camus). And further, while analytic scientists often express themselves in awkward technical language, existentialist authors, particularly Nietzsche, Dostoevski, Sartre, and Camus, are masters of style. Skillfully they use literary genres such as the novel, the short essay, the aphorism, and the play, defying a seemingly clumsy scientific respectability.

Both the analytic science of Man and the theories of existentialism, we thus find, reflect as well as respond to the needs and mood of our time—to a sense of bewildered precariousness of our existence. Therefore it is not surprising that two ways of theorizing about Man, originating from seemingly different traditions of thinking—the one, psychoanalysis, born out of the tradition of natural science; the other, existentialism, born out of a mainly German philosophic tradition—succeeded in greatly influencing and changing the climate of the Western world.

Almost imperceptibly, the basic concepts of psychoanalysis as well as those of existentialism (particularly as represented by Heidegger), repeated, enlarged, popularized, and simplified, have become unquestioned reference points and clichés for many a modern individual's thinking about himself and others—just as in another part of the world the basic concepts of Marxism have become unquestioned guide posts for self-understanding.[1]

Time was needed, however, for the two bodies of theory to come face to face in the field of psychiatry and psychotherapy. For only recently have the ideas and viewpoints of existentialism been

used more extensively to illuminate psychiatry and psychotherapy. This was mainly the work of such psychiatric mediators as
Binswanger, Boss, Straus, and Rollo May.

Each in his individual manner tried to make existentialist
concepts, mainly derived from Heidegger, psychiatrically palatable. As a result, the field of psychotherapy has turned into an arena
in which these two different bodies and traditions of thinking
about Man meet and challenge each other.

How does existentialism present itself in this arena? It presents
itself, we notice at once, in many guises, such as *Daseins*-analysis,
medical anthropology, medical phenomenology, logotherapy, and
others. Often these seem bewilderingly at odds with one another.
And are they, we may ask, genuine offshoots and variations of
existentialism and existentialist therapy? I do not know. Yet
Heidegger and Jaspers themselves, the two persons who publicly
are most strongly identified with existentialism, in their later
years did not want to be called existentialists. Heidegger conceived
of his philosophy as a fundamental ontology; Jaspers referred to
his thinking simply as philosophy. For lack of a better name, I will
keep the label existentialism. In the following I will try to outline
some of the features which I consider most important.

Although both Heidegger and Jaspers may be considered
originators of this existentialist trend in psychiatry, at present
Heidegger's influence on psychiatric thinking in Europe seems
stronger than that of Jaspers. This is somewhat puzzling. For it is
Jaspers who was trained as a psychiatrist before turning into a
professor of philosophy. And it is Jaspers, who, besides many
minor psychiatric papers, wrote a comprehensive textbook on
psychiatry, *Allgemeine Psychopathologie*. But Jaspers, paradoxically,
used his psychiatric knowledge to prevent his "existential"
insights from becoming influential in psychotherapy.

Jaspers, in his psychiatric writings, denied that psychotic, and
particularly schizophrenic developments, could be understood—
that they were *einfühlbar*. He emphasized the gap between

emotional experiences, which are accessible to common understanding, and psychotic experiences, which are not accessible.

But more importantly, he also denied the necessity of scientifically investigating the nature of the interaction between doctor and patient (neurotic or psychotic)—in psychoanalytic terminology, of the transference and countertransference relationship. Such examination, which is characteristic for psychoanalytic procedure, would, he argued, destroy the quality of trust and privacy inherent in a correct doctor-patient relationship.[2] In holding these two positions—that psychotic experiences are inaccessible to common understanding and that the therapeutic interaction must not be subjected to scientific investigation—Jaspers made certain that his "existential" writings remained without direct relevance for psychiatry.[3] Thus, despite the central place of "communication" in his general philosophizing, he greatly limited the possibility of communication with psychotic patients and hindered the study of communication where it counts most in psychotherapy: in the relationship between doctor and patient.

Not surprisingly, he became probably the strongest force in denying to German psychiatry the analytic and dynamic approach developed in the United States. Instead of encouraging psychiatrists to become participant observers, he further entrenched, as I describe in Chapter 3, the position of the distant observer with its strong organic orientation.

Heidegger, on the other hand, suffered no such handicap. Not being a psychiatrist by training, he had no opportunity to disqualify himself in the field of psychotherapy as did Jaspers. But this does not seem reason enough to explain his great influence. How then can Heidegger's influence be explained? The reasons, undoubtedly, are many. But one, I believe, stands out. Heidegger seems to answer the question I referred to in the beginning; namely, what is Man and what should he be like? And this answer seems to arise out of an intriguing firsthand grasp of the phenomena in question, out of a thinking which in some ways appears to be more immediate, more penetrating, and more revealing than conventional formulations about Man, whether they come from a philosophic or a scientific framework.

This is not the place to give a detailed outline and critique of Heidegger's thinking (see References I). The following remarks, geared to the subject of this study, must suffice.

How did Heidegger, we may ask, arrive at his statements about Man? The answer, to oversimplify, is: By a complex detour, an unrelenting preoccupation with Being.

Heidegger affirmed that the quest for the truth of Being, for that which underlies and determines all there is, is the most difficult quest possible. For from whichever angle we attempt this quest, we run into the problem of speech and language. Language is the medium through which Being reveals itself, but, in the very moment of its revelation, is also limited and obscured. To express this differently, any seemingly successful attempt to conceptualize Being in language has already lost sight of the truth of Being. In a way, much of Heidegger's thinking, including that in *Being and Time* (II, 19), is an ongoing comment on this state of affairs, at the same time puzzling, frustrating, and challenging.

One can, I believe, differentiate three aspects of this never-ending quest, all amply reflected in *Being and Time*. Firstly, Heidegger attacks traditional statements about Being, about Man's nature, about human values, etc., in the light of the fact that Being is both illuminated and concealed through language. Thus Western philosophy since Plato, Heidegger concludes, essentially obstructed the grasp of the truth of Being by becoming preoccupied with *Seiendem* instead of with *Sein*.[4] Secondly, intertwined with this more negative approach, Heidegger almost constantly—appearing sometimes pointed, sometimes odd—endeavors to think with and out of a language that is closer to Being than the more traditional and conventional language, including the traditional language of philosophy. Hence his preoccupation with digging up original meanings and roots of words, mainly

German or Greek, which he then uses in an often startling manner to coin words or reintroduce uncommon lines of thought. Best known and most central to his basic thesis—but also most disputed!—is his redefinition and reconceptualization of truth as unconcealedness (*Unverborgenheit*), *a-letheia, a concept that seemingly does away with truth as a representational relation and, as a consequence, also with the subject-object split as a precondition* of human understanding. Thirdly—and this is perhaps the most important aspect—Heidegger's thinking is a relentless, probing argumentation in circles.

This can hardly be otherwise. For this is very much the result of his having committed himself to an obviously unsolvable task: making Being transparent by reconciling the above-mentioned double aspect of language as both revealing and concealing Being. Constant stimulation and frustration appear built into this task. Nevertheless—and this is perhaps Heidegger's uniqueness—he developed an almost monomanic determination to pursue it relentlessly.

The result of this pursuit is rather paradoxical. At the end of the investigation, Being remains as mysterious and elusive as ever. This Heidegger appears to admit himself, yet he also seems to constantly nourish the hope that its discovery is just around the corner. Although Being remains elusive, something, nonetheless, emerges in its pursuit: something that perhaps might best be described as a different climate and way of thinking about Man.

And along with this new thinking about Man, Heidegger comes to design a kind of blueprint of Man's existence, of his "being-in-the-World." Like a Phoenix out of the ashes of the traditional concepts and values, there arises after all, so it seems, the answer to the question: What is Man and what should he be like?

Man's existence, according to Heidegger in *Being and Time*, is embedded in and marked by such central determinants as Man's finding himself thrown into the world—thrownness (*Geworfenheit*)—fallenness (*Verfallenheit*), death, time, and above all care (*Sorge*), concepts which are all given a new and special meaning by Heidegger. On the stage of life, as staked out by these basic determinants or "existentials" (*Existentialien*), Man can live either inauthentically or authentically: Inauthentically in the manner of the great majority of men, in Heidegger's language "one," in the sense of "people" (*das Man*), who is busily immersing himself in chatter and distractions; or authentically in the manner of the few, who dare to face death and their basic loneliness.

It must be added, many of Heidegger's conclusions reached in *Being and Time* stressing and elaborating Man's confrontation with nothingness appear outdated in the light of more recent formulations. In these, for example, Man is conceived as the "shepherd of Being."

Summarizing Heidegger's position, we find it embedded in a peculiar glistening twilight. His fundamental ontology—this seems to be the claim inherent in much of his writings—will supply an answer to the question: What is Man and what should he be like? The analyses of Man's thrownness, of his Being-in-the-World as Being-toward-death, of time and of the other basic concepts elaborated in *Being and Time* appear to verify this claim. Hence also his final differentiation of authentic and inauthentic modes of Being—Heidegger's answer to the question: What should Man be like?

But Being, after all, remains elusive. His arguments often appear questionably tied to his private use of the German language, and his position is shifting. This all invalidates his claim that he has answered the question—although it makes his work intriguing.

And it is this twilight, this intriguing unclarity, which we encounter again when we turn to those schools or trends of "modern existential psychotherapy" which, directly or indirectly, received their main impetus from Heidegger.

Each of these schools, we notice, focuses on certain aspects of Heidegger's thinking and neglects others. Heidegger's work appears like a complex and intriguing symphony. Its various themes and elements are now subject to many interpretations and variations, all carried out with great differences in skill and sophistication. But upon closer scrutiny, we realize that the discords and problems built into the original symphony reveal themselves in these variations. In a way, the application of Heidegger's thinking to clinical problems even seems to bring out more sharply the original inconsistencies and ambiguities.[5]

In the following I want to deal with some of the themes and variations contained in Heidegger's original work, as they have been developed by his followers in their attempt to promote psychiatric understanding. Let me begin with the theme which in many respects has become central. I have in mind that aspect of theorizing about Man which seems most concisely reflected in the term *Dasein*-analysis. The analysis of human *Dasein* in the psychiatric literature is now most strongly identified with Binswanger and Boss. In a way this *Dasein*-analysis is perhaps the most direct psychiatric application and continuation of Heidegger's exposition of *Dasein* (probably best translated "human existence") as "Being-in-the-World," as carried through in *Being and Time*. It was in this exposition that Heidegger arrived at the blueprint of Man's existence, as described earlier.

What then will such a blueprint reveal when used to illuminate a clinical case? In order to answer this question, let me turn to Binswanger's analysis of the case of Ellen West (I, 12). In this case the term "world-design" (*Weltentwurf, Daseinsentwurf*) denotes the framework within which a given patient, Ellen West, is understood and analyzed. Here, as in other *daseins*-analytic writings, the terms "world-design," "*Dasein*," "*Daseinsentwurf*," and "Mode-of-being-in-the-world" appear not clearly distinguishable. Ellen West's world-design, according to Binswanger, is made transparent in the light of such basic concepts as the World (there further differentiated into *Umwelt, Mitwelt* and *Eigenwelt*), Time, and Death. Heidegger's midwifery can easily be recognized. But Binswanger adds color and differentiation. He sees Ellen West, for example, as torn between the Temporality of the Ethereal World and the Temporality of the Tomb World, while failing in the world of practical action. Binswanger tries to grasp what is basic and essential in this girl's life, thus making (he believes) any possible psychoanalytic or other interpretation ephemeral and partial. That which is basic, essential—that which in Heidegger's terms would be ontological as opposed to merely ontic—is described with poetic affluence. But eventually it seems to be something rather simple. Binswanger concludes, "The entire life history of Ellen West is nothing but the history of the metamorphosis of life into mold and death" (p. 318).

Boss (II, 6), similarly, makes us see the world-design of a coprophiliac as his "dark, narrow mode of existence." It is, he writes, "the dirty hole-world of a worm" (p. 60). And von Gebsattel (II, 42)—almost equally indebted to Heidegger, although less outspoken about it—sees his compulsive patients existing in a loveless world of "mire, dirt, and deep holes."

In these and other analyses, different aspects are emphasized and different descriptive terms are used—the focusing on the world of death and mire is, of course, only one among a number of possibilities—but the underlying approach to patients is similar: their neurotic or psychotic symptomatology is seen as the manifestation of an existence in some way gone wrong or undeveloped. However, among these psychiatric writers there is now less talk about authentic versus inauthentic existence than might be expected from an acquaintance with Heidegger. Instead we read of the "unlived, unrealized, and unfulfilled existence," about *"Formen missglückten Daseins"* (modes of being that have failed or gone shipwreck). These modes of a frustrated and crippled existence are then described, often extensively and expressively.

Yet can we, in making such judgments about a given existence, dispense with an explicit standard for such judgments? What, in other words, is the norm, the measuring stick against which the unfulfilled and shipwrecked character of an existence is evaluated? And with this question in mind—central as it is to the understanding of many existentialist writings—we once more have to go back to Heidegger. Trying to answer this question will also permit us to throw light on some other themes which seem essential in existential therapy.

To Heidegger, we must remember, the authenticity or inauthenticity of given modes of existence revealed itself in his analysis of *Dasein* as "Being-in-the-World." The standards for judging authenticity emerged in the process of this analysis. Heidegger's psychiatric followers, particularly Boss, also refer to this analysis as the basis (*Grundlegung*) for all of their clinical considerations. But again, what in the case of Heidegger appears as a perplexingly open-ended and ambiguous web of conceptualizations, in his psychiatric disciples often narrows itself down to a number of closely related arguments and assertions, often brought forward with a dogmatic finality.

Let me, in the following, take up the main argument by which Boss, for example, leaning on Heidegger, tries to make plausible and legitimate his manner of seeing a given existence as either fulfilled or unfulfilled. Existence, or *Dasein*, Boss contends (seemingly following Heidegger), is revealed in the manner in which a light ray sheds light on itself. The light ray, by its very existence, illuminates itself as something both distinct from and related to its environment. In other words: Existence, and the grasp of this existence in a given world, comes all in one package (although this is, admittedly, a somewhat ill-fitting metaphor, as would be any other). In this is reflected the "revealedness of human existence" ("*Erschlossenheit des Daseins*") so central to Heidegger's whole exposition of *Dasein* as "Being-in-the-World." We miss (and that is the next conclusion drawn by Boss) the one-package character of existence when we try to analyze it in the manner of a subject confronted with an object. For once we make ourselves at home in this subject-object split, we already have allowed ourselves to become entangled in the ill-fated analytical and scientific approaches of Western man. We have lost the immediate hold on Being, in which the roles of observer,

participant, and existent are as yet inseparable. Given this state of
affairs, for example, Hora, another *Daseins*-analyst living in the
United States,[6] appears quite consistent in describing existential
therapy as uncausal, unhistorical, unteleological, uninterpretative
and uninterpersonal. For only in this seemingly absurd manner, it
appears, can he emphasize the character of unbrokenness of
existence as revealed in and through Being, as it is experienced in
therapy.

And it is along with this immediate illumination *through* and
rootedness of existence *in* Being that the authenticity or
inauthenticity, the fulfillment or unfulfillment of a given
existence, or Dasein, is revealed. The light ray, through revealing
itself in the world, at once reveals itself, so to speak, also as either a
dim or a shining ray.

Another theme closely related to the above is perhaps
represented best by Erwin Straus (II, 37). Straus' central interest,
sensory physiology, gives it its characteristic coloration. More
than to Heidegger, Straus appears indebted to Husserl, Heidegger's teacher and predecessor at the philosophic chair in
Freiburg.

Straus, in order to elucidate his own position, likes to begin with
a critique of Descartes. Descartes, according to Straus, was the
main philosophic legitimizer of the subject-object split. He
decisively established the tradition within which modern scientific
man learned to think about himself and the world. "The Cartesian
dichotomy," Straus writes, "not only separates mind from body,
but severs the experiencing creature from the world, sensation
from motion" (p. 141). Straus, in contrast, tries to break up, so to
speak, the grooves of theorizing created by Descartes. In order to
achieve this, he emphasizes, from numerous angles, the importance of the unbroken continuum of experience. This unbroken
continuum or "experience-whole," Straus asserts, is the matrix in
which all that traditionally carries the name perception takes
place. The expression "sensory perception," it follows, is

misleading when used in the tradition of Western analytic thought. "At the very outset," Heidegger, for example, points out, "we never hear noises and sound complexes. We hear the squeaking car, the motorcycle. One hears the marching column, the north wind, the hammering woodpecker, the bristling fire" (II, 19). We are therefore led astray, Straus concludes, when we try to break up this immediate experience-whole by introducing such entities as a "perceiving object," "perceptions," and "objects perceived." In doing so, we have already permitted our investigative position to become distorted.

The emphasis on the illumination of the immediate experience-whole, to be grasped without theoretical bias, constitutes the essence of the phenomenological approach. This approach has been applied to a special field of clinical experience designed to illuminate the rootedness of Existence in Being.

This approach lends itself, we notice at once, not only to the investigation of seeing and hearing, but also of feeling (or mood). Mood adds a further dimension. Mood is a central constituent of the immediate experience-whole. In Heidegger's exposition of *Dasein* as "Being-in-the-World," mood is considered an ontic phenomenon: a given mood (*Stimmung, Gestimmtheit*) tunes us to the world, both illuminating and constituting it for us. It is, to extend the metaphor used earlier, an essential element of the light ray which, by its very existence, sheds light on itself and the world.

But this approach—and herewith we observe a further branching out of the above-mentioned themes—may throw light also on areas which seem only more or less remotely related to sensory physiology. Thus, among others, von Weizsäcker (II, 43), Christian (II, 12), and Buytendijk (II, 11) have focused much of their interest on body movement and posture. Gabriel Marcel (II, 22) and Merleau-Ponty (II, 26) tried to throw light, though from somewhat different viewpoints, on the nature of the experience of one's own body.

In the following I want briefly to deal with some aspects of the last-mentioned experience in order to highlight further some features and vicissitudes of this phenomenological approach when applied to the clinical realm.

In trying to understand my experience of my own body I at once find myself entangled in a web of seeming contradictions. What, for example, is the "I" when I speak of "I" and "my body"? Perhaps the most fitting answer, proposed by Gabriel Marcel, is: I am my body. This avoids the necessity of thinking of "I" as something other than my body, such as the soul, consciousness, a sense of self, etc.—all notions resulting in contradictions or inconsistencies. Yet this formulation cannot, it becomes evident at once, altogether do away with the dichotomy I—my body. In many contexts it is meaningful to view the "I" (however it be conceived) and my body as interacting with each other. "I" might be the victim of an illness. "I" suffer from it and reflect about it. This illness, I feel, occurs in deep strata of my body inaccessible to my voluntary control. And yet there seem to exist ways in which I may nonetheless influence this illness. Not only can I decide to take medication, but by undergoing a psychoanalysis or a deep emotional experience, by tuning myself more smoothly, more sensitively, more feelingly to my body, I may also change the course of the illness. Changes in my emotional attitude, occurring subtly and gradually, might just as subtly and gradually alter the manner in which I feel about and through my body. And again, the course of the illness might be changed. But in whatever way I conceive of this interaction, in the final analysis my ties to my body remain elusive, a mystery.

Just as Heidegger found constant stimulation and frustration built into his quest for Being, so we encounter the same while trying to understand our relationship to our body.

And also in this quest, as in the more encompassing quest for Being, we stumble into the formidable problem of language. Here, as there, language appears as both the prime obscurer as well as revealer of truth. The use of words such as conceive, grasp, etc., at once appears inadequate. Words such as these imply a handling or manipulation. They fashion the understanding of our body after the understanding of some mechanical model. Similarly, in stating "I possess my body"—a point analyzed by Gabriel Marcel—I imply an understanding modeled after the possession of tools or instruments. This again proves to be an insufficient formulation. And so it goes on: every formulation I use will be found wanting insofar as it appears chained to its established usage. This immediately dooms its usefulness when applied to the unique problem in question.

Heidegger, we recall, tried to bridge the gap between an understanding of Being and our limited language by developing new words and word conceptions. These new conceptions seemingly gave an altogether new slant to the problem in question. Thus Heidegger attempted to bypass the original gap between Being and language. The authors who are interested in the body problem frequently attempt a similar bypass. They often resort to unusual formulations that give an unfamiliar twist to the problem. Thus Zutt (II, 48), to mention only one example, likes to speak *"vom gelebten welthaften Leibe,"* of a body which is (to translate freely) lived in a world-revealing and world-oriented manner—a formulation that might appear, at first glance, to avoid the pitfalls inherent in understanding the relationship I-body in the more conventional terms mentioned earlier. Similarly, many other problems falling broadly into the realm of psychosomatic medicine appear to reveal a new angle through the use of such new expressions.

Frustrations and stimulations similar to those built into the quest for Being and "my body" are encountered in trying to understand the nature of the therapeutic relationship. This relationship, from the therapist's point of view, can be seen as a peculiar mixture of detachment and involvement. While a relationship evolves, certain transference patterns of the patient can be identified. Part of the identifying process, we know through the studies of E. Weigert (II, 44), M. Cohen (II, 14), and many others, is the therapist's own countertransference reactions. But the analysis of the transference-countertransference dynamics reveals only one among many aspects of the analytic relationship. There is, in other words, more to the relationship than transference and countertransference. For example, there must exist in the relationship something which makes possible a therapeutic relatedness in the first place, which brings into play the elements of trust, growth, and solidarity. And again, it is this "something" which appears elusive, just as Being and the ties to my body turned out to be elusive. And just as in the two aforementioned instances, a new word conception seems to offer a solution. Binswanger (II, 1) and Elrod (II, 16) made perhaps the most successful attempt at coining it. They introduced the term *Tragung* as that which makes possible the *Uebertragung*. The German word *Tragung*—which in this context would be the equivalent of "ference" in "trans-ference"—denotes "holding, bearing, carrying." It thus seems to express quite vividly that which both constitutes and complements a therapeutic relationship within which a transference-countertransference dynamic proper can develop.

This outline of themes must suffice. In applying a *dasein*-analytical and phenomenological approach to illuminate psychiatric problems, we learn that our traditional or more conventional frame of reference is, so to speak, loosened. Old structures of thought suddenly seem to crumble; something truly new and original seems to come within our grasp.

Such experience, however, almost inevitably brings to mind a period in all our lives in which we make new discoveries every day, when the world still has a glow of inexhaustible newness and richness, a sense of promise and unending potentiality. That period is childhood.

During this period words characteristically have a much more magical, world-revealing and world-containing meaning than they have in later life. They have not yet become unquestioned givens, something as available and routinely resorted to as the clothes we wear every day.

And also, such words, newly experienced in childhood, revealing the world while having a magical fascination of their own, seem to promise an immediate communion with the world, an unbroken-ness. It is this unbrokenness which may appear as the promised land to the adult who is painfully aware of the brokenness, fragmentation, and *Heillosigkeit* of the actual world he must live in.

Is not then, we may ask, the above-described existential, *daseins-*analytic, and phenomenological approach a legitimate and perhaps the only way to find a new sense of wholeness? Is not the grasp of a particular "world-design," of the ties to one's body, of the nature of the psychotherapeutic relationship, part of an attempt to establish a new immediacy of experience, a new unbrokenness?

Maybe this is so. But, in whatever way this wholeness and immediacy might be sought, it cannot have the same quality for the adult that it has for the child. The adult has been exposed and accustomed to the experience of abstract thinking, of separate-ness, of the subject-object split. The attempt to undo this state of affairs appears fraught with vicissitudes. And nowhere, it seems, can we better study these vicissitudes than in the endeavors, outlined above, to apply the existentialist approach to psychother-apy. It is these vicissitudes, the problematical aspects of the above-described approaches, with which I have to deal next.

In order to do so, I once again must turn to language. It is a characteristic use of language, we remember, through which Heidegger and his followers succeeded in giving a new slant to the whole problem in question. This use of language we now must study more carefully. We can observe in it (a) an evocative, (b) a reifying, and (c) a de-differentiating element. Let me take them up one after the other.

By "evocative" I mean that quality in language, hardly definable, which sparks in the reader indistinct moods and associations. It is that quality in the wording and form of communication which transmits an immediacy of feeling. Evoking an unconventional feeling-response often requires the breakup and displacement of the word clichés in which feelings have tended to be expressed but also encrusted. This kind of communication often must proceed in a somewhat rambling, groping, and loosely descriptive fashion. It is that element in the style of a poet, that part of his communicative expressiveness, which seems both most effective and most private and elusive. It is also that which may make his production a work of art.

This evocative power of language finds, in a way, its parallel in the personal charisma or style of a psychotherapist—sometimes rather flatly described as his "mode of nonverbal communication"—something which appears almost equally elusive when, for example, studied through some sort of factor analysis. But just as the charisma of the therapist needs to be checked usually by self-analysis, supervision, and other devices outlined by the author elsewhere (II, 34) so as to not degenerate into interpersonal demagogery, so the evocative power of language must be counterbalanced by clarity and precision. And the more we move with our thoughts into that border realm—the realm of the poet and the speculative philosopher—where we try to speak about the seemingly indescribable, the more we need to try for clarity—by defining the scope of relevance and using words which are unequivocal. The German language, more than other languages, seems to lend itself to moves into this border realm and to offer the means to becloud oneself and others by superimposing new shades of meaning on words which are already equivocal.

This use of equivocal language, particularly in the illumination of clinical facts and observations, thus frequently results in formulations which suggest poetry—a process for which Heidegger also provided the model with his *dichtendem Denken*, his poetizing thinking! (II, 27). But, as it turns out, the use of highly evocative and equivocal language in psychiatry very often seems to bring out neither the richness and depth of great poetry nor the clarity that would really deepen our understanding. Instead, not a few of the *daseins*-analytic and phenomenological writings leave with us mainly the impression of a frustrating and wordy ambiguity.

Next I have to deal with the *reifying* quality inherent in the above-described use of language. By reifying I mean a tendency to treat a concept not as representing, but as merging with an object. (Again, it is difficult to describe in the language of the subject-object split something which seems to transcend this split.) A study of the writings of Boss (II, 8), for example, can make clearer what is meant. Boss' whole polemic against Freud appears based on the assumption that Freud, instead of creating with his theories models of understanding which are revisable in the light of new clinical evidence, tried to introduce some sort of mechanical emotional reality. Again his polemic is reminiscent of a child's use of words: the child is not yet clearly aware that a word serves as a symbol or metaphor for something else. For the ability to make distinctions between words and the things they denote develops only gradually as a result of the growth, differentiation, and integration of bodily and mental functions. Only recently— through research in the fields of child and comparative psychology, and last but not least, of schizophrenia—have we come to grasp the enormous intricacy of these processes of growth and differentiation.

The price paid for the often revealing and illuminating use of language as practiced by Heidegger and his followers—and this is probably the most important aspect of this use of language—is therefore a *de-differentiation* in the ability to recognize and distinguish levels of relevance, a kind of reversal of the processes observed in a child's development.[7] A certain richness, immediacy, and expressiveness, in other words, is paid for with a loss of distinctions—between words and things and among related words. Along with this loss of distinctions goes an egotistic narrowing of one's way of experiencing the world, a certain inflated sense of one's own importance—again similar to the attitude of a child who, still unaware of the laws of causality to which he is heir, tends to interpret the happenings in the world in a highly egocentric and anthropocentric manner, just as many primitive peoples might do. (Cf. Piaget, II, 28; Werner, II, 45; and others.)

Certainly, de-differentiation as practiced by Heidegger and his followers is of a different order than the primary lack of differentiation observable in children. And yet it is this comparative lack of differentiation of concepts and of levels of relevance which proves to be most fateful when these concepts are used to illuminate clinical phenomena and the process of psychotherapy. In the following I want to deal with a few aspects of such de-differentiation in the psychiatric realm.

First, a "World-design" or "mode of Being," immediately grasped in its wholeness, excludes the possibility of acknowledging a dimension of the unconscious or the latent. Such an approach addresses itself to what is given, to what reveals itself. It brings forth neither the readiness nor the theoretical tools to cope with those aspects in a person's life or relationships which, in a more dynamic frame of reference, we have come to consider as being out of awareness, dissociated, or repressed. Boss, for example, clearly demonstrates this "neglect of the hidden" in his work *The Analysis of Dreams* (II, 8). Dreams for Boss are just another manifestation of a given person's mode of Being-in-the-World, accessible to an immediate understanding as are the manifestations of that person's waking life. He attacks Freud's notion that dreams reflect wishes which, through the dream, are partially fulfilled as well as coded and disguised. Freud, however, in providing a key for the deciphering of dreams, for translating into the language of rationality (or secondary process) something which had seemed simply irrational and irrelevant, enlarged the human realm of self-confrontation and self-examination. He enlarged the stage on which a person's seemingly hidden and manifest motives could come to grips with each other in increasingly subtle strategies of self-understanding and self-concealment. This "moral dimension," by necessity, is either greatly neglected or diluted by *daseins*-analytic and related approaches. For self-examination worthy of the name requires the ability both to establish distance from oneself and, from such a position of distance, to make distinctions. And it is exactly these distinctions which *daseins*-analytic approaches, in their tendency to de-differentiation, appear to neglect.[8]

Second, the trend toward de-differentiation, evident in the existential approaches, precludes an effective examination of the relationship between doctor and patient. It is characteristic of many modern treatment situations (to repeat a point I have made elsewhere—II, 34) that, because of a climate of change-orientedness and the breakdown of the traditional role concepts of therapist and patient, they invite symbiotic entanglement, obscure manipulations, and the mutual satisfaction of fringe-needs. This is often inevitable or even desirable in order to reach the patient at all. But the more the therapist makes himself vulnerable to such entanglements, the greater the necessity to demarcate himself, in a dialectical process, from the patient. Transference and countertransference patterns must, as soon as they become apparent, be conceptualized and made available for discussion. As part of the matching of sensitizing factors by stabilizing factors (see Chapter 3), the threat and temptation of fusion and ambiguity in the relationship must be counterbalanced by differentiation and clarity about the respective roles and contributions of patient and doctor.

Characteristically, existentialist writers extol the value and significance of the "encounter." Yet they fail to carry through a conscientious and introspectively enlightened examination of the social context of therapy, particularly the dynamics of transference and countertransference. Clearly, the de-differentiation typical of their approach provides neither the intellectual climate nor the theoretical tools to attempt such examination.[9]

Third, this de-differentiation (and this is probably its most important aspect) prevents an articulation with the social sciences and schools of thought which link individual behavior to social and political conduct. The trend toward de-differentiation not only forces the existential analysts into an often unenlightened and defensively rejecting opposition to psychoanalysis and its further development, it also causes them, as Szasz (II, 38) has rightly pointed out, to ignore the significant contributions of social psychology (Dewey, II, 15, Mead, II, 24), empiricism (Bridgman II, 10; Russell II, 31), and the philosophy of science movement (Frank, II, 17, Rapoport, II, 30). The overall result appears to be an isolation of these analysts from the social, political, and scientific stream of life of much of the Western world. They often have become encapsulated in a rather esoteric world of a semi-ideology, which has provided them with both an inflated sense of importance and the possibility of finding an easy confirmation of personal biases.

Heidegger seems to provide a model for this trend also: his philosophy appeared to provide little push or conceptual instrumentarium to deal effectively with the social and political field in which Nazism developed. On the contrary, as evidenced in his speech as newly appointed Rector of the University in Freiburg in 1933, he became spokesman of this regime's irrationalism.[10]

Similarly, in many modern existential and *daseins*-analytic writings, the combination of de-differentiation and a notion that the values and norms of human existence are intuitively given leaves the door wide open to an uncritical perpetuation of one's own biases, vested interests, and prestige needs.

In the field of modern psychiatry, the problems posed by a trend toward de-differentiation seem to be highlighted in our dealings with schizophrenic patients. A peculiar parallel seems to exist between the special human situation commonly called schizophrenia and the more general human situation which is the concern of existentialism. On the one hand, many aspects of the writings of existentialist and *daseins*-analytic writers seem to have direct relevance for understanding essential elements of the schizophrenic condition; and, on the other, problems encountered in schizophrenic patients—on a therapeutic as well as on an epistemological level—may more sharply reveal the value and shortcomings of the existential approaches. In the following I want to mention briefly some of these parallels and problems, confining myself to those aspects which I have outlined above under the general heading of de-differentiation.

In many schizophrenic patients the de-differentiation of the mental organization is striking. Those mental capacities—usually subsumed under the term ego functions—which make possible an effective focusing and structuring of the personality have broken down. Experiences definable in terms of an inner reality can no longer be differentiated from experiences conventionally attributed to outer reality. The result is hallucinations and delusions. The disturbances of thought and feeling, as first described by Bleuler (II, 5)—such as the disorder of association, lack of continuity, and hierarchical structure of ideas—can be seen, among other elements, in many a schizophrenic's behavior as the manifestations of a far-reaching de-differentation. Equally, many other symptoms or traits can be understood as desperate *ad hoc* attempts to control this de-differentiation. These traits serve as a sort of primitive straitjacket, matching in their crudeness the looseness of de-differentiation. This straitjacket makes ideas concrete and overgeneralized. It causes behavior to become frozen in catatonic rigidity. But even so, the underlying chaos and de-differentiation remains prone to erupt at the slightest provocation—in such forms as excitement or hebephrenic fragmentation—unremittingly bringing itself to the observer's notice.

Many a schizophrenic's behavior—and herewith I return to the polarity of the hidden versus the manifest—may therefore suggest the coming to the surface of that which is usually hidden deepest in a person. Incestuous strivings and crude incorporative, cannibalistic, and other "primitive" impulses accordingly seem to be expressed more openly than would be possible in "normal" people.

In its very primitiveness such a patient's *Dasein*, his "mode of Being-in-the-World," may appear immediately revealed. His need for attention, his rage, his loneliness may seem more transparent and thus more accessible to all-encompassing interpretations than they are in normal adults. But such a view, seemingly lending itself to an illumination of schizophrenia, would greatly obscure and make trivial the dimension of the hidden.

On the contrary, it is exactly in the understanding of the schizophrenic patient that this dimension of the hidden takes on a special depth and complexity. In exposing ourselves to this dimension, we find further widened—in ourselves and in the patient—the stage of self-revelation and self-concealment originally staked out for conscious penetration and responsible examination by Freud.

The reasons for the growing significance of this dimension of the hidden are similar to those that make the quest for the "immediate experience-whole" difficult for the adult whose differentiation makes thinking in the subject-object split second nature to him. In the schizophrenic patient who is an adult there does not exist a simple lack of differentiation, as would be more or less the case with small children, but a de-differentiation, experienced out of a position of differentiation already achieved. Consequently, this de-differentiation is uneven. Differentiated and functioning aspects of the personality exist dovetailed with de-differentiated and chaotic ones. Certain abilities and functions, such as interpersonal sensitivity, may be even more highly developed in schizophrenic patients than in more "normal" people.

This can be the result of an adaptation to a stronger person's reality (see Chapter 3). It is in this combination, interplay, and defensive balancing of differentiated and de-differentiated, of overdeveloped and underdeveloped skills and attitudes that a wide panorama of possible human conflicts and modes of self-alienation becomes visible—more deep-seated, more intense, and more complex than we commonly encounter.

This dimension of the hidden is relevant for understanding the intrapsychic realm as well as the family and the larger social field of the schizophrenic patient.

Intrapsychically, we must look behind the manifest attitudes which the patient presents: the dissociated aspects, the need for tenderness behind the outward aloofness, the rage behind the smile, the sensed failures behind the demonstrated achievements, the chaos behind the conventional orderliness. The dimension of the hidden may appear sealed off. Then the firsthand impression is one of more ordinary normal or neurotic behavior. Or the seal, so to speak, may leak, and the hidden may reveal itself in a certain aura of uncanniness and brokenness. The painful, though warded off, realization of not being "whole," of being threatened by disintegration and the breakthrough of dissociated impulses more or less colors such a person's way of behaving or presenting himself. But whether sealed off or leaking, the "hidden" poses a challenge to our ability to become sensitive to the complex, multilevel character of the intrapsychic field.

To the bewildering hidden complexity of the family field of the schizophrenic we have become exposed only recently. It will occupy us in later chapters. The studies of Lidz (II, 21), Bowen (II,9), Wynne (II, 46, 47), and many others have sensitized us to a drama of fateful interpersonal entanglements that lie hidden behind the often conventional facades presented by such families.

The seal (to extend the metaphor used above) which cuts off the hidden, may be seen in the particular way these families have of interacting with one another, which Schaffer (II, 33) and Wynne

(II, 46, 47) variously have described as the "rubber fence" or "pseudo-mutuality." In penetrating this "rubber fence" we recognize, on the family level, a peculiar and precariously explosive integration, both paralleling and reinforcing the uneven differentiation observed on an individual level.

Finally, as I have mentioned in another essay ("The Concept of Cure," unpublished), there exists, on the level of the more general social field, a similar seal. This seal, which also normally prevents or restricts an awareness of the hidden, is our unquestioned identification with many socially sanctioned (but often implicitly conflictual) value standards and modes of defining our feelings and interactions. The poet, who often is most acutely aware of the shallowness, conflictfulness, or inhumanity of these standards and modes, is also, as I tried to show in my comments on Chekhov's *Ward No. 7*, often most prone and qualified to open our eyes to the dimension of the hidden as it prevails in this sphere.

Next, the therapy of schizophrenic patients, more than any other treatment situation, appears to invite symbiotic entanglement and de-differentiation of the roles of therapist and patient. It lends itself, therefore, to be viewed in those existentialist terms which are marked by de-differentiation and emphasize the meaningfulness of the "encounter," but preclude an effective examination of the relationship. Such examination requires us to distinguish clearly between patterns of interaction and to demarcate roles. Such making of distinctions in the treatment of schizophrenic patients is part of the structuring which makes possible the widening of the stage of self-concealment and self-revelation as described above.

Finally, the condition of many schizophrenic patients, unevenly de-differentiated and elusive as it may seem, often invites us to project into it our pet theories about man and life. There exists thus a similarity between the manner in which the de-differentiation inherent in Heidegger's quest for Being seemingly lends support to the greatest variety of notions about man and the way the very vagueness and open-endedness of the Nazi movement made it possible for many to find in it what they wanted.

Such evidence—pointing, as it may, in the direction of organicity, cultural conditioning, or the like—naturally tends to become organized into viewpoints, theories, and ideologies, depending on the needs and abilities of the observer.[11]

These comments point to a seeming affinity and complementarity between the schizophrenic condition and existentialism. But they also point to the difficulties we encounter in trying to illuminate this human condition in the light of the viewpoints which existentialist authors so far have developed.

These difficulties appear typical for the existential approach when applied to other areas of psychotherapy and human life. They cast doubt on the claims made by many of the existentialist authors. The task of grasping more exactly what is essential—in the schizophrenic as in other human conditions—and relating it meaningfully to the totality of our knowledge and actions remains.

Notes

[1] One can draw further parallels. For example, just as Freud needed a Fenichel to demonstrate, in a systematized and relatively plausible manner, his brood clinical applicability to a wider audience, so Heidegger needed a Tillich to become more widely known in this country. In each case the master found his characteristic emissaries, translators, and popularizers, often in the same person.

[2] Jaspers' many bitter attacks on Freud are consistent with these positions. Jaspers thought little of Freud's clinical contributions. He liked to compare Freud to Marx as a provider of an ideology with a wide appeal and as the popularizer and simplifier of insights which were more deeply grasped and movingly expressed by authors like Nietzsche and Kierkegaard.

[3] These comments do not do justice to the complexity of Jasper's psychiatric thinking, particularly to his ability, amply reflected in his *Allgemeine Psychopathologie,* to illuminate clinical phenomena and problems under many different angles. However, one can identify certain central themes and positions which had a most characteristic and fateful impact on German academic psychiatry. Of these, the two mentioned above appear to me the most

important. For a more extensive discussion of Jaspers' psychiatric thinking, especially in regard to his stand on analytic and dynamic theories, see references (40, particularly pp. 296-300), (29) and (35), all in References II.

⁴ At this point the almost insurmountable difficulties in translating the two German words *Sein* and *Seiendem,* so central in Heidegger's thinking, must be taken into account. In ordinary usage, both words stand for "being" or "something existing." But *Sein* in Heidegger's terminology implies a genuine ontological dimension; *Seiendem* less so, or perhaps only derivatively.

⁵ Following Heidegger, his *dasein*-analytic disciples constantly stress the difference between what is considered basic, *grund-legend, a priori,* and that which is merely a derivative or less basic aspect of a phenomenon. This clearly reflects Heidegger's dichotomy between *Sein* and *Seiendem,* the ontological and ontic, known as the "ontological difference." The problems built into such differentiation are obvious. For example, by definition, the empirical observations of clinical psychiatry do not belong in the realm of a basic structure which has an ontological dimension. Hence the necessity to constantly ascertain levels of basicness, to reconcile in some manner the stuff of clinical practice with "that transcendental structure which foremostly or *a priori* underlies all emotional structure as the condition of its possibility" (*die Festigkeit des transzendentalen Gefüges, das allem seelischen Gefüge als die Bedingung seiner Möglichkeit von vornherein und apriorisch zu Grunde liegt*). Out of this dilemma much discussion and many attempts at what seems to me rather unconvincing and sterile differentiation have arisen, (4, p. 304), (20), (36), (37), (38, particularly pp. 300-315), all in References I.

⁶ Speaking at a panel discussion at a meeting of the Washington Psychoanalytic Society on October 13, 1961.

⁷ Harold Searles (II, 32) has extensively elaborated on the significance of this concept in schizophrenia.

⁸ At this point I must mention one work which seems to present an exception to the trend discussed here—at least in some respects. Unlike most others, it reflects an awareness of the drama of self-confrontation and self-concealment as manifest in the polarity "hidden, unconscious versus manifest, conscious." This is the book *Psychotherapie in anthropologischer Sicht,* Stuttgart: Enke, 1961, by Walter Bräutigam, in my opinion a work that stands out among the others mentioned.

Bräutigam uses mainly the poles "depth" and "surface" in order to unfold between them the panorama of a person's precarious existence between self-alienation from and overexposure to what might be considered the deep and hidden in him.

In one respect, Bräutigam makes clear, the polarity between the hidden or deep and the manifest or superficial is relative to a shifting center. This seems in line with much modern theorizing about mental functioning—including such processes as perceiving, memorizing, and thinking. In these theories mental and emotional functioning is a matter of a relative balance of forces. Central to this balance is the concept of focusing. Focusing implies the shutting out of the unessential. The unessential then, to some degree at least, becomes the hidden. The ability to focus, in other words—and along with it the ability to shut out—also structures the realm of the hidden or unconscious, preventing adequate mental functioning. Psychotic states, for instance, as observed either in cases of fragmented schizophrenia or in LSD experiments, reflect an upset of this balance by an uncontrolled flooding of the mental arena with the normally hidden or unconscious.

But also, in order that the conscious mental functioning not become dried up, stereotyped and, eventually, equally inefficient, channels to the hidden or unconscious must be kept open. A sort of dialectical communication of the conscious personality must be maintained with its hidden, unconscious parts. In the framework of psychoanalytic thinking, this dialectical communication with the usually hidden has been conceptualized in various ways. One aspect, for example, can be understood as regression in the service of the Ego (Kris).

On the other hand, Bräutigam emphasizes, there exists a more hierarchical relationship between surface and depth. And it is in this respect that we speak more properly of an arena of self-confrontation as mentioned above. But it is this hierarchical relationship which appears also more elusive. This is the case particularly when the "deep" becomes more identified with bodily feelings and processes, with more archaic sensations. The "deeper" these seem to be, the harder they can, it seems, be conceptualized in everyday rational terms (or secondary processes) and be illuminated in operational frameworks. In trying to illuminate these more elusive aspects, Bräutigam also seems to resort more to the de-differentiation of concepts, thereby becoming increasingly vulnerable to the critical considerations outlined above.

[9] Again, Bräutigam's book appears in this area also as an exception. It provides a very perceptive account of the physician's complex and peculiarly two-sided relationship with his patient, in which involvement and distance, expertness and ignorance, participation and analysis of this participation are all significant elements—although here also some of the above critical considerations apply.

[10] And although in 1935 he felt the need to dissociate himself from the "philosophy" of the party hacks, there is nothing to suggest that the Nazis' systematic inhumanity appalled him. W. Kaufmann discusses Heidegger's relationship to Nazism (I, 11, p. 343).

[11] Many existentialist and *daseins*-analytic interpretations of schizophrenia, although implying or professing an immediate grasp of the essentials of another person's existence, nevertheless often continue to reflect in this grasp the attitudes of the organically oriented observer, which I described in another essay (II, 35), as characteristic for much of the present European scene. Binswanger, for example, after having analyzed Ellen West in a *daseins*-analytic framework, seems to conceive of her illness nonetheless as a process in the Kraepelinian tradition. He writes, "in our case (Ellen West) we see no other possibility than this: an unknown something, which cannot be entirely explained from heredity, milieu and experience, appears to initiate and maintain this process" (p. 355).

References I

Numerous books about existentialism and existential psychotherapy have been published in English. The following introductory treatments, in addition to the references mentioned in the text of this essay, can be

recommended. These references contain ample bibliographies of the
works of Kierkegaard, Nietzsche, Sartre, and Camus.

1. Barret, W. *Irrational man*. New York: Doubleday, 1958.
2. Grene, M. *Introduction to existentialism* (first published as *Dreadful freedom*). Chicago: Phoenix Books, University of Chicago Press, 1959.
3. ———. *Heidegger*. New York: Hillary House, 1957. (A readable introduction to Heidegger.)
4. Heidegger, M. *Existence and being*. London: Vision Press, 1968.
5. Jaspers, K. *The way to wisdom*. New Haven: Yale University Press, 1951.
6. ———. *Man in the modern age*. London: Routledge, 1933.
7. ———. *The perennial scope of philosophy*. London: Routledge, 1950.
8. ———. *The origins and goal of history*. New Haven: Yale University Press, 1953.
9. ———. *Reason and anti-reason in our time*. New Haven: Yale University Press, 1953.
10. Kaufmann, W. *Existentialism from Dostoevsky to Sartre*. New York: Meridian Books, 1956. (Contains an introduction written by Heidegger to the essay "What is metaphysics?", translated by Kaufmann.)
11. ———. *From Shakespeare to existentialism*. New York: Doubleday, 1960. (This book contains a bibliography of the works of Martin Heidegger which appeared up to 1958.)
12. May, R., Angel, E., and Ellenberger H. F., eds. *Existence: a new dimension in psychiatry and psychology*. New York: Basic Books, 1958. (This work contains an extensive introduction by the editors, as well as representative samples of the writings of L. Binswanger, E. Minkowski, E. Straus, V. E. von Gebsattel, and others.)
13. May, R., ed. *Existential psychology*. New York: Random House, 1961. (This work contains a bibliography of most of the important works on existential psychotherapy and phenomenology presently available to the English reader. It was arranged and annotated by Joseph Lyons.)
14. Rossman, K., and Kolle, K., eds. *Offener Horizont, Festschrift für Karl Jaspers*. Munich: Piper, 1953.

15. Schilp, P., ed. *The philosophy of Karl Jaspers.* Library of Living Philosophers. New York: Tudor Publishing, 1957. (German edition. Stuttgart: Kohlhammer, 1957.)
16. Weigert, E., Existentialism and its relations to psychotherapy. *Psychiatry* 12: 399-412, 1949.

References II

1. Binswanger L. *Grundformen und Erkenntnis menschlichen Daseins.* Zurich: Niehaus, 1953.
2. ———. Geschehnis und Erlebnis. In *Ausgewählte Vorträge und Aufsätze.* Bd. I. Bern: Huber, 1947.
3. ———. *Schizophrenie.* Pfullingen: Neske, 1957.
4. ———. *Ausgewählte Vorträge und Aufsätze.* Bd. II. Bern: Francke, 1955.
5. Bleuler, E. *Dementia praecox or the group of schizophrenias* (1911). New York: International Universities Press, 1950.
6. Boss, M. *Meaning and content of sexual perversions: a daseins-analytic approach to the psychopathology of the phenomenon of love.* New York: Grune and Stratton, 1949.
7. ———. *Psychoanalyse und Daseinsanalytik.* Bern-Stuttgart: Huber, 1957.
8. ———. *The analysis of dreams.* New York: Philosophical Library, 1958.
9. Bowen, M. A Family concept of schizophrenia. In *The etiology of schizophrenia,* ed. D. D. Jackson. New York: Basic Books, 1960.
10. Bridgman, P. *The way things are.* Cambridge: Harvard University Press, 1959.
11. Buytendijk, F. *Allgemeine Theorie der menschlichen Haltung und Bewegung.* Heidelberg: Springer, 1956.
12. Christian, P. *Das Personverständnis im modernen medizinischen Denken.* Tubingen: J. C. B. Mohr, 1952.
13. ———. Zur Phänomenologie des leiblichen Daseins. *Jahrbuch für Psychologie, Psychotherapie und Medizinische Anthropologie* 7: 2-9 Freiburg-Munich: Alber, 1960.
14. Cohen, M. Countertransference and anxiety. *Psychiatry.* 15: 231-245, 1952.
15. Dewey, J. *Human nature and conduct: an introduction to social psychology.* New York: Henry Holt, 1922.

16. Elrod N. Unglück steckt an. *Psyche* 14: 336-359, 1960.
17. Frank, P. *Modern science and its philosophy.* New York: George Braziller, 1955.
18. Heidegger, M. *Die Selbstbehauptung der deutschen Universität.* Breslau: Korn, 1933.
19. ———. *Sein und Zeit.* Halle: Niemeyer, 1927; *Being and time.* Translated by J. Macquarrie and E. Robinson. New York: Harper & Row, 1962.
20. Kunz, H. Die Bedeutung der Daseinsanalytik Martin Heideggers für die Psychologie und philosophische Anthropologie. In *Martin Heideggers Einfluss auf die Wissenschaft.* Bern: Francke, 1949.
21. Lidz, T. Schizophrenia and the family. *Psychiatry* 21: 21, 1958.
22. Marcel, G. *The mystery of being.* Chicago: Regnery, 1960. Gateway edition. 2 vol. (Cf. particularly Vol. I, pp. 127-153.)
23. ———. Qu'attendez-vous de medicine? Paris: Librairie Plon, 1949.
24. Mead, G. *Mind, self and society: from the standpoint of a social behaviorist.* Edited with an Introduction by Charles W. Morris. Chicago: The University of Chicago Press, 1936.
25. Merleau-Ponty, M. *Phenomenologie de la perception.* 4th ed. Paris: Gallimard, 1945.
26. ———. *La structure du comportment.* Paris: Presse Universitaire de France, 1949.
27. Muschg, W. Zerschwatzte Dichtung. In *Die Zerstörung der deutschen Literatur.* Bern: Francke, 1956.
28. Piaget, J. *The construction of reality in the child.* Translated by M. Cook. New York: Basic Books, 1954.
29. Pfister, O. Karl Jaspers als Sigmund Freuds Widersacher. *Psyche* 6: 241, 1952/1953.
30. Rapoport, A. *Operational philosophy: integrating knowledge and action.* New York: Harper, 1954.
31. Russell, B. *Human knowledge: its scope and limits.* New York: Simon and Schuster, 1948.
32. Searles, H. Integration and differentiation in schizophrenia. *Journal of Nervous and Mental Diseases* 129: 542-550, 1959.
33. Schaffer, L., Wynne, L. C., Day, J., Ryckoff, I., and Halperin, A. On the nature and sources of the psychiatrist's experience with the family of the schizophrenic. *Psychiatry* 25: 32-45, 1962.
34. Stierlin, H. Individual therapy and hospital structure, In *Psychotherapy of the psychoses,* ed. Arthur Burton. New York: Basic Books, 1961.

35. ———. Contrasting attitudes toward the psychoses in Europe and the United States. *Psychiatry* 21: 141-147, 1958.
36. ———. Verstehen und wissenschaftliche Theoriebildung in der Psychoanalyse. *Psyche* 6: 389-400, 1952/1953.
37. Straus, E. Aesthesiology and hallucinations. In *Existence,* ed. Rollo May. New York: Basic Books, 1958. (See pp. 139-160.)
38. Szasz, T. *The myth of mental illness.* New York: Hoeber-Harper, 1961.
39. Szilasi, W. Die Erfahrungsgrundlage der Daseinsanalyse. *Schweizer Archiv für Neurologie und Psychiatrie* 67: 74, 1951.
40. Thiel, M. Die Distanzproblematik in der Philosophie. *Studium Generale* 4: 297, 1951.
41. Thomas, H. *Anorexia nervosa.* Stuttgart: Klett, 1961.
42. von Gebsattel, V. Die Welt des Zwangskranken. *Monatsschrift für Psychiatrie und Neurologie* 99: 1074, 1938. Abridged English translation by Sylvia Koppel and Ernest Angel in *Existence,* ed. Rollo May. New York: Basic Books, 1958. (See pp. 139-160.)
43. von Weizsäcker, V. *Der Gestaltkreis.* Stuttgart: Thieme, 1947.
44. Weigert, E. Countertransference and self-analysis. *International Journal of Psychiatry* 35: 242-247, 1954.
45. Werner, H. *Comparative Psychology of Mental Development.* 2nd rev. ed. New York: International Universities Press, 1957.
46. Wynne, L., Ryckoff, I. M., Day, J., and Hirsch, S. I. Pseudo-mutuality in the family relations of schizophrenics. *Psychiatry* 21: 205-221, 1958.
47. ———. Day, J., and Ryckoff, I. M. Maintenance of stereotyped roles in the family of schizophrenics. *Archives of General Psychiatry* 1: 109-115, 1959.
48. Zutt, J. Vom gelebten welthaften Leibe. Congress Report. 2nd International Congress for Psychiatry. Zürich, 1957. Vol. IV: 444-445.
49. ———, and C. Kulenkampff. *Das paranoide Syndrom in anthropologischer Sicht.* Berlin-Göttingen-Heidelberg: Springer, 1958.

Chapter 2

Bleuler's Concept of Schizophrenia

A meaningful concept allows us to approach the essential. It ties specific insights to the totality of available knowledge. It makes for increasing differentiation and integration of this knowledge, and it exerts a dynamic push which leads to new concepts, new perspectives, and new questions.

Schizophrenia is a concept with such meaning and dynamic strength. It was Eugen Bleuler who put it before the scientific world in 1911. Since then this concept has guided countless psychiatrists, causing them to focus on certain aspects of the disturbance while excluding others.

Bleuler's concept of schizophrenia is still meaningful; this I have tried to show elsewhere (8). However, as much as this concept has enriched and stimulated our thinking, it has also tended to confuse crucial issues.

This confusion remained almost unnoticed because many people knew only part of Bleuler's work. Thus, the English- and German-speaking publics, as a rule, built up different notions of Bleuler. Most American and English readers are familiar only with Bleuler's monograph "Dementia Praecox or the Group of Schizophrenias." Originally published in 1911 as a volume of

Aschaffenburg's *Handbuch*, its English translation by J. Zinkin appeared in 1950 (5). This translation had five printings in rapid succession. In Germany, however, the monograph was never reprinted. Bleuler's ideas on schizophrenia became known to German students and psychiatrists mainly through his textbook of psychiatry, of which six editions appeared during Bleuler's lifetime. Compared to what we find in the monograph, his textbook account of schizophrenia is not only very condensed but also suggests different perspectives. The question poses itself: What was Bleuler's real view of schizophrenia?

This question is difficult to answer. Bleuler's work on schizophrenia, multilayered and complex, offers many aspects. While reflecting a strong integrative trend, it nevertheless seems fragmented at times. Not without justification did Freud point out that Bleuler, the originator of the concept "ambivalence," appeared himself ambivalent and half-hearted in many of his utterances (6). And further, Bleuler's position on schizophrenia shifted between the inception of the concept in 1911 and his death in 1939. These shifts, reflected in his articles in German psychiatric journals and in the statements of his textbook, are now all well known.

In the following remarks, I shall try to give a short overview of the central propositions which Bleuler held in regard to schizophrenia, but I shall also mention some shifts and unclarities by which he eroded these propositions. I consider this an attempt to balance the account of Bleuler's concept of schizophrenia which I gave elsewhere (8).

Bleuler appears situated in the center of two psychiatric mainstreams, one safely embedded and widely recognized, the other precariously turbulent and far from being acknowledged. Kraepelin was the chief proponent of the former, Freud of the latter. In Bleuler's concept of schizophrenia, these two streams meet. Bleuler acknowledges this in the foreword to his 1911 monograph, where Kraepelin and Freud receive equal tribute.

Bleuler, in a sense, seemed destined to become the mediator between these two psychiatric traditions. Like nearly all other continental psychiatrists, he was exposed to the spell which Kraepelin cast. He considered Kraepelin's delineation of the psychoses as the decisive step toward a scientific psychiatry. But he also recognized Freud's genius. In his own publications he took notice of Freud's analytic writings as early as 1906, and it was at about the same time that Jung and Abraham, in his Burghölzi hospital in Zurich, began to apply analytic insights to the understanding of psychotic disturbances.

By and large Bleuler accepted Kraepelin's delineation and subdivision of the clinical entity "dementia praecox." This means he accepted the subgroups catatonia, hebephrenia, paraphrenia, etc. (which Kraepelin, in his turn, had taken over from Kahlbaum and others), and the corresponding well-known symptomatology: hallucinations, delusions, stereotypies, catatonic stupor, catatonic excitement, as well as dementia and others. He accepted Kraepelin's underlying notion that some organic alteration or process—most likely a brain disease on the order of progressive paresis or Alzheimer's disease—was at the root of this symptomatology. And he accepted, finally, Kraepelin's assumption that the disease, in general, had a downhill course.

While Kraepelin thus provided the nosological framework, Freud supplied the main ideas with which Bleuler could build a psychological theory. In his *Interpretation of Dreams*, Freud had elaborated the mechanisms of displacement, condensation, turning into the opposite, etc., whereby certain wishes and conflicts of the dreamer are both concealed and—to the analytically perceptive observer—revealed. These wishes and conflicts gave evidence of powerful affective constellations or "complexes." Of these, the sexual complex was the most important.

Bleuler found these same mechanisms and complexes at the root of the schizophrenic's symptomatology. The latter's delusions, hallucinations, stereotypies, mannerisms, etc., began to make sense when viewed in this light. Bleuler adduced example after example to prove this. In so doing he outlined a rich clinical phenomenology of the disturbance. He paid particular attention to how the pathogenic complexes overpowered and perverted the balancing impact of language. Instead of tying the individual to a cosmos of conventional meanings, obligations, and expectations, language served to provide a shortcut to wish-fulfillments and to spin out a web of private fantasies. Bleuler's concept of "autistic thinking," similar to, but not identical with, Freud's concept of the primary process, served to emphasize this point.

Bleuler pointed to the essential similarity between dreams and schizophrenic symptomatology. There existed only this difference: dreams provided a legitimate sanctuary for the (relatively) undisguised reign of the complex and for the abuse of conventional logic and language; the dreamer will, after all, return to waking life. The schizophrenic, in contrast, remains stuck with the consequences of such abuse. In making his logic and his expressions persistently idiosyncratic, he runs the danger of spoiling them for ordinary communication. His nightmare then remains his reality.

This analytic view of schizophrenic symptomatology brought meaning to what until then had appeared a potpourri of freakish or bizarre derangements. As a theory it was at once comprehensive and simple. But a crucial problem remained: How could this view be reconciled with the tenets of the Kraepelinian nosology as outlined above?

The analytic theory, conceived on a purely psychological level, provided no bridges to the anatomy and chemistry of the brain. Freud recognized this clearly but was unconcerned with it as an immediate problem. Not so Bleuler. He seemed compelled to do justice to Kraepelin's propositions. Thus, he looked for a complementing theory which, if it could not establish such bridges between psychology and brain pathology, would at least open the way to them. This had to be a kind of metapsychology which could fit in with the analytic theory but which would, at the same time, be more fundamental and closer to physiology than the latter.

Bleuler believed he had found the theory which could be made to suit this purpose. This was Semon's theory of psychic engrams (*Engramme*) and their associative links (2). Semon's psychology of associations appeared to Bleuler more comprehensive and explanatory then the one which Wundt and his disciples had made popular. In particular, it seemed to fit the facts of schizophrenia. Thus, Semon must be mentioned along with Kraepelin and Freud when we try to understand Bleuler's thinking about this disturbance.

In following Semon, Bleuler distinguished within the human psyche two basic entities: the engrams and the associative links. The former are stable while the latter are variable; consequently, only the latter can be used to explain symptoms which in themselves vary.

The associations are formed as a result of our experiences. They integrate themselves into clusters which, under certain conditions, can be evoked and be integrated with other clusters. In order to serve our cognitive adaptation, the associations must have a certain looseness; but they also must lend themselves to becoming ordered, "steamlined," and hierarchically organized; that is, they must become goal-directed. Variations exist among individuals and circumstances as to how this adaptive integration is achieved. The associations are normally loosened in dreams, during states of fatigue, lessened attention, and other conditions.

The various associative trends are assumed to compete constantly with each other. The trend with the greatest affective charge (or energy) is bound to win out but might also, under certain conditions, "break loose." These circumstances prevail when there is a weakness or defect in the switches which tame and coordinate the associations. Bleuler speaks of a weakening of the *Schaltspannung* or *Assoziationsspannung,* that is, of the tension which keeps the associations bound and coordinated. But such weakening implies a loosening of associations, and along with it a loss of hierarchic structure and goal-direction of thinking. If such loosening is severe, affects will become fragmented and the inner unity of the personality will be lost. In other words, there will be schizophrenia.

This theory of the weakness of the associative links, of the decreased *Schaltspannung,* when applied to schizophrenia appeared to mediate between the Kraepelinian tenets and psychoanalytic theory. The way was cleared to give due credit to the organic genesis postulated by Kraepelin and his like. "We can assume a decrease in *Schaltspannung,*" writes Bleuler, "which corresponds to the nature of the illness, namely one which is not functional but which is the direct consequence of a direct chemical or anatomical or molecular brain alteration" (2). But also analytic theory (so Bleuler thought) could find its place in the conceptualization. The loosening of the associations, as facilitated by the brain alterations already mentioned, prepared the ground for the free reign of the complexes and, along with that, for the flourishing of schizophrenic symptomatology. This symptomatology could now be seen as either a manifestation of or an attempt at restitution of the loosened associations.

However, this integration of different viewpoints had an unexpected result: it led to a change in, as well as a widening of, the concept of schizophrenia. Thus it raised new perspectives and problems.

While developing this theory of schizophrenia, Bleuler was forced to reshuffle the schizophrenic symptomatology. He had to distinguish between primary and secondary symptoms, and this distinction ran counter to common expectation and usage. Bleuler considered primary the loosening of associations and secondary most of those other symptoms which, in the description of dementia praecox, had up to that point taken the limelight: the delusions, hallucinations, gross stereotypies, and so on.[1] This reshuffling of symptoms thus had the effect of depriving schizophrenia of much of the awe-inspiring, bizarre flamboyance which it had had in the eyes of laymen as well as of professionals. Bleuler's analytic approach to schizophrenia had similar consequences. It tended to tear down that barrier of strangeness which had separated the schizophrenic from so-called normals. In citing example after example of how complexes in one way or the other made persons behave in a schizophrenic manner, he made the schizophrenic look "much more human than otherwise." He therefore refuted the claim of Jaspers and other German psychiatrists that schizophrenic experiences were inaccessible to common understanding. Bleuler put the schizophrenic disturbance into the panorama of everyday human experience. He led the reader to see the schizophrenic disturbance of thinking and affectivity as differing from normal experiences in quantity but not in quality. "Even normal persons," he wrote, "show a number of schizophrenic symptoms when they are emotionally preoccupied, particularly inattentive, or when their attention is concentrated on a single subject. Among these symptoms are peculiar associations, incomplete concepts and ideas, displacements, logical blunders, and stereotypies" (5). At one point he mentions a scientist of his acquaintance who appeared catatonic when preoccupied. And he stated further: ". . . the individual symptom in itself is less important than its intensity and extensiveness, and above all, its relation to the psychological setting" (5). He repeated this statement in his textbook.

Thus Bleuler not only humanized the concept of schizophrenia—that is, linked it to common experience—but also widened it. In accordance with such widening, he noticed the frequency of so-called latent schizophrenia. "There is," he wrote, "also latent schizophrenia, and I am convinced that this is the most frequent form, although admittedly these people hardly ever come for treatment" (5). Schizophrenia, in mild and embryonic forms, was seen as all-pervasive. Bleuler notes that ten of his schoolmates later developed schizophrenia.

This widening further implied a relativizing of the concept. The border between schizophrenia and other psychic conditions became blurred. Schizophrenia, which Bleuler had undertaken to delineate more clearly and, so to speak, more microscopically than had ever been attempted before, seemed to dissolve as a clear-cut entity. In emphasizing that schizophrenic symptoms exaggerated normal experiences, that the psychological setting was all-important, and that there existed many abortive and latent forms of schizophrenia, Bleuler indeed threatened the very Kraepelinian edifice which he had set out to complete and underpin. That was the paradoxical result of his efforts. This result, when taken seriously, would open new and exciting perspectives. But for a long time it did not. The main reason for this lay with Bleuler.

Did Bleuler recognize this paradoxical result of his conceptualizations, and did he reorient his thinking accordingly? I believe that he did so only to a minor degree and that he became increasingly bogged down in the contradictions and complexities which he himself had engendered or laid open. We may remind ourselves at this point that Bleuler had made the splitting the main characteristic of the disturbance, and it became associated with his name. "The splitting," he wrote, "is the prerequisite condition of most of the complicated phenomena of the disease. It is the splitting which gives the peculiar stamp to the entire symtomatology" (5). Could it be that he himself was split in regard to what he "knew" and what he acknowledged about the disturbance? In order to bring some light into this situation, we must understand how this work on schizophrenia was received by his contemporaries.

Bleuler was soon reminded by his colleagues that he was on slippery ground. Along with praise, he incurred vehement criticism. Overwhelmingly the criticism was directed against his psychological theory of schizophrenia, in which he had applied the ideas of Freud. Gruhle, Bumke, Hoche, and nearly all the other stars of contemporary German psychiatry repudiated it in whole or in major part. This was understandable, for not only had Bleuler allowed psychoanalysis to creep into "respectable" psychiatry by the back door, so to speak, he had also implicitly questioned many of the assumptions of this kind of psychiatry. We notice, therefore, bitter emotional undertones in the criticism launched at him, held in check only by respect for his generally recognized stature.

In this situation Bleuler could have sided with Freud and his small group of analysts, who wooed him to join them in a more straightforward manner. But Bleuler did not do so. Thus he saw himself under (more or less veiled) attacks from the two sides he had set out to reconcile. Both sides came to see him as lukewarm and ambivalent with regard to their own cause.

Bleuler found himself in a charged field. In contrast to Freud, who usually disregarded his critics and pursued his lonely path of theory-building, Bleuler became involved in many arguments. It would exceed the intent of this paper if I tried to trace their content in detail. But this much can be said: Bleuler's stand became more and more uncertain and vacillating. Frequently he appeared to contradict or tone down what he had said only a few moments before. Also, from approximately 1913 on, Bleuler began to move away from Freud and to come closer to academic psychiatry. He began to sound defensive about his Freudian leanings. In response to criticism from academic quarters, he wrote, for example: "The illness (schizophrenia) is in my opinion not due to psychic causes (*psychogen*), but a great many of its symptoms are; and some of these come about in ways which Freud and Jung have demonstrated" (1). This over-cautious statement seems a far cry from what he had stated in his 1911 monograph. Or, we read: "Critics should realize that far too much in my theory has been considered Freudian" (1). Numerous such examples could be given.

Along with deemphasizing Freud's contributions, Bleuler asserted his basic agreement with Kraepelin. He became more insistent in claiming organic causes for the disturbance. Although we read in his text-book, "We do not know as yet on what the pathologic process is based," we learn immediately thereafter:

In acute stages various kinds of changes in the ganglion cells are found. In old cases the brain mass is reduced a little; many ganglion cells, especially in the second and third layer, are changed in various ways; sometimes the fibrils of the cells and the axis cylinder look diseased. The glia is regularly involved: various changes of its cell varieties, increase of the small cells; there is a deposit of pigment and other catabolic materials, increase of the finer glia fibers and other things besides (3).

Although he qualified the meaning of these statements, Bleuler's message to the reader seems clear.

Still later Bleuler emphasized the hereditary basis for the disease—again to be conceived along organic lines. In the sixth edition of this textbook, the last one which he himself prepared, we read: "The essential cause, which most likely is necessary to schizophrenia, lies in an inherited disposition" (4).

Thus in the older Bleuler, the organic, Kraepelinian orientation clearly won out over the psychoanalytic. Bleuler demonstrated this in his stand on therapy. He wrote, for example: "Most schizophrenics are not to be treated at all, or at any rate outside of asylums," and

Expensive treatments, that are of no use anyway, should be cautioned against, above everything. Moreover, the economic and moral interests of the healthy members of the family should not be sacrificed for a hopeless treatment. On the other hand, the supreme remedy which in the majority of cases still accomplishes very much and sometimes everything that can be desired is training for work under conditions that are as normal as possible (3).

We note the absence of any recommendations for some sort of analytically oriented psychotherapy, and we note also an attitude toward the schizophrenic's family which seems curiously at odds with many modern insights (7, 9) and the tenets of the following chapter.

Despite Bleuler's increasing detachment from Freud, he continued to acknowledge his debt to the latter from time to time. He praised Freud outspokenly in the foreword to the fifth edition of his textbook (although not in the foreword to the sixth edition). In a sense he never seems to have given up on the task of reconciling the two psychiatric traditions, but this task clearly overtaxed him. Reconciliation remains to be carried out. But where such reconciliation seems impossible, we must revise our concepts.

Note

[1] There was, of course, something even more primary than the loosening of associations: the brain alterations which gave rise to them. Accordingly, Bleuler differentiated at times between "organic" and "psychic" primary symptoms, of which the former were in a sense more "primary" than the latter.

References

1. Bleuler, E. Kritik der Freudschen Theorien. *Allg. Z. Psychiatrie* 70: 665-718, 1913.
2. ———. Störung der Assoziationsspannung/Ein Elementarsymptom der Schizophrenie. *Allg. Z. Psychiatrie* 74: 1-21, 1920.
3. ———. *Textbook of psychiatry.* Translated by A. A. Brill from *Lehrbuch der Psychiatrie.* 4th ed. New York: Macmillan, 1924, p. 442.
4. ———. *Lehrbuch der psychiatrie.* 6th ed. Berlin: Springer, 1937, p. 316.
5. ———. *Dementia praecox or the group of schizophrenias.* Translated by J. Zinkin. New York: International Universities Press, 1950.
6. Freud, S. Selbstdarstellung. *Gesammelte Werke.* Vol 14. London: Imago Publishing Company, 1948, p. 77.
7. Lidz, T., Fleck, S., and Cornelison, A. R. *Schizophrenia and the Family.* New York: International Universities Press, 1965.

8. Stierlin, H. Bleuler's concept of schizophrenia in the light of our
    present experience. In *International Symposium on the Psychotherapy of
    Schizophrenia* (Lausanne, 1964). New York/Basel: Karger, 1965, pp.
    42-55.
9. Wynne, L., and Singer, M. T. Thought disorder and family
    relations of schizophrenics. *Archives of General Psychiatry* 9: 191-198,
    199-206, 1963.

The Adaptation to the "Stronger" Person's Reality

"Independence is a middle-class prejudice," said George Bernard Shaw, "for we are all dependent on each other." Yet we are dependent in different ways, in varying degrees, and with varying awareness. In the following pages, I want to deal with some of the problems and vicissitudes inherent in human interdependence, hoping thereby to throw some light on the human condition in which this interdependence seems to take its most tragic and destructive form—schizophrenia.

Interdependence between two organisms is often called *symbiosis*. This term derives from biology, where it covers, as a rule, three phenomena: commensalism, mutualism, and parasitism. The second of these characterizes an interdependent relationship which is productive for each partner, and it is an extension of this meaning which I shall be using here. That is, I propose to let symbiosis denote a relationship of intense interdependence between two people, having the potential of becoming mutually beneficial, mutually harmful, or both, in a wide scale of variations and gradations. This differs from the way in which the term is frequently used in psychiatric thinking, to denote *only* mutual harm—a usage which has become so common that the question arises whether it is wise to try to force the word back into a wider and nonjudgmental meaning. I think, however, that much confusion has arisen from restricting the word to mean mutual harm, and that this often obscures the intricate nature of the relationship in question.

An example of a human symbiosis which is predominantly beneficial is the normal relationship between mother and child. The partners in this relationship are indispensable to each other for the fulfillment of many vital needs: the child fulfills the mother's need for mothering and the mother the child's need for being mothered.

Such a relationship is more a moving, dialectic process than a static interchange. As Therese Benedek has stated, "Parallel with the developmental processes which lead to confidence in the infant, the mother, through introjecting the gratifying experience of mothering, establishes *her* self-confidence, her trust in her motherliness. These are reciprocal ego-developments" (2). Such a healthy, changing symbiosis permits mutual growth. It will lead to a deeper mutual self-confirmation, accompanied by an increase in mutual esteem and love. It will foster each partner's individuation and relative autonomy.

A static and pathological symbiosis, however, might best be described as a mutual enslavement. It leaves no room for developmental change. The partners form a closed symbiotic system which by its very nature is self-perpetuating and self-petrifying. A separation becomes increasingly difficult.

How do closed symbiotic systems come into being? What is it that prevents growth? There is undoubtedly a strong tendency inherent in any living organism to get stuck in a certain developmental equilibrium and in a certain constellation of available need fulfillments. Thus, there are many human cultures which, left to themselves, today remain stuck in a stage that corresponds to the stone age. Similarly, each human life seems to be characterized by the everpresent threat of getting stuck. But this threat seems to become greatest when there is a culturally sanctioned amassing of power and exploitative ability in one person or group of persons. For it very often removes for the "privileged" and more powerful person the stimulus to gear his actions to the needs of his subordinate partner. This fact seems to underlie Lord Acton's famous statement that power corrupts, and absolute power corrupts absolutely; for power makes it unnecessary for its wielder to respect and appreciate the needs of other persons. In other words, the exploitation of his power provides him with enough secondary gain to make any change in his own personality appear unnecessary. Corresponding to the degree of his own rigidity, the wielder of power will then tend to force, by the threat of heavy and frightening sanctions, the dependent person to adapt himself to the interpersonal status quo—that is, to the stronger person's reality.

There are many such interpersonal constellations characterized by rigidity and controlling power in one partner and adaptive maneuvers in the other. Examples are found in the relationship between subordinate and boss in a totalitarian system, between husband and wife in a patriarchic household, and between master and slave, some aspects of this relationship being relevant in the traditional relationship between whites and blacks in the southern United States. In these examples, the greater the dependency of the underprivileged partner on the stronger one, the more encompassing the adaptation required.

Characteristically, this adaptation includes a psychological outwitting of the stronger person. The black servant, for instance, is often described as developing, behind the facade of the childishly servile blockhead, into a far more perceptive observer and clever practitioner of human psychology than his white master. The outwardly dominated Southern woman traditionally makes psychological weapons out of the very attributes of her weakness, using her fragility, her doll-like and playful charm, and so on, to manipulate her flattered protector. Similarly, the dependent

Communist, harassed by the necessity to adjust to a constantly shifting party line, is reported to develop a peculiar kind of *Zwiedenken* (double thinking)—a mixture of opportunistic manipulation and ideological self-confusion (10)—in order to survive. These manipulations can all be described as the weaker partner's effort to make himself as indispensable to the more powerful person as the latter is to him. They are his attempts to symbiotize the relationship.

However, successful as this kind of psychological outwitting often may be, it is also crippling and anxiety-laden. It does not lead to increasing experiences of greater respect, mutual confirmation, and gratefulness, but rather thrives on a ground of bitter resentment and hate. Further, although the weaker person often gains perceptivity, manipulative ability, and consequent psychological power through his adaptive endeavors, he may use up all his creative abilities by "living on a volcano." (With almost these words did Khrushchev, in his famous speech delivered at the Twentieth Party Congress, describe life around the aging Stalin.) Therefore, the secondary manipulation of the stronger person by the underprivileged one is not conducive to a mutually liberating relationship, but to a mutually crippling enslavement; that is, to a static and unhealthy symbiosis.

SYMBIOTIZATION IN SCHIZOPHRENIA

I now propose to examine another significant constellation which throws further light on certain aspects of the adaptation to the stronger person's reality—almost an experiment of nature which one can observe in the study of human psychopathology. This is the special kind of early interpersonal relationship which many psychiatrists today—basing themselves on studies made by Sullivan (15), Hill (6), Fromm-Reichmann (4, 5), Lidz (9), and many others—recognize as an essential factor in the later development of a schizophrenic way of life. Lidz, for example, considers schizophrenia an extreme form of asocial withdrawal, specifically characterized by efforts to modify reality into a more tenable form by distorting the internalized symbolization of reality. The distortion of symbols separates the patient from the remainder of his culture, since his perceptions and his modes of communication are idiosyncratic.

In the ideal-typical situation, which prepares the ground for this later asocial withdrawal, reality for the little child is basically represented through one parent, usually the mother or the mothering one. Later the whole social power field of the family clan, as shown particularly by Lidz, contributes to the formation of the schizophrenic's "minority reality." This field may, for example, reinforce the mother's needs for the child, or it may structure a situation in which the child's sickness fulfills a role essential for the family's functioning. In the present context, however, I am primarily interested in the mother. She often needs the child, because of her own pathology, as a means of self-justification and self-confirmation. She therefore puts the child under pressure to experience and interpret reality as she, the mother, wants it to be. This applies most significantly to the perception and interpretation of inner, psychological reality; that is, of the actions, feelings, and motives which determine the character of the mother-child relationship. Regarding this perception and interpretation, one can probably establish one general rule: however strongly the mother may make the child the recipient of her anxious overprotectiveness, of her desperate strivings for self-confirmation, and however much she may use him as an instrument for her own erotic, prestige, and mothering needs which she cannot satisfy otherwise, the child, on his part, must strongly believe and confirm by his actions that all of the mother's behavior is an outgrowth and proof of love. The child is thus forced into the dilemma which is typical for the interpersonal climate in a totalitarian environment. He is confronted with the alternative of either accepting the mother's crippling definition of reality or losing her protection. It is a dilemma that Bateson (1) recently described as a "double bind," characterizing it as a central element of a schizophrenic way of life.

If one now compares this adaptive pattern, taken from clinical psychopathology, with the subordinate-boss, husband-wife, and master-slave situations, several points emerge.

First, the reality to which the weaker partner had to adapt, as described in these earlier examples, was more culturally than psychologically determined. That is, the specific form of enforced adaptation arose from such general sociological factors as the given political and ideological climate and the culturally defined roles of the participants. In the case of the schizophrenic, however, this reality is decisively determined by the personal character and needs of the mother or mothering one. The mother's needs are, in turn, determined by the sociological field in which she is living. That is, her own interpersonal relations, the given family situation, and the possibilities for growth and satisfaction open to her within the framework of her culture have their impact on these needs. Nevertheless, it is, after all, her own individual, rigid, and—in relationship to her child—powerful personality which, in a most important sense, represents to him the prototype of human reality. It is precisely this fact that determines the unavoidable collision one day between this reality orientation, geared to the mother of the family, and the other, conventional reality orientation, represented by the given culture. This child will, in other words, some day have to face the stressful fact that he, equipped only with his mother's edition of reality, has to live in a world in which most people act, feel, and value differently.

It is known from clinical experience that most schizophrenic breaks—the transformations of a precarious schizoid adjustment into a state of psychotic maladjustment—occur during late adolescence. This is, in one respect, a period of biological upheavals and reintegrations. But it is also the time at which the person has to adjust to an adult reality of interpersonal relations and professional responsibilities. He has to learn to manage new types of intimate encounters and practical problems of living, tasks that require radically different interpersonal techniques from those he had learned previously. Adolescence is, in other words, the time at which the person can no longer postpone the collision between his mother-geared minority reality and the conventional majority reality. A patient suffering from schizophrenia of long standing said, "I could have easily lived in the world had it turned out to be as Mother represented it to me. But growing up I realized the world was different. And I broke."

This unavoidability of conflict between two reality orientations does not, in any comparable degree, exist for the previously outlined cases. The roles of the black servant, of the woman in the patriarchal family situation, and of the member of a totalitarian society often force the person into an extremely difficult schizoid way of life, but he is frequently spared the stress of an unavoidable and radical reorientation. The double bind becomes somewhat neutralized by the fact that it is widely experienced and culturally accepted. Through the absence of comparisons (and thereby of situations that could tempt him), his adaptation to "living on a volcano" presents itself as a culturally defined normalcy. For no man is free to choose and likely to be tempted by what he has never heard or dreamed of. It is only when he gets in touch with, or makes himself susceptible to, a different way of life, that personal upheavals and states of crisis occur that in many respects suggest an experience of psychotic disintegration.[1]

A second point emerges when one compares the culturally determined adaptation to the stronger person's reality with this adaptation in the early situation of the schizophrenic. In the latter case, the pressure to accept reality as it is embodied by the mother—in this case a clear-cut minority reality—hits the child at a very early and critical stage of his development. It is at this time that the emotional and intellectual basis is laid for the kind of inner stability and integratedness which may be called ego strength. Ego strength is an integral part of a character structure which is able to stand stresses, to grow, and to relate productively to the surrounding world, even through one's life situation and personality may change—for example, through aging. Much in this area has still to be clarified. Important, however, among the many factors necessary for the development of this ego strength is certainly the capacity for testing reality, for understanding complexities, and for differentiating one's own and other people's actions, feelings, and motives. It is exactly during this stage of the beginning differentiation and development of the instruments of reality testing, a phase of tender susceptibility and plasticity, that the child becomes a target of the mother's indoctrination. From this follows a further essential difference from the culturally determined situations. For the pressures which foster a schizoid conformity, distorting and warding off important aspects of outer and inner reality, occur at a time when the person is incomparably more susceptible and malleable, and so much more vulnerable.

Therefore, the chances of the child's symbiotizing, without personality damage, his relationship with the mother appear to be comparatively small. For he lacks many of the cognitive facilities by which the differentiated adult obtains and organizes his observational data. In the cultural examples, these facilities were a part of the weaker partner's self-protecting tools in the symbiosis. The little child headed for a schizophrenic break stands unprepared.

Thus there are two factors—the unavoidability of the conflict between the two reality orientations, and the much earlier and more deeply exerted pressure for adaptation to the stronger one's reality—which may explain the decompensatory, ego-disruptive nature of the schizophrenic break, in contrast to the still compensated, though difficult and crippling kind of adjustment outlined in my first examples.

However, these two factors seem insufficient to explain a

specific schizophrenic development. Among other factors, constitutional or hereditary disposition may be assumed. Such a disposition is not only postulated by most organically oriented psychiatrists, and especially such geneticists as Kallmann (7), but also acknowledged by such analysts as Sandor Rado (11) and Melanie Klein (8). Klein, for example, characterizes this disposition as an inability or deficiency in the child to gratefully accept the mother's breast. In the child's ability for joyful and grateful acceptance of the breast she sees the prototype of that significant human ability which permits one to accept goodness from others, in the widest sense of the word. This is the basis for all later capacity to accept love and experience joy in doing so. However, if this capacity remains underdeveloped, destructive and hostile impulses gain dominance in the child. He becomes fixed in the increasingly unbearable dilemma of having to destroy what he basically wants. He will be unable to incorporate that love and goodness which he so urgently needs to build up a strong feeling of self-worth. Thus the primary love offered by the mother in the form of the breast, as well as all later love he may find, will be devalued, fought, and distorted by him in a paranoid way.

This assumption, however, seems to do justice to only a part of the observed phenomena. I would like to suggest the plausibility of regarding the hereditary or constitutional element as a potential for maximal responsiveness of the child to the pressure for symbiotization as it is exerted by the mother. The child headed for schizophrenia is, in other words, unusually vulnerable to the mother's needs and demands; they take on for him great depth and meaning—almost an all-or-nothing quality; and he reacts to them with more intensity than do other children. He is more geared to an interpersonal emotional exchange and thus, comparatively, more dependent on it. This explains, partially at least, the frequently amazing intensity that one encounters in the transference relationships of schizophrenics. This intensive element will, in turn, be experienced by the schizophrenic as such a threat that he has to defend himself against it by mechanisms which suggest great distance, aloofness, and withdrawal; that is, by the seemingly exact opposite of an intense relationship. Something like this was suggested by Frieda Fromm-Reichmann shortly before her death, when she characterized schizophrenics as people who have a disposition to give and need more love than others (5).

The early onset and the magnitude of the pressure for symbiotization as exerted by the mother, together with a readiness of the child to respond to this with particular intensity, throw some light on the frequent unavoidability of the schizo-phrenic catastrophe. This symbiotic process has, however, still another aspect which may clarify some characteristics of the schizophrenic way of life and the therapeutic problems resulting from it.

The child predisposed to schizophrenia and pressured by maternal indoctrination has, as was shown above, less chance of consciously integrating complex data than the differentiated adult. He is thus, one may say, weaker than the adult. It may be assumed, however—and here is an important point—that the undifferentiated child has also capacities for obtaining and organizing data which most adults have lost. Among these capacities, the one which appears to be of the greatest significance is the ability to assess, in a particularly immediate and astute way, feelings and moods in another person who may not be fully aware of them. This capacity seems to correspond closely to what Sullivan called "empathy." There are grounds for believing that this is a capacity related to a preverbal and prelogical developmen-tal stage, akin to certain innate, instinctive capacities of animals. Schachtel (12, 13) most convincingly described how, along with the crystallization and development of conceptual thinking, one's ways of sensing, perceiving, and experiencing reality become increasingly stereotyped and zombilike. Thus the adult no longer experiences the immediate, intense, and colorful quality radiating toward him from life and nature itself, as he once did, but mainly that which is suggested in him associatively by his already formed and more or less petrified ways of thinking and perceiving. Only occasionally—for example, during the analysis of dreams—may he rediscover something of the lost intense quality of moods and experiences, through the lifting of that crust of concepts and structures which has increasingly overlaid and denaturalized his experiences.

This capacity of the child's (in connection with the maternal pressure for symbiotization and the child's particular vulnerability to it) may throw some light on a significant trait of schizophrenics which has been increasingly emphasized by authors such as Sullivan, Hill, Fromm-Reichmann, and Searles (14). I have in mind the often amazing capacity of these patients to sense the unconscious of another person. Thus the therapist encounters an almost seismographic sensitivity to his own (often unrecognized) anxiety and the defense mechanisms he is employing against it. Here a particularly important role seems to be played by introjection—that is, the unconscious incorporation of the therapist's attitudes and anxieties by the patient. The patient may then, in turn, express these introjected attitudes and anxieties in the form of behavioral peculiarities or possibly even hallucinations, thereby making the therapist aware of them.

Thus in the schizophrenic the capacity for communication with another person's unconscious has in his early life been overdeveloped and has been maintained longer than in more "normal" people. His characteristic sensitivity to unconscious processes is a kind of subtle emotional radar system that developed under the specific conditions of early dependency to intercept the danger signals from the mother or other important persons. This warning system made it possible for him to respond to the threats embodied in his mother with adaptive maneuvers that would lead to the best possible symbiotization of the relationship.

I characterized the three culturally determined adaptations to the stronger person's reality as living on a volcano. In the case of the schizophrenic, this quality of the adaptation is even more marked. He has become a superspecialist in understanding unconscious communications. At the same time, however, his intellectual tools for understanding and mastering the complex conventional reality, a reality as unavoidable as death, have remained weak and warped, this being the price he has had to pay for his extremely early and all-encompassing adaptation. Thus he finds himself in a tragic situation. Hill (6) exemplified it in stating that the schizophrenic is aware of what is deeply unconscious in his doctor, while remaining unaware of his conventional and conscious orientation. For the schizophrenic this creates a grotesque, deeply perplexing, and threatening situation. Lacking the instrument for integrating the knowledge he has obtained through unconscious communication with the facts of conventional reality—that is, being unable to give these insights their meaning, scope, and perspective within the framework of everyday living—he is thrown into an abyss of utter confusion and anxiety. Being unable to recognize, for example, that the ambition and infantile curiosity he diagnoses in his doctor are being checked by the control mechanisms of daily life, he sees them in a terribly destructive and devouring dimension, making him withdraw in panic. The doctor, understandably, at first will react to this in a negative manner, thereby increasing the schizophrenic's dilemma. The patient cannot grasp the reasons for his doctor's reactions. Even less can he communicate about this, and so he becomes more and more deeply convinced that his own feelings and attitudes, and particularly his knowledge gained through empathic communication, are wrong, contemptible, and destructive. He becomes more and more fixed in a vicious circle. More and more he barricades himself within a world of his own, until, sooner or later, his very empathic abilities atrophy from lack of stimulation. This, the clinical picture of chronic, deteriorated schizophrenia, is the last consequence of his inability to cope with the challenge of adaptation against insurmountable odds.

IMPLICATIONS FOR THERAPY

If the foregoing is right, several important consequences for the psychotherapy of schizophrenia follow. In many respects, the psychotherapist of the schizophrenic is expected to make possible the impossible. For the therapist is supposed to be receptive to the unusual, subtle as well as intense, radiations of his patient's anxiety; but, at the same time, he is expected to tolerate this anxiety. He is supposed to be able to communicate with the unconscious of his patient, but, at the same time, he is expected to know where the requirements of conventional reality have practical priority. While he is expected to be strong and independent, he is supposed also to possess the kind of sharpened sensitivity which is often the by-product of a weaker partner's successful attempt at symbiotization. He is supposed to have a deep and sympathetic understanding of what it means to be adapted to a minority reality, yet he is supposed to be a representative of the broader, encompassing majority reality.

Thus the psychotherapist must do the seemingly impossible, and the patient, having his doctor as a model, will be able to experience that the impossible—within limits—*can become* possible. This, it seems, can be brought home to him in two ways. First, he will find in the personality of his therapist vivid proof that a set of problems similar to the ones that vex him have been solvable in one concrete human existence. Second, the process of therapy itself will provide him with a lively demonstration how a sensitivity that is primarily an attribute of weakness may finally become an element of genuine strength.

To consider the first point, it must be remembered that the therapist arrives at psychological understanding mainly by reflecting about his own feelings and motives which he, in turn, finds confirmed as typical in other persons. Thus he can, for example, understand the subtle dynamisms of a schizophrenic's anxiety only insofar as he can relate it to his own experience, either actual or potential. He must, in other words, in his own life have become sensitized to an experience of this kind. However, this experience must also differ from the schizophrenic's, at least to the degree to which it is re-enacted. To make possible this decisive difference, something significant must have happened: to some degree at least, his anxiety and the measures employed against it must have been brought into awareness, so that the anxiety could become integrated into the personality and thereby become tolerable and controllable.

Exactly this process of bringing anxiety into awareness is, however, at the same time a process of breaking up the pathological, static symbiosis, of transforming it into a dynamic symbiosis, within which the demarcation of himself from the stronger one may now gradually become possible. It is the process through which the boundaries of his ego become crystallized. This process, building on the therapeutic relationship as a dynamic symbiosis instead of re-enacting through it the pathological, static symbiosis, is the basis of any necessary relinquishing of mother-geared satisfactions, of facing up to his real-life situation, in order to make possible further growth and genuine productivity. Yet it is concomitantly the basis for discovering and testing out new, enduring satisfactions and for building up new sublimations, which have been precluded by emotional adherence to a *static* symbiotic relationship. This, in turn, makes possible the development of self-esteem, of an inner freedom, permitting him to give up the broken personality typical of the weaker partner, while at the same time maintaining at least part of the sensitivity that developed in the battle for symbiotization. This process will, as a rule, be fostered by the therapist's own analysis. The therapist who reflects this experience in his own personality has thus, at least within certain limits, proved that the original weakness of the underprivileged partner of the symbiosis may become a point of genuine strength. He has proved that one can make use of one's own neurosis.

To come to the second point: this process leads to greater inner freedom and strength. But also it will increase the therapist's ability to bring his anxiety into his own awareness. This, finally, makes it possible for him to prove to the patient, in an even more important manner, that the seemingly impossible can be made possible. For his strength and inner freedom now allow the therapist to expose himself to his patient's world of anxieties and conflicts incomparably more readily than would have been possible otherwise. He now introjects the anxieties and conflicts of his patient and, by, so to speak, being able to endure them because of his own strong ego, gives the patient a most vivid example of how his seemingly unsolvable problems may find a solution. It is the therapist's very sensitivity, developed under the conditions of his own fight for survival but molded into an instrument for treatment and diagnosis, that makes him, in a therapeutic way, responsive to the specific dynamisms of the schizophrenic's anxiety.

SENSITIZATION AND STABILIZATION

From this another important fact becomes apparent: in a therapist dealing with schizophrenics, two countervailing forces must operate jointly. I would like to call one of these a *tendency for sensitization.* It is represented by all those factors which make for involvement with the schizophrenic as the basis for an understanding that is subtle and intense at the same time, including those factors which drive the therapist to a kind of psychological outwitting similar to that typical of a weaker partner's attempt at symbiotization. But such sensitivity and capacity for outwitting are therapeutically useless (and possibly dangerous) when they have been too important a part of one's own efforts at survival. In order to make this tendency therapeutically useful, there must exist, therefore, a strong opposing force, which I would call a *tendency for stabilization.* In this I count all factors which make for a disinvolvement, detaching the above-mentioned sensitivity and capacity for outwitting from their object. The tendency for stabilization makes, in other words, for a desymbiotization, thereby allowing the sensitivity developed in this process to become available for therapeutic and sublimatory purposes, for growth and individuation.

This is not altogether new. From psychoanalytical studies there is the well-known concept of "free-floating attentiveness" (*freischwebender Aufmerksamkeit*)—a state in which the analyst is supposed to be optimally geared to his patient. It has been repeatedly described by, among others, Edith Weigert (16) as a quick change between empathic-intuitive participation and self-reflecting consciousness, as a constant alternation of—to use Freud's terms—primary and secondary processes in the analyst. This corresponds, in a certain way, to the just-described counterplay of tendencies for sensitization and stabilization. But it appears that in order to reach the schizophrenic patient therapeutically, this counterplay must work with an intensity and persistence that is unusual in classical analysis. That is, there must be forces operating which make for a particularly intense and persistent emotional investment, for a strong motivation that again and again creates in the therapist a subtle sensitivity to and understanding of the patient's specific anxieties and defensive maneuvers. But, at the same time, there is needed a counterforce, operating with the same strength, that again and again detaches this intensity from the patient, that objectifies it and elucidates it in self-conscious reflection.

It appears now that it is exactly the capacity for experiencing and maintaining such an intensive counterplay of these two forces within oneself which forms an essential personal trait of any therapist who deals successfully with schizophrenics. But further, there is the question whether such forces can work, not just in the individual therapist, but in a hospital where intensive psychotherapy of schizophrenics is carried on over longer periods of time, providing a kind of additional, institutionalized motivation for the doctor. And this seems quite characteristically to be the case in at least one hospital that I have been familiar with, Chestnut Lodge in Rockville, Maryland.

Sensitization, on this hospital level, involves all the factors which cause a therapist to concentrate with special intensity on a particular psychotic patient, and the threshold of attention and participation in regard to this patient is thereby lowered. Here I refer, in other words, to those factors which increase the doctor's readiness to incorporate the anxieties and conflictual strivings of his patient; that is, to make them his own. Stabilization, on the other hand, appears to consist of those factors which again cause a neutralization of this enforced intensity. They make, in other words, for detachment, objectivity, and self-control. The counter-play of these opposing tendencies on an institutional level becomes particularly evident in a hospital such as Chestnut Lodge, geared strongly to the intensive psychotherapy of schizophrenic patients.

The relatively small number of patients forming the caseload of one therapist makes possible an incomparably stronger invest-ment of therapeutic energies than would be the case even in a selective psychoanalytic practice. This is a strong factor for sensitization. Further, Chestnut Lodge selects therapists who find a particular challenge in the treatment of very sick patients—a trait that, of course, has its basis in the particular history, needs, and motivations of the therapist. Both factors, the small number of patients and the specific selection of therapists, create a climate in which the self-esteem of a therapist comes under severe stress if "nothing is moving" in therapy. Thus a strong pressure is exerted on the therapist for a symbiotization of his relationship to the patient. And it seems to be this very pressure for symbiotization which brings into being an oversensitivity for the partner's (in this case the patient's) particular problems. In other words, there are strong forces which drive the therapist to an overinvestment in his patient similar to that of the "schizophrenogenic" mother in the patient when he was still a child. Only under these or similar circumstances, it seems to me, can a situation of "therapeutic despair" arise, highly stressful to both doctor and patient, as it has been described by Leslie Farber (3).

Yet, quite characteristically, there are in this therapeutic environment stabilizing factors of no less strength which, in turn, tend to desymbiotize, alleviate, and objectify this intensive relationship. One such factor is the high degree of supervision the therapist receives. At Chestnut Lodge he usually receives it on three different levels: First, in the case of a younger therapist, he receives individual supervision by more experienced therapists of the hospital. Second, it is provided in the form of discussion groups, comprising about five doctors and taking place twice a week. Third—and this is probably the most important way in which the young therapist receives supervision—it comes from a personal training analysis which he has to undergo at the nearby psychoanalytic institute. But that is not all. The stress brought about by these intensive relationships seems to be made further bearable by the fact that they are, so to speak, imbedded in a matrix of constant self-confirmation offered by other members of the hospital community. This is expressed, for example, in the frequent statement, "Don't worry—we all have similar experiences." But in addition, scientific research—that is, the reflective clarification of the processes at play in an interpersonal relationship—can in itself function as a powerful factor for stabilization. For this research, too, necessitates a constant re-establishment of distance, of self-critical awareness, and of objectivity toward oneself and the patient. This factor of stabilization is also institutionalized in the hospital.

This study, then, leads to the conclusion that, in order to counteract the schizophrenic dilemma, the combined effect of two intensive and persistent forces, operating on the individual as well as hospital level, is needed. I have called these forces the tendency for sensitization and the tendency for stabilization. This state of affairs was expressed in a strikingly simple formula by Sullivan when he stressed the attitude of the "participant observer" as a basic psychiatric prerequisite, thereby indicating the paradoxical counterplay of these two forces. The analysis of this attitude and of the human situation necessitating it may provide a key for the understanding not only of a very pertinent aspect of the schizophrenic's dilemma, but also of a broader human problem.

Note

¹ Richard Wright (17, 18) for instance, has vividly described the emotional crisis that accompanied both his break with communism and his emancipation from many of the racial barriers with which he grew up.

References

1. Bateson, G., Jackson, D. D., Haley, J., and Weakland, J. Toward a theory of schizophrenia. *Behavioral Science* 1: 251-264, 1956.
2. Benedek, T. Contributions to the libido theory: parenthood as a developmental phase. Paper presented at the meeting of the Washington Psychoanalytic Society, March 8, 1957.
3. Farber, L. The therapeutic despair. *Psychiatry* 21: 7-20, 1958.
4. Fromm-Reichmann, F. *Principles of intensive psychotherapy.* Chicago: University of Chicago Press, 1950.
5. ———. Private communication.
6. Hill, L. B. *Psychotherapeutic intervention in schizophrenia.* Chicago: University of Chicago Press, 1955.
7. Kallmann, F. *Heredity in health and mental disorders.* New York: Norton, 1953.
8. Klein, M. *Envy and gratitude.* New York: Basic Books, 1957.
9. Lidz, T., and Terry, D. The intrafamilial environment of the schizophrenic patient. I. The Father. *Psychiatry* 20: 329-342, 1957.
10. Milosz, C. *The captive mind.* New York: Vintage Books, 1955.
11. Rado, S. et al. Schizotypical organization: preliminary report on a clinical study of schizophrenia. 225-235. In *Changing concepts of psychoanalytic medicine*, ed. Rado and G. E. Daniels. New York: Grune and Stratton, 1956.

12.   Schachtel, E. On memory and childhood amnesia. *Psychiatry* 10: 1-26, 1947.

13.   ———. The development of focal attention and the emergence of reality. *Psychiatry* 17: 309-324, 1954.

14.   Searles, H. F. The schizophrenic's vulnerability to the therapist's unconscious processes. *Journal of Nervous and Mental Diseases* 127: 247-262, 1958.

15.   Sullivan, H. S. *The Interpersonal Theory of Psychiatry*, ed. H. S. Perry and M. L. Gawel. New York: Norton, 1953.

16.   Weigert, E. Counter-transference and self-analysis of the psycho-analyst. *International Journal of Psycho-Analysis* 35: 242-246, 1954.

17.   Wright, R. *Native son*. New York: Modern Library, 1942.

18.   ———. *The god that failed*. New York: Harper, 1950.

Chapter 4

Lyrical Creativity
and Schizophrenic Psychosis
in Friedrich Hölderlin's Fate

The year 1770 witnessed the birth of three seminal personalities, all Germans: Georg Wilhelm Friedrich Hegel, Ludwig van Beethoven, and Friedrich Hölderlin (2).* Yet while the genius of Hegel and of Beethoven was soon recognized, that of Hölderlin had to await its time in order to receive its due acclaim. Today, however, Hölderlin's star shines brightly, as many Germans have come to consider him their country's greatest lyrical poet. No other poet writing in German has become the subject of a similar renaissance or, perhaps more correctly, discovery. This discovery was made possible through some of the most painstaking philological research ever devoted to any writer. Once discovered, Hölderlin has fascinated authors with diverse backgrounds— Martin Heidegger (who devoted a volume of essays to Hölderlin), Bertolt Brecht, Paul Celan, Karl Jaspers, Theodor Adorno, and Walter Benjamin, to name only a few.

The reasons for the increasing interest in Hölderlin are many. If

---

* Quotes after F. Hölderlin: *Grosse Stuttgarter Ausgabe* (F. Beissner and A. Berk, eds.). Stuttgart, Kohlhammer, 1946.

I were asked to name the main one, I would single out his *timeless modernity*, using a paradoxical phrase of the kind that Hölderlin often coined. It is, above all, the works of his late creative period, spanning approximately the years 1800 to 1806, that have this quality in greatest measure. And it is also these late works that had to wait longest—more than 150 years—for their extraordinary quality to be appreciated.

The expression "late works" must, however, be qualified. For Hölderlin, who lived to the age of seventy-three, was only in his mid-thirties when he wrote them (17). We speak here of late works because Hölderlin, during his final, incredibly creative period, became mad—and stayed mad until the time of his death thirty-six years later. Following a year in a psychiatric hospital (the Autenriethsche Klinik in Tübingen), he led a restricted life in a tower in the same city from 1807 until 1843, cared for by a carpenter by the name of Ernst Zimmer. Hölderlin wrote only a few, relatively short poems during these last thirty-six years of his life. In their seemingly childlike simplicity, they would never suggest to the uninitiated that they were written by one of Germany's greatest lyric poets.

Hölderlin's madness has unanimously been diagnosed as a form of schizophrenia. The concept *schizophrenia* (split mind) as a diagnostic term has remained tainted by controversy (4, 14; see also Chapter 2). Still, there can be no doubt that Hölderlin was deeply disturbed mentally, if not deranged, and that the label of schizophrenia best fits his disturbance (20). From 1802 on he became irritable and prone to uncontrollable rages. Later he appeared withdrawn and subdued. He seemed unable to focus his attention for any length of time; he was mannered, servile in a mocking, exaggerated way; and he referred to himself by different names, such as Scardanelli or Scaliger rosa. It is questionable, however, whether he had any extensive delusional ideas. Neither is it certain that he hallucinated.

I want now to consider some aspects of the ways in which the development of Hölderlin's mental disturbance may have inter-locked with his lyrical creativity. I do so with trepidation, however. For, in attempting to link what appears as psychopathology with creative achievement, I must cope with two dangers. First, there is the danger of impoverishing the creative work by being overexplanatory. Here I speak of the temptation to explain in psychiatric or psychodynamic jargon what by its nature cannot be explained through psychiatric concepts—those qualities that make any creative work outstanding and unique. Such psychiatric overexplanations easily become another instance of what Whitehead has called the "fallacy of misplaced concreteness" or, in blunter terms, of an irreverent, as well as inappropriate, reductionism. On the other side, there is the danger of becoming overawed by the genius and everything that pertains to him. This, then, can induce an idealization of many aspects of his work and life. Freud (5), in his essay on Leonardo da Vinci, has shown how a biographic study can avoid these twin dangers. While bringing to light important aspects of da Vinci's life and works through a psychoanalytic interpretation, he also has carefully delimited the validity of this interpretation.

Regarding the dangers just mentioned, Hölderlin has had, I believe, little luck with his psychologically inclined biographers. While his psychiatric pathographers—such as Lange (11), Treichler (19), but also Jaspers (9)—have tended to investigate him with outdated reductionist models of psychopathy and schizo-phrenia in their minds, his nonpsychiatric biographers have tended to view his personality and personal relations through rose-colored, idealizing glasses (3, 7, 15, 22). In their need to find in or near him only the sublime, the heroic, the loving, and the positive, these scholars have often closed their eyes to many negatively tinged features that are important from a humane and psychological point of view, such as the intrapsychic and interpersonal drama of hatred, jealousy, ambivalence, and destructiveness with which Hölderlin, no less than other persons of creative genius, confronts us. I shall try here to do justice to the positive as well as to the negative features of the poet's life and work—as much as the limited intent of this chapter will permit. But before taking up these features, I must briefly reflect on some aspects of schizophrenia that seem relevant to my topic.

This cannot be the place to review the many complex and, to a large extent, unresolved issues pertaining to the concept of schizophrenia. Suffice it to say that we have good cause to view schizophrenic disorders as the outcome of a life process which—contrary to views held by Jaspers and by many other European psychiatrists—can be understood. In this process we see, from the moment of birth and even before, an individual disposition interacting with a given human environment. This life process is circular insofar as disposition and environment affect and modify each other on ever-new levels, creating new transactional configurations which, in turn, imply changing dispositions and changing environments.

Although from this theoretical vantage point it appears problematical to use the concepts *disposition* and *environment* in an unqualified (that is, undialectical) manner, let us do so for a moment and consider separately these two ingredients in any human—and hence potentially schizophrenic—development.

Regarding the disposition for schizophrenia, most available evidence suggests that it is relatively weak and unspecific. We must think of it at present as a rather common vulnerability to a wide range of stresses out of which a wide range of disorders might develop. For these latter the term *schizophrenic spectrum disorders* has been suggested. These disorders include not only cases of bona fide schizophrenia, but also character disorders, so-called inadequate personalities, schizoid states, and others. In monozygotic twin pairs with one schizophrenic member, we find a probability of only 25 to 45 percent that the other member—who supposedly has the same hereditary endowment—will some day also be diagnosed as schizophrenic (10, 12, 18). Moreover, careful studies of biologic and adoptive relatives of schizophrenics, which were carried out in the United States and abroad, suggest that the same disposition that may give rise to these schizophrenic spectrum disorders may also—and this seems important in our present context—give rise to creativity. For example, L. Heston (8), an American researcher, compared two groups of approximately fifty adopted children who had grown into adulthood. One group came from biologic parents of whom at least one parent had been diagnosed as schizophrenic. The other group of adoptees came from biologic parents without any diagnosis of schizophrenia. Among the children from schizophrenic parents Heston found five cases of schizophrenia and, in the control group, none. However, in the group of subjects who had schizophrenic parents, he also found a sizeable number of individuals with an artistic and unconventional bent and life-style. In contrast, the individuals in the control group appeared uniformly mundane and conventional.

Observations such as these make us ask: Can we discern also in Hölderlin a disposition that harbors the potential for creativity *and* schizophrenia? Can we find in him clues as to how the ingredients for creativity and schizophrenia may become perhaps inextricably mixed? I believe we can, although, admittedly, these clues are crude and provide, at best, circumstantial evidence. So let us, with this question in mind, briefly look at the personality of the poet as it has been described to us by him and by persons who knew him well.

In a letter to his mother that Hölderlin wrote after he had broken off his engagement to his first girl friend, Luise Nast, he resisted his mother's wishes that he marry and settle down as a Protestant minister. In this letter we also find him reflecting on his peculiar character, on his whims, on his penchant for unrealizable projects, on his ambition, and, above all, on his fear of anything, any position or relationship, that might tie him down. From Hölderlin's adolescence on we find many further references—by himself and by others—to his mood swings, to his lacking joy in life, to his loneliness, and to his eternal, melancholic worrying. His fellow students at the Tübinger Stift (theological seminary at Tübingen) noticed his suspicious recalcitrance and called him *Holz* (wood). Hölderlin described himself in those days as a *Klotz* (blockhead). But some of these same fellow students have also transmitted an altogether different portrait of Hölderlin, that of a charming youth of incredible radiance and amiability. In Christoph Theodor Schwab's Hölderlin biography, we read (7:399):

> *Die Freundschaft mit Hölderlin gewann schon durch seine körperliche Schönheit etwas Idealisches; seine Studiengenossen haben erzählt, wenn er vor Tische auf und abgegangen, sei es gewesen, als schritte Apollo durch den Saal.*

> (Friendship with Hölderlin gained an ideal quality by his physical good looks alone; his schoolmates told of how, when he would walk up and down before their table, it seemed as if Apollo were passing through the room.)

We are made aware of the young poet's tender imagination, of his passion for heroic metaphor, of his enthusiasm for all that is truly great (here we remind ourselves that the etymological origin of the word "enthusiasm" lies in the Greek *en theos*—"the God in us") and, perhaps most important, of his compulsion constantly to objectify, to express, and to reflect on his inner experiences, experiences which often seem to have baffled him. Note, for example, the piece of self-reflection from his early twenties in which he writes (in a letter to Immanuel Nast 6: 8-9, No. 5) that, sitting between his dark walls, he calculates how abysmally poor he is in terms of inner joys, and that he admires his resignation.

We thus get a glimpse of completely intermixed personality traits; and, judging from our present enlightened perspective, it seems fair to assume that they reflect a disposition to become a poet and/or a schizophrenic. Our next question, then, must direct itself to the second ingredient in the circular process I mentioned earlier: the human environment with which Hölderlin interacted during the formative and crucial periods of his life. This human environment consists, first, of his family and, second, of those important persons outside his family who engaged him while he seemed to be reaching a cross-roads in his artistic and psychological development. Let me briefly comment on this environment, beginning with his family.

Hölderlin, who was born into a small-town, middle-class milieu, lost his father at the age of two. His mother remarried two years later. Her new husband, the poet's stepfather, died of pleurisy when Hölderlin was nine years old. As an adolescent Hölderlin described movingly how much this death had shaken him. He had a sister, who was two years younger, and a half brother, who was six years younger. He corresponded with both siblings rather frequently but irregularly up to the time of his madness. His most important family tie was clearly that to his mother. Four times during his adult life he returned to her—at least twice abruptly— when, for one reason or another, he had failed to establish himself professionally. After his last return home, his mother arranged for his institutionalization as a psychiatric patient. Unfortunately, we know little concerning what his mother was like, since only a few documents from her own hand—such as one letter written to the poet after her final will—have been transmitted to us. We know, however, a good deal about how Hölderlin reacted to her, as he wrote her numerous letters, of which many are extant. Here is the only preserved letter to the poet from his mother (HW 6: 371-372):

Allerliebster Sohn!
Ob ich schon nicht so glücklich bin auf mein wiederholtes Bitten auch
einige Linien von Dir mein Lieber zu erhalten, so kann ich es doch
nicht unterlassen, Dich manchmal von unserer vordauernden Liebe

und Andenken zu versichern. Wie sehr würde es mich freuen und erheitern, wenn Du mir nur auch wieder einmal schreiben wolltest, dass Du die l. Deinige noch liebst und an uns denkest. Vielleicht habe ich Dir ohne mein Wissen und Willen Veranlassung gegeben, dass Du empfindlich gegen mich bist, und so bitter entgelten lässest, seie nur so gut, und melde es mir, ich will es zu verbessern suchen. . . .

Besonders aber bitte ich Dich herzlich, dass Du die Pflichten gegen unser l. Gott und Vater in Himmel nicht versäumest. Wir können auf dieser Erde keine grössere Glückseligkeit erlangen, als wenn wir bei unseren l. Gott in Gnaden stehen. Nach diesem wollen wir mit allem Ernst streben, dass wir dort einander wieder finden, wo keine Trennung mehr sein wird.

Ich sende Dir anbei ein Wamesle und vier Paar Strümpf und ein Paar Handschuh als einen Beweis meiner Liebe und Andenken, ich bitte Dich aber, dass Du die wollene Strümpfe auch trägst. . . . Nebst unserm allerseitigen herzlichen Gruss und Bitte, dass Du mich auch wieder mit etwas erfreust und bald schreibst, schliesse ich mit der Versicherung, dass ich unverändert verharre.

Nürtingen

Deine

d. 29. Oktober 1805   *getreue M. Gockin.*

(My dearest Son:
Although I am not so fortunate as to have received even a few lines from you, after begging you repeatedly, my dear one, I cannot help assuring you how much I love you and think of you all the time. How joyous and delighted I would be if only once again you would write me that you still love and remember me, your dear mother. Maybe I have, without my knowledge or intent, given you reason for being so easily hurt and so bitterly vengeful. If this should be the case, please let me know and I shall try to improve matters. . . .

Most of all I beseech you with all my heart not to become remiss in your duties toward our dear God and Father in heaven. We can on this earth obtain no greater bliss than to stand in the grace of our dear God. Toward this God let us strive with mighty seriousness so that we shall find each other again in the Beyond where there shall be no more separation.

Enclosed I am sending you a woolen undershirt and four pairs of socks and a pair of gloves as proof of my love and thought of you. Yet please—do not forget to wear the woolen socks after I have sent them to you. . . . In adding my most heartfelt regards and the request that you will again make me a little happy and write me soon, I am closing with the assurance that I remain unchanged as ever.

Nürtingen,   Your
October 29, 1805   faithful M. Gockin.)

This letter has touched many readers because of its seeming childlike simplemindedness (which comes out even better in the German original than in my slightly streamlined English translation). Yet in order to grasp some of the psychological impact and implications of this letter for Hölderlin, we must remind ourselves that it was written when the poet was thirty-five years old, when he had already been intermittently disturbed and in deep emotional turmoil. (It was only a short time later that he was institutionalized permanently.) To judge from this letter, the mother seems to have been unable to acknowledge, and empathize with, her son's emotional disturbance. Instead, she views his silence vis-à-vis her as evidence that he wants to hurt her and take his revenge on her. She projects a picture of herself as the one who is being unjustly slighted but who continues to love and to forgive. Yet in so doing, she clearly induces guilt in her correspondent. At the same time she admonishes him to believe in God according to her own narrow, fundamentalist notions. The reward for such belief will be their reunion in heaven.

Certainly there is the danger that we make too much of this one extant letter written by the mother. In reading it and trying to put myself into the poet's situation at the time it was written, however, I could not help being struck by its imperviously binding, possessive, and guilt-inducing qualities.

And yet on the basis of Hölderlin's own extant letters to her (as well as on other grounds), we have reason to believe that this mother-son relationship also had many positive elements. In my book *Conflict and Reconciliation: A Study in Human Relations and Schizophrenia* (16), I have tried to speculate on those features of an early mother-child relationship that may give rise to a creative variety of schizophrenia. I have there reflected on that often strange mixture of responsive tenderness and imperviousness, of rich, maternal giving and tyrannical, guilt-inducing enslavement that— sometimes!—seem to be at the root of simultaneous schizophrenia and creativity. Most of the mother-child interaction, crucial from this perspective, seems to occur during what I have called the *dawn of knowing individuation;* that is, during the child's first three years of life, when he is still most symbiotically enmeshed with his mother, most dependent, most moldable, and hence most receptive to the good as well as to the bad that comes to him from her. I shall later have more to say about how Hölderlin eventually, in trying to return to his (internalized) mother, overreached himself and became schizophrenic.

The loss of two husbands in short succession seems to have further channeled the mother's binding love to her oldest son, increasing her importance to him. Thus, while the image of the mother—in all its contradictory intensity—became strongly implanted in the poet, that of his father (or fathers) seems to have been more shadowy. As models for identification, these fathers must have seemed only precariously available. As Oedipal rivals they must have appeared weak and vulnerable. His two younger siblings, in contrast, appeared to offer the poet, relatively speaking, the most unambivalent and enduring family relationships available to him. This may be the reason for the apparently (and again, relatively) conflict-free nature of Hölderlin's association with his peers throughout his life. Outside of his family circle, I can mention here as his perhaps most important friends only such significant figures as the philosophers Hegel and Schelling; further, Neuffer, Magenau, and Sinclair; Schiller, his mentor in Jena; and, perhaps most important of all, Susette Gontard, who provided his fateful experience in love.

After outlining the two ingredients of the interactional process which may result in schizophrenia *and* creativity, I had originally intended to trace this process to and through the poet's last creative period. But the more I immersed myself in the period, the more I felt compelled to give up my plan because of the sheer richness and complexity of the material. In order to stay within the bounds of a limited study, I had to restrict my focus. I finally settled on a theme which presents one aspect of the transactional process just mentioned—the seemingly inextricable interlocking of self-destructive and self-healing processes in certain creative persons, of whom Hölderlin appears a prime example. This theme does not imply the simultaneous presence of creativity and schizophrenia in all creative persons. On the contrary. However, in Hölderlin's case at least, the schizophrenic disorder seems to have cast into unusually clear relief how that which may destroy us may also save us, and vice versa.

Lyric poets, more than other artists, have, I believe, alerted us to such tragic dilemmas. Many of them tend to demonstrate through their lives that the very same intrapsychic or interpersonal configuration that allows creativity to flourish also seems to promote the creator's eventual destruction. Such, for example, seems to be the case with Dylan Thomas, whose exuberant, apparently inexhaustible, orally tainted productivity of earlier years appeared to interlock with the alcoholism that finally killed him.

When we reflect on the kind of configuration that specifically underlies lyrical creativity, adolescent sensitivity and proneness to conflict appear as important prerequisites. In lyric poets who have been creative throughout their adult lives, such as Goethe, a repeated renaissance of adolescence has been noted. But many and perhaps most great people, we notice at once, have not been as fortunate and successful as Goethe, who—admittedly, amidst frequent crises—could integrate an ever-renewed adolescence into a richly unfolding and maturing life. For most of these poets either died young, or their inner sources of inspiration dried up after they had reached a certain age. Keats, Shelley, Novalis, Trakl, Pushkin, to name only a few, all died young. And their biographers have in many instances produced good evidence for suspecting a self-destructive bent in their lives which contributed to such early death. Rimbaud stopped writing poetry in his late teens and then disappeared in the jungle, and Wordsworth, Hölderlin's exact contemporary, seemed to lose his lyrical inspiration about the same time that Hölderlin became mad.

Creativity in the lyric poet frequently implies, however—and this seems important here—not only a tendency toward self-destruction but also one toward self-healing. And for longer or shorter periods of time, the creator's fate may hang in the balance as to whether the self-healing or the self-destructive forces will win out.

The notion of self-healing through creativity is, of course, not new. This notion implies that creativity—and lyrical creativity in particular—is the creative person's royal and only road to solving unbearable personal conflicts and dilemmas. It becomes, then, a by-product of his unique, personal attempts at conflict resolution that this person creates new meanings and Gestalten, possibly a new consciousness and new sensibility, and very possibly a new vision of man's inner and outer worlds.

Let us now look more closely at four of the elements inherent in lyrical creativity that paradoxically may link the creator's self-healing and self-destructive tendencies. The principle of attempted salvation through creation implies, first, that the creative effort is frequently so total and so exclusive that it thrives only at the expense of almost everything else. Nietzsche once said that any great talent tends to turn into a vampire: it feeds on everything—on friends, on the family, on the artist's physical and mental health. For this reason, the world in which creative persons move often becomes a human disaster area. It is strewn with the wreckage of ruined and exploited lives and hopes. From this point of view, it can rightly be said (and has been said by Philip Weissman, 21, among others) that creativity is neither constructive nor adaptive in a conventional sense. The creative drive does not align itself with an ego that obeys a so-called reality principle but seems, rather, captive to an unusually exacting and idiosyncratic superego which disregards what may seem most important for survival, as well as most elementary in human decency.

Such self-healing through creation seems, second, frequently to thrive on precarious life situations and human relationships which the artist himself did not want or could not control. Bertolt Brecht is a case in point. Again and again this author—who was great as poet *and* as playwright—decried the cold, competitive climate of capitalist America. He called it his misfortune that the advent of Nazism and the outbreak of World War II left him no choice but to live in the States. But it was exactly in the oppressed loneliness of his American days that he created some of his most important plays—*The Life of Galileo, Mother Courage and her Children, The Caucasian Chalk Circle*—and poetry. In Communist East Germany, in contrast, where he was put in charge of an excellent theater and was acclaimed (at least publicly) as that country's most distinguished author, he produced no major play and wrote only sycophantic rhymes in praise of Stalin and the regime.

Third, the poet, in order not to allow his creative inspiration to dry up, must again and again expose himself to the spontaneous life within and outside himself which, by its very nature, is full of danger and conflict. This seems tied to the needed renaissance of adolescence mentioned earlier. Yet in such exposure to life, the artist's ego might be overwhelmed.

Should he finally succeed in his poetic effort (and this is a fourth point), he may strike such an immediate and powerful chord in his contemporaries that he can feel confirmed. But often such reception remains for a long time in doubt. The poet's contemporaries may be repelled by or insensitive to the truth and power of his creations. They need time to catch up with his ideas. Only later generations can begin to appreciate his works—if he is lucky enough to have his works preserved. Such a fate implies that there is little or no feedback to the creator that could boost his self-esteem, relieve his loneliness, and sustain his vision. Without such feedback, the self-healing potential inherent in his creative attempts is further negated.

Let me now take up these four points with Hölderlin as my specific focus.

First, the totality of Hölderlin's creative effort seemed to conflict ever more sharply with the demands for adaptive survival, this conflict reaching its crescendo and climax in his last five productive years. Most of the elegies and hymns on which his fame as a timeless modern rests were written between 1800 and 1806. This was clearly the most unsettled period of the poet's life, the period when he showed increasing signs of schizophrenic disturbance. He seemed less and less able to work as a tutor in well-to-do households, which he had started to do after his earlier plans to start a literary journal had failed. The exact reasons for his failure in this and related enterprises are unclear. We can plausibly assume, however, that he became so obsessed with his creation that few, if any, energies were left for ordinary living. The only thing that really counted to him seems to have been to reach ever higher levels of artistic precision, construction, and craftsmanship. All else seems to have faded into insignificance. When composing the hymn "Der Rhein," one of his latest completed works, for example, Hölderlin jotted down in the margin of the manuscript (2: 722):

> *Das Gesetz dieses Gesanges ist, dass die zwei ersten Partien der Form nach durch Progress und Regress entgegengesetzt, aber dem Stoff nach gleich, die zwei folgenden der Form nach gleich, dem Stoff nach entgegengesetzt sind, die letzte aber mit durchgängiger Metapher alles ausgleicht.*

(It is the principle of this poem that its first two parts, in terms of progression and regression, are opposed to each other as regards their form, while they are alike in content; the two following parts are alike in form but opposed in content; while the last part reconciles everything in pervasive metaphor.)

He appears to have feverishly written one version after another of a given poem, never seeming really satisfied with the end result. While he was being driven to ever more complex self-expression as a poet, the inner as well as the outer foundations of his life seemed to crumble. His ego seemed to break down almost visibly under the strain of having to reach ever higher degrees of artistic reconciliation. He seemed to implore his God, as in Empedokles' last great soliloquy (4: 138):

> *O Geist, der uns erzog, der du geheim*
> *Am hellen Tag und in der Wolke waltest,*
> . . . .

Nun nicht im Bilde mehr, und nicht, wie sonst,
Bei Sterblichen, im kurzen Glück, ich find
Im Tode find ich den Lebendigen
Und heute noch begegn' ich ihm, ...

(O Spirit, you that reared us, secretly
Both in the cloud and in the bright noon govern,
. . . .
No longer in the image now, nor yet,
As formerly, with mortals, in brief joy,
No, but in death I find the Living One
And this day shall confront him, ...)

Yet, despite his metaphysical anxiety, he seems to have been unable to seek his salvation in any other way than through his creative work.

It is therefore not difficult to find the taint of schizophrenia in Hölderlin's late poetry, as this poetry suggests a loosening of associations and a breakdown of the hierarchical organization of thought processes which Eugen Bleuler (4) considered central to the schizophrenic disturbance. Hölderlin tended more and more (as has been noted by Friedrich Beissner (1) and others) to shake together different historical periods, different associative contexts, different things near and distant. This makes for the frequently terse and dissonant quality of his later poetry and for a seemingly disjointed, multilevel complexity. But also, I believe, this makes for the modernity of his poetry. When reading Hölderlin's late poems we feel—despite their frequent references to ancient gods and mythologies and their often elevated style— much closer to the world of Arnold Schoenberg, Anton von Webern, or James Joyce than to that of Goethe, Schiller, or even Beethoven, who were his contemporaries.

While Hölderlin thus introduces us to a dissonant, multilevel complexity, he also opens our eyes to the new harmonies, new lyrical patterns, and new modes of reconciliation that seem feasible and necessary to cope with this complexity. He not only gives us glimpses of the pristine chaos in us, but also shows how this chaos—through a singular devotion to craftsmanship—can, in unorthodox ways, be harmonized without being squelched.

Second, we have to focus on the precarious and transitional state of related unrelatedness that seems to underlie Hölderlin's most intensely creative efforts, particularly his late works. We notice here that Hölderlin tended to become most productive after he had broken off an important relationship but could still feed on it creatively. This holds true, above all, for his latest creative period which, from the viewpoint here presented, must also be considered his latest phase of related unrelatedness.

In order to document this viewpoint, I must briefly turn to Hölderlin's fateful love relationship with Susette Gontard, the wife of a Frankfurt banker, for whose children he served as tutor. He held this tutorial position from 1796 to 1798, but continued a clandestine correspondence with Susette throughout the following two years. Susette was immortalized as Diotima (named after the priestess of love in Plato's *Symposium*) in Hölderlin's poetry and paramountly in his novel *Hyperion*. As far as we know, the relation between Hölderlin and Susette remained sexually unconsummated, but it had for both partners an incredible emotional intensity. The sudden separation of the lovers in 1798 seems to many Hölderlin scholars to be the event that set the poet on the road to final emotional wreck and madness. This may be so, but we cannot overlook the immense sense of liberation that Hölderlin seems to have experienced—for a while, at least—when circumstances finally forced him to give up his love. This sense of liberation, I think, sustained the near frantic productivity of his late period. Note, for example, these lines from the elegy "Menons Klagen um Diotima," which express his strange bliss in the midst of deepest suffering (2: 75-76):

Festzeit hab ich nicht, doch möcht ich die Locke bekränzen;
  Bin ich allein denn nicht? aber ein Freundliches muss
Fernher nahe mir sein, und lächeln muss ich und staunen,
  Wie so selig doch auch mitten im Leide mir ist.

(Cause have I not to be festive, but long to put on a green
  garland;
  Am I not quite alone? Yet something kind now must be
Close to me from afar, so that I smile as I wonder
  How in the midst of my grief I can feel happy and
blessed.)

Thus, while there can be no doubt that Hölderlin grieved deeply
over his loss, as an artist he seems to have benefited from this loss
in at least three ways: (1) he underwent the kind of emotional
experience that allowed him to drench his elegies with his life's
blood, as it were; (2) having obtained a respite from a deeply
entangling relationship, he could devote himself anew and totally
to his work, to the extent, as indicated earlier, of disregarding his
everyday survival; and (3) this loss seems to have induced the kind
of ego growth that Freud (5) must have had in mind when he
referred to the ego as the precipitate of past object losses. The ego,
according to this view of Freud's, can erect the lost person as a part
within itself and can, as Hölderlin's case seems to indicate, become
stronger and richer in ways that make for heightened creativity.
However, it is important to note that we deal here at best with an
uneven, one-sided ego growth which does not necessarily enhance
one's chances for a happy life or even for simple everyday survival.

Now to my third point: the poet must expose himself to life's
most conflict-ridden currents with suspended defenses—and in so
doing risk being torn asunder by them. In the following passage of
the letter to Böhlendorff of December 4, 1801, Hölderlin seems to
show how aware he is of the extent to which he was subject to this
dilemma (6: 426):

Denn das ist das Tragische bei uns, dass wir ganz stille in irgendeinem Behälter eingepackt vom Reiche der Lebendigen hinweggehn, nicht dass wir in Flammen verzehrt die Flamme büssen, die wir nicht zu bändigen vermochten.

(For this is the tragic element in our lives: that we, completely silenced, packed away in some container, depart from the realm of the living; rather than that we, consumed by flames, atone for the very flames we were unable to tame.)

And in a letter to his friend Neuffer, written November 12, 1798, we read (6: 290; No. 167):

... weil ich alles, was von Jugend auf Zerstörendes mich traf, empfindlicher als andre aufnahm, und diese Empfindlichkeit scheint darin ihren Grund zu haben, dass ich im Verhältnis mit den Erfahrungen, die ich machen musste, nicht fest und unzerstörbar genug organisiert war. Das sehe ich. Kann es mir helfen, dass ich es sehe? Ich glaube, so viel. Weil ich zerstörbarer bin als mancher andre, so muss ich um so mehr den Dingen, die auf mich zerstörend wirken, einen Vorteil abzugewinnen suchen, ...

(... because from youth on I have reacted more sensitively than other people to what could destroy me, and this sensitivity seems to have to do with the fact that I, considering the experiences I had to endure, was not organized solidly and indestructibly enough. So much I see. But will the fact of seeing it help me? To this extent, I believe: because I am more easily destroyed than other persons, I must try all the harder to obtain an advantage from those things which have a destructive influence on me, ...)

What, then, were the things that were destructive to Hölderlin and that, nonetheless, he had to seek out in order to realize himself as an artist? In the letter to Neuffer just quoted he was not very specific about it. I, for my part, am inclined to find these destructive influences chiefly in the realm of his inner, subjective experiences, as these had come to be shaped by his past and reactivated in his current personal relationships. And because family associations are so central, it is, above all, these on which we must focus in order to understand what may have been at once destructive and conducive to creation in his subjective experience.

Our family relationships, and among them specifically our long dependence on our mother, we cannot help carrying with us through our lives even after we have left home or our parents have died. And when we make new human contacts, it has to be through that inner mold and matrix of conflicts and expectations that our parents have bequeathed to us. In my book *Conflict and Reconciliation* (16) and elsewhere, I have dealt with the complex dynamics which here come into play. At this point I can only touch on a few of those dynamics in Hölderlin's inner experience that seem most relevant here.

I have in mind perhaps the deepest conflict, which seems rooted in the poet's early psychic ties with his mother and which, to some extent, was reactivated through his later relationships. This conflict constitutes, I believe, a part of those aforementioned experiences that Hölderlin felt he had to undergo, although he doubted whether he was (as he expressed it in the letter to Neuffer) *"fest und unzerstörbar genug organisiert"* (organized solidly and indestructibly enough) not to be harmed by them (that is, he doubted whether his ego was strong enough to stand them).

This most central conflict seems inherent in Hölderlin's recurring wish to return to a mother earth who promises to gratify and protect him totally, while he simultaneously fears that any such return will destroy him. This, of course, is the schizophrenic's core conflict. Both sides of this conflict appear richly elaborated in Hölderlin's late work. There is hardly another poet who has so intensely evoked the nourishing, peace-giving, enlivening aspects of the earth, which he expressly linked with the image of the mother. The expression *Mutter Erde* occurs, according to Pierre Bertaux (3), more than one hundred times in the late work (after March 1799). Passages like the following two, both taken from his play *Der Tod des Empedokles,* seem typical. In the first passage we hear Empedokles in his great opening soliloquy in the fragmentary third version (4: 122):

> Und wenn . . . ihren Arm
> Die Mutter um mich breitet, o was möcht
> Ich auch, was möcht ich fürchten.

(And when . . . the Mother
With her own arms enfolds me, O what could I,
What could I fear.)

In the second passage, from the same late version, Empedokles' faithful companion Pausanias addresses him (4: 129):

> Und wagtest dich ins Heiligtum des Abgrunds,
> Wo duldend vor dem Tage sich das Herz
> Der Erde birgt und ihre Schmerzen dir
> Die dunkle Mutter sagt, o du der Nacht
> Des Aethers Sohn! ich folgte dir hinunter.

(Daring to trend the sanctum of the abyss
Where, patient, Earth conceals her heart from day
And the dark Mother will confide to you
Her sufferings, her griefs, O son of Night,
Of Aether, even then I'd follow you down.)

We note in this context that Hölderlin has chosen the pre-Socratic philosopher Empedokles of Akragas as the hero of his only play—the same Empedokles who tried to save mankind and himself by throwing himself into the volcano Etna. But also, in the "Thalia-Fragment" of *Hyperion*, in the definitive novel, as well as in a large number of his poems, we find passages that strikingly reflect his longing for death through reunion with the mother. (We have heard how Hölderlin's actual mother, in the letter quoted earlier, hoped for a reunion with her son in heaven.) How much it must have tempted but also terrified Hölderlin when the woman who had stirred up the deepest layers of passion and conflict in him, namely Susette Gontard—Diotima—expressed a longing for a reunion through mutual death. For example, we read in one of Susette's last letters to Hölderlin, written at the end of December 1799:

> *Ich musste gestern noch viel über Leidenschaft nachdenken. Die Leidenschaft der höchsten Liebe findet wohl auf Erden ihre Befriedigung nie! —— Fühle es mit mir: diese suchen wäre Torheit ——. Mit einander sterben! ——Doch still, es klingt wie Schwärmerei und ist doch so wahr ——, ist die Befriedigung.*

(Yesterday I had to think a lot about passion. The passion of the highest love will probably never find its fulfillment on earth! —— Feel it with me: to seek this would be folly ——. To die united! —— Yet stop, it sounds like a romantic wish and yet is so true ——, it is fulfillment.)

Critics have also speculated on the prophetic significance of the death of Diotima in volume 2 of *Hyperion*, especially since Hölderlin, in one of his very few extant letters to Susette, apologizes to her for letting the heroine of the novel die. We have almost no evidence on how this development in *Hyperion* affected Susette, unless the letter just quoted be construed as pertinent evidence. But I am willing to believe that it must have shaken Hölderlin deeply and stirred up unconscious guilt when Susette died in 1802, having seemingly wasted away in her frustrated passion.

But—and this brings into focus the other side of Hölderlin's perhaps deepest ambivalence—while he sought to be reborn through death and return to the mother earth, he seems to have become increasingly aware that such death would not necessarily mean blissful union and rebirth, but would rather mean madness, nothingness, or both. I know of no poem in Hölderlin's oeuvre that develops this point so movingly as his last completed hymn, "Mnemosyne," from which I quote the concluding stanza in the wording of the third and final version (2: 198):

> *Am Feigenbaum ist mein*
> *Achilles mir gestorben,*
> *Und Ajax liegt*
> *An den Grotten der See,*
> *An Bächen, benachbart dem Skamandros.*
> *An Schläfen Sausen einst, nach*
> *Der unbewegten Salamis steter*
> *Gewohnheit, in der Fremd, ist gross*
> *Ajax gestorben,*
> *Patroklos aber in des Königes Harnisch. Und es starben*
> *Noch andere viel. Am Kithäron aber lag*
> *Elevtherü, der Mnemosyne Stadt. Der auch, als*
> *Ablegte den Mantel Gott, das Abendliche nachher löste*
> *Die Locken. Himmlische nämlich sind*
> *Unwillig, wenn einer nicht die Seele schonend sich*
> *Zusammengenommen, aber er muss doch; dem*
> *Gleich fehlet die Trauer.*

(Beside the fig-tree
My Achilles has died and is lost to me,

And Ajax lies
Beside the grottoes of the sea,
Beside brooks that neighbour Scamandros.
Of a rushing noise in his temples once,
According to the changeless custom of
Unmoved Salamis, in foreign parts
Great Ajax died,
No so Patroclus, dead in the King's own armour.
And many others died. But by Cithaeron there stood
Eleutherae, Mnemosyne's town. From her also
When God laid down his festive cloak, soon after did
The powers of Evening sever a lock of hair. For the
Heavenly, when
Someone has failed to collect his soul, to spare it,
Are angry, for still he must; like him
Here mourning is at fault.)

We are indebted to Beissner (1) for having alerted us to the ways in which this extraordinary poem, right through its various versions with their many rich and overdetermined images, expresses a despair beyond despair—that is, that state of mind which, so it seems, allows only for suicide or massive schizophrenic disintegration and retreat.

Hölderlin invokes here, among many other things, the futility of heroic enterprises and heroic death; the despair, madness, and suicide of Ajax; the end of friendships; the failure of reconciliation between gods and mortals; the pointlessness of artistic efforts; and, perhaps most frightening, the end of all memory.

After this last hymn there followed only fragments before his madness (almost) silenced him.

I can be brief about my fourth and last point: of all artists who were misunderstood in their own time, Hölderlin probably fared worst. Yet the fate he feared most, as indicated in these last lines, that his work would be totally wiped out and forgotten, has not materialized—yet. He seems rather to have provided proof for the truth of one of his best-known lines: *"Was bleibet aber, stiften die Dichter"* (But what is lasting the poets provide [2: 189]).

References

1. Beissner, F. Hölderlins letzte hymne. In *Über Hölderlin*, ed. Jochen Schmidt. Frankfurt: Insel, 1970.
2. Beissner, F., and Beck, A., eds. *F. Hölderlin Grosse Stuttgarter Ausgabe*. Stuttgart: Kohlhammer, 1946.
3. Bertaux, P. *Hölderlin und die Französische Revolution*. Frankfurt: Suhrkamp, 1969.
4. Bleuler, E. *Dementia praecox oder gruppe der schizophrenien*. Leipzig and Vienna: Deuticke, 1911.
5. Freud, S. *Leonardo da Vinci and a memory of his childhood (1910)*. SE X, 57-137. London: The Hogarth Press, 1957.
6. ———. *Mourning and melancholia (1917)*. SE XIV, 237-258. London: Hogarth Press, 1957.
7. Hàussermann, U. *Friedrich Hölderlin in Selbstzeugnissen und Bilddokumenten*. Hamburg: Rowohlt, 1961.
8. Heston, L. Psychiatric disorder in foster-home reared children of schizophrenic mothers. *British Journal of Psychiatry* 112: 819-825, 1966.
9. Jaspers, K. *Strindberg und van Gogh. Versuch einer pathographischen Analyse unter vergleichender Heranziehung von Swedenborg und Hölderlin*. 3d ed. Bremen: Storm, 1951.
10. Kringlen, E. *Heredity and environment in the functional psychoses. An epidemiological-clinical twin study*. Oslo: Universitetsforlaget, 1967.
11. Lange. W. *Hölderlin. Eine Pathographie*. Stuttgart: Enke, 1909.
12. Pollin, W., and Stabenau, J. Biological, psychological and historical differences in a series of monozygotic twins discordant for schizophrenia. In *The transmission of schizophrenia*, ed. S. Kety and D. Rosenthal. London: Pergamon Press, 1969.
13. Ricoeur, P. *Freud and philosophy*. New Haven and London: Yale University Press, 1970.

14. Rosenbaum, C. *The meaning of madness.* New York: Jason Aronson, 1970.
15. Ryan, L. *Friedrich Hölderlin.* Stuttgart: Metzler, 1962.
16. Stierlin, H. *Conflict and reconciliation.* New York: Doubleday-Anchor and Jason Aronson, 1969.
17. Szondi, P. *Hölderlin-Studien.* Frankfurt: Suhrkamp, 1970.
18. Tienari, P. Psychiatric illness in identical twins. *Acta Psychiatrica Scandinavica* 39, 9-195, 1963.
19. Treichler, R. Die seelische Erkrankung Friedrich Hölderlins in ihren Beziehungen zu seinem dicterischen Schaffen. *Zeitschrift für die gesamte Psychiatria und Neurologie* 155: 40-144, 1936.
20. Waiblinger, W. *Friedrich Hölderlins Leben, Dichtung und Wahnsinn. Neue Ausgabe.* A. Beck, Marbach: Turmhahn-Bücherei, 1951.
21. Weissman, P. Theoretical considerations of ego regression and ego functions in creativity. *Psychoanalytic Quarterly* 36: 37-50, 1967.
22. Wells, F. Hölderlin. Greatest of schizophrenics. In *The literary imagination,* ed. H. M. Ruitenbeck. Chicago: Quadrangle Books, 1965.

Chapter 5

Relational Dynamics in the Life Course of One Schizophrenic Quadruplet

Identical twins and other multiple births (such as triplets and quadruplets) have long interested researchers on schizophrenia. These monozygotic siblings promise to throw new light on the vexing question of how heredity and environment might interact in bringing about the schizophrenic disorder. While, as of today, twin studies have not succeeded in settling this question, they have alerted us to many relevant data. In so doing, they have opened up new perspectives and raised new questions.

This chapter takes up one of these questions. It addresses itself to a finding that seems borne out by all the relevant literature: If identical twins are discordant for schizophrenia, the nonschizophrenic twin usually turns out to have been the leader, heavier at birth, first-born, more energetic, and more self-assertive. And in a pair that is concordant for schizophrenia, the first-born and more energetic twin develops, as a rule, a less severe schizophrenic disturbance than the other (2-8, 12, 13, 15, 16). Any exception to the above rule must arouse our interest, as it might bring into focus the schizophrenogenic impact of certain experiential constellations. Such an exception is provided by the patient we shall consider. This patient belongs to that set of schizophrenic multiple births most thoroughly studied in the psychiatric literature: the Genain quadruplets, whose story was published in 1963 under the editorship of David Rosenthal (9). The patient is Nora, the first-born of the quadruplets. The question is then: Why did Nora become and stay more seriously schizophrenic than Myra (her "twin")?

Nora was recently rehospitalized at the Clinical Center of the National Institutes of Health for a period of approximately one and a half years (9). During this time I was her psychotherapist and could begin to see in a "longitudinal" perspective Nora's attempts to grow up and to separate herself from her family. It is, above all, this perspective which permits a new look at the above question. I shall describe my psychotherapy with her only insofar as it bears on this question.

DIFFERENT LIFE COURSES OF NORA AND MYRA

With the above question in mind, let us first trace briefly the different life courses of Nora and Myra. For the present purpose I shall consider the girls as twins in a quad system. While such a point of view may seem problematical, I believe it makes good sense: Nora and Myra saw themselves as a twin pair and were seen as such by their parents and sisters. The many positive as well as negative aspects of this pairing became major topics in Nora's and Myra's psychotherapies.

Nora was born the eldest of the quadruplets. Her sisters, Iris, Myra, and Hester, were born next in that order. Nora weighed four pounds, eight ounces at the time of her birth. Myra tended to refer to Nora, the "strongest" and "first-born," as the "oldest." She described Nora and her relationship with the latter in the following words, as recorded by Dr. S. Perlin:[1]

> I think Nora was the leader. I mean, she was the first to talk, or rather I guess she sometimes felt that she was the first, and she did. And then, of course, I sort of waited for

her to do that. Although I wanted to talk ever so bad (laugh) but I just sort of waited, being sort of polite. You know she was the first born. She was first . . . . and I was the second because I catered to Nora. We got to liking each other a lot, you know. So as I say, first and third held together.

In school Nora worked hard and made the honor roll. Her intelligence was average, and her IQ scores and her school performance were better than those of her sisters. But, despite her assets, relatively good performance, and early leadership, Nora's later schizophrenic development was more serious and debilitating than Myra's.

Nora showed the first signs of this development at age 20 when she complained about shoulder and chest aches which had no organic basis. Appearing pressured, anxious, and unable to concentrate, she was forced to resign from her job at age 21. The following year she stayed at home doing very little and vacillated between a despairing apathy and anxious agitation. She developed a number of delusions, mostly of a somatic nature, and talked about people pursuing her and talking behind her back. Suicide was repeatedly on her mind and at one time was attempted.

From age 22 to age 24, she was intermittently hospitalized and received several courses of EST. As time went on, she appeared more withdrawn, delusional, and hallucinated. At the Clinical Center of the National Institutes of Health, where she was hospitalized with her sisters for approximately three years between the ages of 25½ and 28½, her course was, on the whole, not encouraging. "After a half year at NIH," we read, "her symptoms increased; she had delusions, hallucinations, marked fatigue, and lack of energy, was unable to engage in activities and unwilling to eat" (9).

After leaving the Clinical Center, Nora was transferred to a state hospital, where she stayed more than a year and a half. Here her condition gradually improved, and after her discharge, she took a business refresher course and subsequently passed an examination, which entitled her to work with the state tax department. The first several years she worked with modest competence. But she had difficulties with superiors and colleagues and could not deal well with complex and pressuring situations. Gradually, she became more stereotyped and restricted. She would stand in a corner, say "think, think," and be unable to sit down to do her work. Her performance deteriorated so badly that she was finally discharged for medical reasons. She would now stand for many hours in her mother's house, crying "kitchen, kitchen," and pulling her hair out. In so doing, she gave the impression of a chronic schizophrenic patient. Throughout these years she was seen about once every two weeks by a psychiatrist who prescribed varying amounts of Thorazine® and Trilafon®.

Nora's rehospitalization at the Clinical Center was arranged after Dr. Rosenthal, on one of his regular visits to the Genain home, had mentioned this possibility.

After her readmission to NIMH, she was often seen standing by herself and crying in a stereotyped manner: "I must be happy, I must be happy," or "don't worry, don't worry, don't worry," or "thought, thought, thought." In mumbling to herself, she would pull her hair out and make rhythmical, sneezing movements. (Her constant hair-pulling resulted in a partial baldness.) With her back rested against the wall of her room and seemingly impervious to the goings on around her, she appeared often lost in hallucinations.

Myra, the third-born quad and Nora's "pairing partner," weighed four pounds and four ounces at birth. As a child Myra appeared to be less aggressive, less domineering, and less competitively jealous than Nora. Also, Myra seemed to have had a "sweeter disposition" and was, in general, considered more outgoing and popular with people. Although once diagnosed as schizophrenic along with the rest of the quads, Myra appeared always less seriously disturbed and more "reachable" than the other girls. Myra had three and a half years of psychotherapy with Dr. Seymour Perlin, first as an inpatient and later as an outpatient at the Clinical Center.[2] After ending her therapy, Myra married and later gave birth to one child. Her husband, who is unstable and tends to drink excessively, is in the armed forces. Repeatedly Myra has thought of divorcing him, but at the moment the marriage still holds. She has, on the whole, managed her household competently and seems to get along with her neighbors on the Army base where she presently resides. Her continuing problems notwithstanding, Myra has thus (until now) mastered her life far more successfully than has Nora.[3]

DIFFERENT STRATEGIES FOR INTERPERSONAL SURVIVAL

How could Nora, the first-born, the "leader," and seemingly the strongest member of the tetrad, become more schizophrenic and more restricted than Myra? A key to an answer lies in the operation of so-called vicious or virtuous circles through which a minor deviation might lead to a major result. Hilde Bruch (3) and Paul Wender (17), among others, have illuminated the role of such vicious or virtuous circles in human development.[4]

In the case of the Genain quadruplets, we find at birth minor deviations such as differences in birth weight, in ordinal position, in sensitivity, and in energy level, and we can assume that these differences, through the mechanism just mentioned, could give rise to the major differences that are reflected in each quad's later personality and life course. What then caused some of such presumed minor differences to beget in Nora a more schizophrenic and in Myra a less schizophrenic development?

With this question in mind, we turn to those features in the transactional (or interpersonal) system which, in the cases of Nora and Myra, could amplify some and wipe out other deviations so as to either promote or counteract a schizophrenic disturbance. This transactional system is complex and comprises the relationships of each parent with the other, of each parent with the two girls in question, and finally of the girls with each other and with the other quads. I shall, at this point, not attempt to do justice to this relational complexity and shall mainly focus on the two sisters' relationships with their parents, but in particular with their mother. I have elsewhere (14) elaborated in detail why I consider the mother-child relationship to be fatefully formative.

Unfortunately, much of the two sisters' early relationship with their mother eludes a clear reconstruction because of missing, unverifiable, or even contradictory reports, despite the thorough research done by Dr. Rosenthal and his associates. Still, the following features emerge: The mother favored Nora and Myra over Iris and Hester, and she favored Myra over Nora. In favoring Nora and Myra, she recognized and affirmed in each girl some of those traits which she cherished in herself. In Nora this was chiefly a certain perfectionist and controlling compulsivity, a certain "hard-nosed over-adequacy," as it were; in Myra, in contrast, she seemed to affirm a softer, more amiable, and more sharing quality. Also, she seemed to appreciate in Myra a capacity for independent and flexible action. Thus, she recognized and encouraged in Myra a part of herself that "could get out and could get what she wanted." (Iris and Hester were, on the whole, negatively delineated. The mother affirmed in these girls mainly those negative traits, such as "dirty" sexuality, which she kept dissociated from her own awareness while fighting and disapproving of them in her husband.)

It appears that the mother's delineations[5] of Nora and Myra found some basis in the girls' actual appearance and disposition at birth. It seems likely that these delineations became hooked onto such minor, neonate deviations as Nora's presumable energetic assertiveness and Myra's "softer" emotional responsivity. But, also, it appears that these maternal delineations became a projective cast into which the girls had to fit themselves or risk losing their mother's approbation. This, then, staked out for each girl a characteristic "strategy for interpersonal survival" which further amplified certain aspects of her original dispositions while it minimized others.

Nora's strategy for survival consisted in molding her personality toward a symbiotic bond wherein she related to her mother in a preambivalent, idealizing, and submissive sweetness while she used her energy and "leadership qualities" to supervise the other quads (particularly Hester) and to set a model of perfectionist achievement. Myra's strategy for survival capitalized instead on her greater ability to attune herself to her mother's moods and concerns and, most important, on her capacity, supported by the mother, "to get out and get what she wanted." Thus, Myra appeared to build into her relationship with her mother a "counterbinding" element. These different survival strategies had different implications for the separation drama that awaited the girls in their adolescence and early adulthood.

VICISSITUDES OF THE SEPARATION DRAMA

In turning now to this separation drama, we find that some of Nora's seemingly greater assets, such as her skills and her leadership within the family, turned into liabilities. While she acted as the quads' leader and spokesman, her sisters had no love for her role (9).

> They suffered it more than they appreciated it. On the other hand, the tetrad was vital to Nora. Without it she was nothing, had nothing. She became dependent on the tetrad and had to maintain its integrity and its public image, but the dependency was not reciprocal. Her social position had no firm ground. Unlike Myra, she was more concerned with maintaining her dominance among the quads than in developing a personal link to the outside world.

Nora's assets, in other words, did not help her to draw increasingly on resources outside the family, while Myra could more and more avail herself of such resources.

Even more fateful for her separation efforts appears the manner in which Nora related to her parents. Here Nora's relationship to her father appears particularly important. Nora had always been her father's "favorite." As an adolescent and young adult, she became even more tied to him. "He wanted," in Myra's words, "all of her attention, in some respects the kind of attention he would get from another wife, not sexually of course, but just in other ways: time, compliments, devotion, homebody sorts of things" (9). In a veiled way, we must add, he also wanted her sexually. (Up into her early twenties, he would watch her, as well as the other girls, dress, change sanitary pads, and occasionally fondle Nora's breasts and perform similar sexually tainted acts. Yet he disavowed any sexual interest and instead indicated that he wanted to test the girls' innocence.) Along with affording Nora special attention, he forbade her to pay attention to other men. In his exhortations about the dangers of dating boys, he was inconsistent: he often told Nora about the horrors of being raped by boys, but when she on one occasion was actually subjected to a rape attack, he dismissed this episode as trivial. When Nora worked as a typist after her graduation from high school, he made sure that she never had lunch with a boy. Instead he himself lunched with her most of the time.

Myra, by contrast, who had always been more distant with him, could disregard such injunctions. She dated behind his back, learning to make herself attractive to other men. This later made it possible for her to attract and hold first a devoted therapist and later a husband. This is another instance of how, in the separation drama, a seemingly small initial advantage may provide the leverage for a major breakthrough.

In order to understand further the implications of Nora's and

Myra's different father relationships, we must once more turn to the mother. When the girls were eleven years old, the mother suffered an angina attack. According to Dr. Rosenthal, this event became critically important in that the mother now made Myra even more her favorite. Myra took over the household duties Mrs. Genain usually performed. She designated Myra "the sweet, dependable one, the maid," and appointed her the arbiter in family squabbles. Also, she made Myra her quasi-confidante. The stage was thus set for Myra to become more positively identified with her mother in a manner that fostered eventual self-determination while it lessened dependence on her father. (This did not eliminate many serious problems for Myra, but it improved her chances of later having rewarding and growth-inducing relationships outside her family.) Nora's fate was the opposite. While she lost status with her mother, she gained favor with her father.

This, however, had for Nora consequences beyond a mere "father fixation." The father was a weak man, drunkard, slacker, and philanderer. But further, he was treated by the mother in a contradictory fashion, depending on whether he was present or not. When he was present, Mrs. Genain mothered him; she pampered, babied, appeased, and took gentle care of him. "When she was with others, she presented," in the description of B. Basamania (1), "her husband as a cruel, hostile, raging man who was sexually immoral, perverted, and impotent."[6] Thus, Nora faced a special separation dilemma. While the mother "ceded" Nora to Mr. Genain, she also undermined any respect or love Nora could have for him. (The mother "ceded" Nora and, to a lesser degree, the other quads, to her husband also in the sense that she covertly tolerated and even encouraged Mr. Genain's veiled sexual advances toward them.) Therefore Nora found herself locked to a father whom her mother—the stronger parent, to whom she remained symbiotically captive—alternately treated as a baby and decried as a monster. I believe it is this bind which accounts for many features of Nora's subsequent breakdown and development and which makes understandable why she failed where Myra seemed to succeed.

IMPLICATIONS OF NORA'S SEPARATION DILEMMA

Let us now trace some implications of Nora's separation dilemma for her later experiences with men and, among those, with male therapists. This will lead us to take a look at her subsequent psychotherapies and relationships with "boy friends."

We begin with the psychotherapy she received during her first stay at the Clinical Center. Here her first therapist saw her for seventeen months. This was the time when the novelty and uniqueness of the quads' hospitalization tended to make the psychotherapeutic situation unusually complex and often competitive. Her first therapist made a point of waiting for Nora in his office and of abstaining from anything that could look like an active pusuit of his patient. Nora initially seemed eager to meet with this therapist, but soon began to see him less and less. In retrospect, it appears that Nora experienced this therapist's strategically employed passivity as a rebuff and lack of interest. Evidently, this was the second such blow for her, because she had already competed with Myra and the two other quads for Dr. Perlin (who had made the first home visit to the Genain family) and had lost for reasons intimated earlier.[7]

Nora saw a second therapist for nine months and responded postively in the beginning. After about six months this therapist challenged Nora's compliance and sweetness, and he did not feel discouraged when Nora, as happened in her later therapy with me, withdrew into confusion and hallucination. However, the progress stopped when, in the spring of that year, Nora's discharge from the Clinical Center was set for the end of the year. From this point on, Nora did little more in psychotherapy than mark time.

We note here that Nora, while being treated by male therapists without much success, remained strongly tied up with her father. We read in *The Genain Quadruplets* (9) that of all the quads, Nora was the most interested in her father's visits and often appeared deeply preoccupied with him. Toward the end of her stay at the NIMH, her father died. We read that she met the news of his death with stony silence and some depression. After the funeral, she appeared less simpering, smiling, and complaining, and became increasingly stern, depressed, and resentful.

Let us next trace how Nora, seemingly liberated from and yet internally bound to her deceased father, fared with her "boy friends."

NORA AND FRED

The first of these "boy friends" was a long-time hospitalized patient with whom Nora would often disappear while she was hospitalized at a state institution following her discharge from the Clinical Center. This relationship petered out before she met Fred. It is Fred who subsequently played a central role in her life and who sheds most light on her attempts to liberate herself from her dead father *and* from her living mother.

Fred, in his late fifties, was a friend of her mother, who was financially indebted to him. He ran a dance studio and owned a workshop in her home town. For some time, Nora worked for him as an assistant dance instructor. After a while she started irregular sexual relations with him. Fred was the active, pressuring partner; she would comply without enjoying these relations. More and more she appeared pressured and was made uneasy by them. There can be little doubt that this relationship contributed to, or even triggered, Nora's latest psychotic regression.

We notice here a repetition of the dynamics[8] that led to Nora's first psychotic breakdown, with Fred now being cast in the role of her father. As had happened in her early twenties, Nora could not move away from the family field and was, in effect, made more dependent on her mother, whose approval for the continuation of her relationship with Fred she needed. The more this dependence grew and the more she had to adopt a servile, helpless, idealizing position toward the mother, the more she had also to defend herself against the underlying rage, the disassociated and unexpressed side in her relationship to her mother. Again, it seems, she could only fight this rage by becoming ever more helpless, whining, dependent and yet withdrawn, thus finally approaching the state of the chronic, washed-out, passively stewing schizophrenic patient described earlier.

In one further important respect, Nora seems to have repeated an earlier family experience: Fred's daughter became Nora's teacher and rival as a dance instructor. With her, Nora developed an ambivalent (that is, partly adoring and partly jealous) relationship similar to the one she had with her sister, Myra.

Along with the similarities in interpersonal constellation, we also note significant differences.

Fred, a man in his late fifties, certainly seemed to resemble her father in many respects: he was not far from the latter in age and, according to Nora's account, was similarly intrusive and pressuring. However, Fred seems to have differed from her father in that he, Fred, appeared to be more generous, less jealous, and less paranoid than her father. Also, Fred was more accepted by Nora's mother than her father had been. As an adolescent and young adult, Nora had had to listen to her mother's constant tirades about her father's meanness and ineptness. Now she heard her mother praise Fred as a helpful and generous gentleman. Never in Nora's presence did the mother seem to disapprove of Fred, although she must have been aware of the fact that he had sexual relations with Nora. Nora thus got involved with a substitute father who, while resembling her real father, appeared in some respects an improvement over the latter. And this substitute father was not devalued by her mother. However, while this interpersonal constellation seems to have given Nora some opening for growth, it mired her, paradoxically, also more deeply in her separation dilemma. Even though her father's death seems to have made it possible for Nora to get involved with a man like Fred, it appears also that now, with Mr. Genain out of the picture, Mrs. Genain could even more unabashedly foster an "incestuous" relationship between Nora and her new quasi-husband. (There are indications that Fred, with covert encouragement from the mother, also tried, and possibly consumated, sexual relations with the other quads.) Thus, Nora found herself again in a familiar predicament: the incestuous elements in her relationship with a father figure, along with the reactivated dependency on and closeness to her mother, subjected her to those very conflicts which had triggered her first schizophrenic breakdown.

THE SEPARATION DILEMMA
REFLECTED IN NORA'S PSYCHOTHERAPY

Let us, finally, consider how Nora's separation dilemma shaped my psychotherapy with her. For this purpose I shall present at first a brief overview of this therapy, which lasted for one and a half years and comprised 133 sessions of approximately fifty minutes duration each.

Throughout many of her therapeutic sessions, Nora related to me in a stereotyped, stale, and boring manner. She made the same point hundreds of times and seemed to make little or no attempt to tune herself into my wavelength, to share a common focus with me, to make lively, visualizable, and interesting what concerned her.[9] I experienced myself as a replaceable sounding board and often wanted to withdraw or to end the sessions. Frequently, I felt close to erupting in frustration. Yet, when I withdrew or showed irritation, Nora's hold on reality seemed to become precarious. She then talked, in a voice increasingly whining and meek, about her vision becoming blurry, about peculiar "light lines" arising in her head, about a "funny loneliness" taking possession of her, and similar topics. Often she would also mention some somatic trouble, such as pains in her chest or her arm, some headache or itching. (We know from her previous history that she tried to make sense out of strange and disintegrative experiences by placing them into some somatic framework.)

Nora could switch within one session, often several times, from a restricted and restrictive state to one where her experiences seemed to become blurry and uncanny. Often these changes occurred from one therapeutic session to the next. At times they appeared almost predictable.

Whenever Nora had to find her way in a complex interpersonal field which elicited ambivalence and conflict, she felt quickly lost. This became apparent, for example, when Nora was attracted to the father of her roommate, a schizophrenic girl, and then could not understand why the latter behaved angrily. She could not understand that her roommate might be jealous.

When the ward staff at times viewed and treated her withdrawal as stubbornness and resistance, Nora felt more overwhelmed, confused, and prone to get the "rush, rush" feeling. She would then use many individual therapy sessions to express her consternation and anger about her treatment on the ward. But also in so doing, she would use me primarily as a sounding board for endlessly repetitive complaints, and would "shrink" if I indicated that the nurses might have a point or could offer her something.

My dilemma was, thus, that I would either serve Nora as her interpersonal anchorage for a restricted yet "workable" hold on reality or that I, by reacting more "naturally," would cause her to withdraw into a shadowy, semipsychotic existence. If I listened captively to what she said, I could, to a degree, ensure that she would remain fairly organized; if I indicated inattention, irritation, or even puzzlement, she would appear to "shrink," to "loosen," and to become unreachable.

This, however, was not the whole picture. As our work progressed, longer, more varied exchanges took place. But these more varied, lively, and "sharing" transactions remained precariously embedded in a relationship in which either Nora made me captive to her restriction or I, in trying to break out of such captivity, seemed to erode her hold on reality.

A dilemma similar to the one that pervaded her individual therapy marked also her interactions with her fellow patients and nurses. Nora often reached out to these persons in the manner of a submissive little girl. But when the latter responded by offering advice or criticism, she was quickly overwhelmed. She would feel panicky, have a "rush, rush" feeling, withdraw into her room, and stand there seemingly paralyzed, her head pressed against the wall and, it appeared, absorbed in hallucinations. Often Nora would try to flee from her ward into the structured peacefulness of her typing office; or she would simply run out of the building, go on walks, and avoid people as much as she could.

Nora passed her Civil Service examination approximately ten months after her admission to the Clinical Center, and she then began an enthusiastic job search. Unfortunately, this search was unsuccessful despite sustained and heroic efforts on her part. After dozens of rebuffs at the hands of prospective employers, her morale began to wane. She felt herself now more pressured by the nurses, whose advice and help she earlier had eagerly sought and appreciated. Also, she felt herself becoming lonelier and lonelier. It happened around this time that all the other patients in her own age group left the ward, which then became populated with adolescents. I heard more and more of Nora's wish to return to her home town in order to be close to her mother, her sisters, and those friends whom she had made while she was a young adult. In addition to finding herself thus demoralized in her job search and alienated from her fellow patients, she had to cope with a long

separation from me. I could not forego a long-planned two-month
trip to Europe. During my absence she was seen by Dr. Rosenthal.
When I returned from my trip, I fell ill and was bed-ridden for
another four weeks. When I finally saw Nora again, she appeared
anxious, restless, and deeply shaken by a recent rejection at the
hands of an employment agent. She could no longer conceive of
becoming an outpatient and finding a typing job in Washington
within the foreseeable future.

Thus it came as no surprise when Nora decided to return to her
home town, where she expected to resume life with her mother
and to find a nearby job. For some time the mother, in a more or
less veiled manner, had asked Nora to return home. Finally, the
latter responded. Immediately after Nora made her decision, she
seemed to feel only triumph and relief about having been able to do
so. However, her subsequent letters to me indicated that, by
leaving the NIMH and her therapist, she had suffered a great loss.

TRANSFERANCE ASPECTS OF THE SEPARATION DILEMMA

In the above overview, I have focused on Nora's restriction and
restrictiveness as the central aspect in her psychotherapy with me.
This restriction and restrictiveness, I believe, are the offshoot of
Nora's earlier-mentioned strategy for interpersonal survival,
wherein she related to her mother in a preambivalent, idealizing,
and submissive sweetness. This had become Nora's way of coping
with her mother's dominating and intrusive behavior. She had
learned to adopt the position of the obedient little girl who tries
always to be good, to work hard, and who never dares to question
the idealized image of her mother. The entrenchment of this
defensive position had presented the greatest obstacle in her first
psychotherapy at the NIMH. It proved similarly formidable in this
second attempt at psychotherapy. Again and again, I was
impressed by the unshakable rigidity of Nora's idealization of her
mother and, by way of transference, of me. Once I asked Nora
whether she could conceive of a situation in which her mother

might be wrong. With an expression of fright and disbelief, she ruled this possibility out. At one time the mother called her sister, Myra, the sicker of the two, and Nora accepted this unquestioningly and literally. In line with idealizing her mother, Nora perceived the latter as the unwavering pillar of the family. Also, she considered her a martyr, who had sacrificed herself for the quads and, in so doing, had had to cope with a mean, drunken, and inept husband.

During the psychotherapy, much of what I experienced as Nora's restrictiveness resulted, without doubt, from her casting me in the role of her idealized mother. Nora idealized me from the beginning. And, in making me near perfect, she restricted and deadlocked me in the manner described earlier. It was only gradually that this deadlock lessened.

To the degree that this happened, our interchange became more varied. Even some humorous and gentle note could then enter it. When this occurred, I became more aware of a childlike wooing, which seemed erotically tinged. Nora cared more about making herself attractive.

While this happened, I heard more about her father. Usually she would speak about him in grim terms: he was a drunkard who possessively shut her off from all joys in life (not once would he allow her to go to a movie) and who made her mother miserable. While she thus debunked (evidently parroting her mother) her own father, she talked longingly about Fred and about the father of her roommate whose home she had visited repeatedly. She had tears in her eyes when she talked about these possible father substitutes, emphasizing their warmth and givingness as against her own father's harshness. Also she commented more and more about me as the kind of father she would have liked to have had. Several times she grasped the picture of my little daughter in my office and intimated that she would like to be in the latter's place. "Oh, your daughter is such a darling, she looks so happy, she is so fortunate in having a father like you."

At this point in the therapy, it seemed that Nora, while drawing a dark picture of her father, could yet bring some positive aspects of her father relationship into the transference. Partly, she seems to have acted on a wish, in the sense that she related to me and the above-mentioned father surrogates in the way she would have liked to relate to her own father; and, partly, she seems to have been able to build on the base of an earlier good father-daughter relatedness. But this good relatedness, it appeared now, could never be enjoyed and appreciated because of the mother's devastating undercutting of the father.

Along with this activation of the father transference, there was now some movement, and the therapeutic relationship became more varied. Nora slowly became able to express criticism of me and to become aware of some resistance. Several times during this period she was late, and one time she missed her session altogether. She could admit that there might have been something about the sessions that made her reluctant to come. While the thaw in her restriction thus got underway, Nora talked more about her sister, Myra. She made it clear that she expected to follow in Myra's footsteps—to move, like Myra, from NIMH into a halfway house and to find, like Myra, a husband in the Lutheran church in downtown Washington, D. C. In bringing up Myra, Nora revealed her intense ambivalence toward her sister.

TERMINATION

As it turned out, none of these themes and transference feelings could be developed in depth, as Nora left the Clinical Center after approximately one and a half years. As I indicated earlier, Nora had reasons to be dissatisfied with Washington, with the Clinical Center, and with her psychotherapy. However, the main reason for her leaving psychotherapy and the Clinical Center was, I believe, her mother.

There were unmistakable signs that the mother began to withdraw her support of Nora's therapy after Nora had stayed at the NIMH for about nine months and had clinically improved. While I received several grateful and rather obsequious letters from the mother during this first period, later such letters stopped. Instead, I learned from Nora that the mother indicated through her letters and telephone calls to her that she, the mother, needed and wanted Nora at home. The mother felt particularly lonely after Myra, following a lengthy stay in the parental home, had left in order to follow her husband to a foreign country. The mother also felt more burdened by the demands that Iris and Hester, both hospitalized in a nearby state institution but increasingly able either to visit the mother or to invite the latter's visits, made on her time and energies. Nora appeared as the one who could ease these burdens. The more responsive Nora became to the beckonings from her mother, the more hopeless she felt about ever establishing herself in the Washington area.

It appeared, in brief, that Nora could only stay in therapy with a male therapist as long as her mother gave her permission. When the mother began to withdraw this permission, Nora remained captive to her real mother, as she had remained captive to the latter's restricting, internalized views and prohibitions. Thus, while Nora *had* progressed during her last hospitalization (that is, appeared more energetic and much better organized when she left the Clinical Center than when she came), this progress must be judged with caution.

SUMMARY

I have tried to give an overview of those relational vicissitudes which may have caused Nora, the first-born of the Genain quadruplets, to become and remain more seriously schizophrenic than her sister, Myra, despite the fact that Nora earlier seems to have presented the lesser risk. In giving this overview, I have described strategies of interpersonal survival in Nora and in Myra. These survival strategies appeared forced on the girls by the manner in which their parents related to them. In the case of Nora, her survival strategy exposed her to characteristic conflicts and binds. These binds and conflicts became revealed in what I have described as her separation dilemma. This dilemma was at first structured in her relationship with her parents and sisters and was later reenacted in other important relationships, modeled after the earlier ones. All these relational vicissitudes, I believe, make understandable why Nora became more seriously schizophrenic than Myra.

Notes

[1] Perlin, S.: The psychoanalytic therapy of a schizophrenic quadruplet. A case report. Unpublished monograph, National Institute of Mental Health, 1969.

[2] A shortened report on this treatment is contained in *The Genain Quadruplets* (9); the original can be obtained from D. S. Perlin on request.

[3] D. Rosenthal will soon publish a follow-up report on the Genain family.

[4] Wender (17) used the term "deviation amplifying feedback" (DAF) (derived from cybernetics) to describe this well-known mechanism. He quotes the following example, taken from the nonhuman sphere, which was first introduced by Maruyama: A boulder in a temperate climate is likely to be replaced by gravel once a minor deviation, in the form of a crack caused by random perturbation, is introduced. For, with the succession of seasons, rain will fall, freeze, and expand the crack into a fissure. As this fissure enlarges and new ones form, organic material or plant seeds will find their way into the interstices, grow further, enlarge the cracks, cause new ones to form, etc. In a similar manner we can conceive that, given a certain interpersonal (or transactional) environment, minor deviations might eventually lead to major effects.

[5] The concept of delineations, as here intended, has been introduced and elaborated by R. Shapiro (10).

[6] B. Basamania (1) has described how these contrasting attitudes in Mrs. Genain grew out of her childhood experiences with her own parents.

[7] Dr. Perlin chose Myra as his patient at the time when he, as the representative of NIMH, made the first contact with the Genain family. He comments on this choice as follows: "Myra was selected by the therapist at that early date (prior to an only apparently haphazard mode of assignment at the NIMH). The reasoning for choice included her social adjustment, work history, and clinical status. Hester was felt to be the most regressed, and the least amenable to any form of therapy. Iris, severely catatonic, seemed potentially a person who might respond to electroconvulsive therapy on a temporary basis. Nora seemed the most anxiety-ridden but also the most productive of anxiety in the therapist."

⁸ In addition to similar interpersonal dynamics, we find similarities in Nora's work situations preceding her first and last psychotic breakdowns. In her life and work after her discharge from the state hospital (subsequent to her first stay at NIMH), Nora manifested the same wish to please people, the same relatively high energy level, the same perfectionism that she had shown as an adolescent and young adult. At that time, this perfectionism and wish to please had made her a promising secretary, but had also contributed to her psychotic downfall; the more anxious and disturbed she got and the harder she tried, the more she became incapable of sitting back and taking stock of herself. She finally had to resign from her job and had to be hospitalized at the local state hospital. She was then in her late twenties. After Nora was again discharged from another state hospital, at the age of 29, she worked similarly hard and perfectionistically in her job at the state tax department and in so doing became gradually more anxious, panicky, and insensitive to what other persons and her job situation required—only this time her psychotic disintegration occurred less acutely. Nora simply seemed to get more and more into an obsessive stew, which immobilized and incapacitated her.

⁹ In so doing, she exemplified many of the core features in a schizophrenic's transactions, as described by M. T. Singer and L. C. Wynne (11).

References

1. Basamania, B. The development of schizophrenia in the child in relation to unresolved childhood conflicts in the mother. In *The Genain Quadruplets*, ed. D. Rosenthal. New York: Basic Books, 1963.

2. Bruch, H., and Palombo, S. Conceptual problems in schizophrenia. *Journal of Nervous and Mental Diseases* 132: 114-117, 1961.

3. ———. The insignificant difference: discordant incidence of anorexia nervosa in monozygotic twins. *American Journal of Psychiatry* 126: 85-90, 1969.

4. Gifford, S., Murawski, B., Brazelton, T. B., and Young, G. C. Differences in individual development within a pair of identical twins. *International Journal of Psycho-Analysis* 47: 261-268, 1966.

5. Kringlen, E. Schizophrenia in male monozygotic twins. *Acta Psychiatrica Scandinavica Supplement* 178: 1, 1964.

6. Lu, Y. Mother-child role relations in schizophrenia: a comparison of schizophrenic patients with non-schizophrenic siblings. *Psychiatry* 24: 133-142, 1961.

7. Pollin, W., Stabenau, J. R., Mosher L., and Tupin, J. Life history differences in identical twins, discordant for schizophrenia. *American Journal of Orthopsychiatry* 36: 492-509, 1966.

8. Pollin, W., and Stabenau, J. R. Biological, psychological and historical differences in a series of monozygotic twins discordant for schizophrenia. In *The transmission of schizophrenia*, ed. D. Rosenthal and S. S. Kety. Oxford: Pergamon Press, 1968.

9. Rosenthal, D., ed. *The Genain quadruplets.* New York: Basic Books, 1963.

10. Shapiro, R. Action and family interaction in adolescence. In *Psychoanalysis*, ed. J. Marmor. New York: Basic Books, 1968.

11. Singer, M. T., and Wynne, L. C. Principles for scoring communication defects and deviances in parents of schizophrenics: Rorschach and TAT scoring manuals. *Psychiatry* 29: 260-288.

12. Stabenau, J. R., and Pollin, W. Early characteristics of monozygotic twins discordant for schizophrenia. *Archives of General Psychiatry* 17: 723-734, 1967.

13. ———, Tupin, J., Werner, M., and Pollin, W. A comparative study of families of schizophrenics, delinquents, and normals. *Psychiatry* 28: 45-59, 1965.

14. Stierlin, H. *Conflict and reconciliation.* New York: Doubleday, 1969.

15. Sydow, G., and Rinne, A. Very unequal "identical twins". *Acta Paediatrica* 47: 163-171, 1958.

16. Tienari, P. Psychiatric illness in identical twins. *Acta Psychiatrica Scandinavica Supplement* 39: 9-195, 1963.

17. Wender, P. Vicious and virtuous circles: the role of deviation amplifying feedback in the origin and perpetuation of behavior. *Psychiatry* 31: 309-324, 1968.

Chapter 6

The Functions of "Inner Objects"

This chapter introduces the concept of inner-object functions, conceived to be comparable to, but not identical with, ego functions. This concept promises to illuminate several aspects of psychoanalytic object-relations theory which have remained unclear or controversial.

The inner objects of psychoanalysis can be viewed as fulfilling three main functions.

First, they perform an *inner referent function*. In this sense, inner objects are best described as object representations: they represent external objects within the psyche in a manner which emphasizes the former's congruence with these external objects. They thus serve cognitive reality orientation. They presuppose memory and the capacity to symbolize. They resemble Semon's engrams in that they allow us to tie a new percept to a familiar image. They provide a file for mental recall and make possible an adaptive intelligence which can rely on differentiated inner structures.

Second, inner objects serve as guideposts for interpersonal relationships, present and future. In this sense they appear best defined as object images. They provide an inner anticipatory set which narrows the selection of possible outer objects. This applies mainly to potential partners in relationships. Inner objects as anticipatory sets correspond partly to what Boszormenyi-Nagy, among others, has called "need templates" (3). Sutherland (29) speaks of the inner objects as "a scanning apparatus which seeks a potential object in the outer world" (p. 117). Novey (21), in treating object representations as dynamisms, also suggests this function. The young girl, in seeking a marital partner, is unconsciously guided by an inner object which has the features of her father. The masochist searches and finds his needed sadist— which he carries as an inner object. And so on. The inner objects determine our relational course like a gyroscope, a steering device which minimizes the distracting impact of weather conditions. Therefore I shall refer to their *gyroscopic function*, using the metaphor of the gyroscope somewhat as did Riesman (22) when he wanted to characterize the inner-directed personality. In addition to the stabilizing function of the gyroscope, I want to emphasize the dynamic, directing moment inherent in inner objects.[1] (An inner object in this sense is similar to a concept. A concept also, as Lidz, 18, has pointed out, serves as an anticipatory set for expectations and thus fulfills a dynamic steering role. For example, in the concepts "infectious mononucleosis" and "leukemia"—both referring to blood diseases—different expectations, attitudes, and courses of action as to treatment and outcome are structured.)

Finally, the third function of inner objects is to contribute to the relative autonomy of the individual. They enable him to fall back on himself by relating to some part within. They constitute inner resources and facilitate an inner dialogue. I shall therefore refer to their *autonomy-furthering function*. When we have this third function in mind, we focus primarily on intrapsychic events rather than external objects.

To a degree these three functions are interdependent, reflecting different aspects of one total situation and suggesting, within limits, common psychic correlates or structures.

This raises next the question as to how far inner-object functions, as defined here, can be related to well-known ego functions. The intent and scope of this chapter preclude a detailed pursuit of this question, but some orienting and clarifying remarks seem in order.

INNER-OBJECT FUNCTIONS AND EGO FUNCTIONS

The inner-object functions, as defined here, for the most part presuppose or are identical with well-known ego functions. This is evident in the case of what I called the referent function of inner objects. The cognitive mastery of reality—requiring, among other things, the ability for sharp and rapid discrimination, for the differentiated handling of memories and percepts, for choice, and for task-appropriate dissociation—can be viewed as a manifestation of ego functions as well as inner-object functions. The same, to a considerable degree, holds true for the gyroscopic and autonomy-furthering functions of inner objects: here also we note an overlap[2] with well-established ego functions such as anticipation, goal-directed thinking, and integration and organization with regard to many intrapsychic and interpersonal processes. Still, a focus on inner-object functions (as against a focus on ego functions) entails a somewhat different position of our searching telescope that is bound to bring into view different distinctions and different perspectives. For example, the gyroscopic (or steering) function of most objects seems much more tied to superego phenomena (e.g., the early internalization of parental "whole" or "part" objects) than to ego phenomena, as these are currently conceptualized. This would be in line with Hartmann and Loewenstein's (15) conceptualization of "direction-giving" superego functions.

This different perspective comes into view also when we compare the geneses of ego and inner-object functions. Since Hartmann, we distinguish between ego functions which grow out of the conflict-free area[3] and those resulting from intrapsychic conflict. Similarly, we can speak of inner-object functions, such as the referent functions, which seem to develop (relatively) independently of the vicissitudes and patternings of early identifications and introjections (as these vicissitudes have been described by Freud, Fenichel, Sandler and Jacobson, among others) and those, such as the gyroscopic function, which are shaped and colored largely by these vicissitudes and patternings—not least, of course, by the vicissitudes of the oedipal period.

Considerations such as these make it evident that there are different theoretical thrusts and different potentials for conceptual linkage and leverage inherent in an ego-functions, as compared to an object-functions, approach. A brief look at Hartmann's basic theoretical vantage points makes this understandable.

Hartmann's ego psychology can be seen as partly explicating and partly enlarging the conceptual potential of Freud's structural theory in the direction of a drive control system. Under this main viewpoint he developed his detailed analyses of ego apparatuses, structures, and functions, out of which grew his elaboration of the concepts of secondary autonomy of the ego, the crucial role of neutralization, the conflict-free area, and others. Hartmann chose, we might say, to develop those features of Freud's structural theory which could be most easily reconciled with the basic tenets of Freud's theory of drives. Insofar as he took off from the same theoretical framework (Freud's structural theory) and hence largely from the same clinical phenomena as did the object-relational approach presented here, it is not surprising that his ego psychology should bring to light functions similar to those implied in the term object functions. Still, the differences revealed in these two theoretical approaches seem significant. They will become clearer in the following exposition.

DISTURBANCES OF INNER-OBJECT FUNCTIONS

In the organic as well as in the psychological realms, it is usually a disturbance in a function which exposes and highlights the latter's nature. In order better to understand disturbances in inner-object functions, we must remind ourselves that human relationships unfold dialectically in a manner which affects the inner as well as the outer objects: the inner objects, as they are affected by outer objects, are constantly remodeled and restructured.[4] But, to a degree, the inner objects, through the efforts of an actively adapting subject, also affect outer objects. This accounts for the dialectic, expanding circularity of the relationship. A disturbance of inner-object functions then implies that, on one level or the other, this dialectic circularity is interfered with. It is above all the psychotherapy of schizophrenic patients which reveals disturbances of inner-object functions.

Many seemingly undifferentiated schizophrenic patients are extreme examples for the disturbance of the *referent functions of inner objects*. They appear unable to connect, enduringly and distinctly, with their inner frame of reference what they experience and perceive externally. Hence nothing seems to sink in to them; inside and outside, past and future, they and their therapists, merge blurrily into each other. Their file of inner percepts appears amorphous and jumbled. As long as the referent functions of their inner objects remain thus chaotically disturbed, they are bound to experience their therapists as blurred, discontinuous, and disjointed. The latter, in turn, are themselves prone to feel useless and fragmented.

In these extreme cases the dialectic circularity of a therapeutic relationship, as mentioned earlier, appears aborted from the beginning: there seems to exist little or no nodal point from which a therapeutic dialogue could germinate. When trying to relate, patient and therapist seem to tread on quicksand.

A disturbance of the gyroscopic function of inner objects can present itself in contrasting ways—which nonetheless herald a similar negative relational outcome: they prevent the individual from experiencing an enduring and dialectically unfolding relationship. In the first case the inner objects, or object images, appear too rigidly entrenched. This allows little leeway for the above-mentioned circular process to occur. The possibility for remodelling and refitting these inner objects through an ongoing dialectic, i.e., through new relational experiences, is therefore slight. Instead, the subject feels driven to match his unchangeable inner objects with outer objects which are perceived as equally unchangeable. This condemns the individual to tread a rigid and narrow relational path with only scant hope of reaching his goal. For this subject will have only very limited object choices available to him. He appears committed to chase an unalterable ideal. His inner gyroscope sets his course too rigidly.

This is the case in many so-called father or mother fixations, where the internalized parental image allows for little or no correction through relational experience, with the result that many of these people wind up endlessly searching for the ideal partner. This "jamming" of the inner gyroscope, of course, often grows out of an unresolved oedipal conflict: ambivalence towards an over-cathected and hence too rigidly internalized parent has been defused through the idealization of the latter. This idealization, in turn, makes any realistically available partner appear wanting.

In the other variety of disturbance of the gyroscope function, the object images, instead of being too rigidly entrenched, appear too loose and changeable. They have then too little gyroscopic valence and are too unspecific as anticipatory sets. They fit themselves effortlessly into a wide variety of outer objects. Thus they no longer steer the subject effectively towards a manageable range of suitable partners. Such a person appears rudderless in his (or her) relational quest. He resembles a German Dachshund which follows any master who happens to beckon him. This, for example, applies to certain (often amorphous) hysterical patients, who seem constantly driven to incorporate (and become infatuated with) the power and magnetism of so-called strong personalities.

Also, in these instances the oedipal conflict usually appears unresolved. We may speak now of a constant jolting of the inner gyroscope in an attempt to cope with the reactivated ambivalence towards the oedipal parent through rapid decathexis and recathexis, i.e., through a quick swinging around of the inner rudder.

Whether the inner gyroscope is set too rigidly or too loosely, a circularly unfolding and yet enduring dialectic with external objects will be impossible in either case.

While disturbances in the referent and gyroscopic functions of inner objects bring to light mainly an individual's precarious intrapsychic base for his relating to external objects, the disturbance in the autonomy-furthering function of inner objects highlights the importance of what we might describe as the intrapsychic drama. These disturbances appear most important from a clinical point of view, but also seem difficult to understand and describe.

Freud (7) opened up such understanding by introducing the concept of narcissism and by subsequently differentiating primary from secondary narcissism. It is chiefly secondary narcissism which brings to light disturbances in the autonomy-furthering function of inner objects.

The subject resorts to secondary narcissism when, for some reason, he has found outer objects either unsatisfactory or too difficult to cathect. The cathexis is then rechanneled within the subject. The cathexis does not there cease to exist, and a typical intrapsychic relational drama can thus unfold. The ego (according to Freud, the chief actor in this drama) assumes now the role of a frustrated lover and offers itself as a love object to the id.

Only an established and differentiated ego can do this. Hence secondary narcissism can only become a reality once the ego has matured. Only within a relatively complex and differentiated psychic arena can the inner relational drama be acted out.

In enacting this inner drama, the subject can find relative

independence and autonomy by relating to an integrated inner world which is rich and meaningful to him. He can fall back on his own resources and enter into a dialogue with himself. Up to a degree, he can do without others, i.e., without outer objects.

But only up to a degree! When this degree is exceeded, the inner drama becomes dangerously overinvested. And this is the more likely the less assimilated, the less anchored in a "true self" these inner objects are. The subject then undergoes torture and frustration, agony and bliss, by merely relating to his inner objects. It is at this point that relative autonomy turns into alienation and secondary narcissism becomes pathological: The inner objects—often (as in certain types of schizophrenia) in the form of frightfully concretized, unassimilated and "split" inner voices[5] and "things"—will now exclusively engage the subject's love and hate and cause him to take a detached and often schizoid stance towards the world of real human relations.

For, in a sense, this inner drama is all shadowboxing. The subject is trapped within himself. He becomes egocentric like a small child. In being hung up on his inner drama, outer objects cease to matter to him. Having become a fortress unto himself, he can no longer be touched by their possible loss. He becomes exempt from common human suffering, grief, and mourning and thereby misses out on life. And, along with shying away from life, he loses his chance for ego change and ego growth via abandoned object cathexis (or object loss) as described by Freud. Here also we find thus an interference with an unfolding relational dialectic.

Such a pathological narcissism Freud found in melancholia, as well as in other serious narcissistic syndromes, such as schizophrenia and hypochondriasis. Freud noted further an important implication of this libidinal withdrawal from the outer object world: the individual's inability to establish meaningful and lasting transference relationships. Seriously narcissistic patients, in Freud's opinion, disqualified themselves from psychoanalysis.[6]

INNER-OBJECT FUNCTIONS IN THE LIGHT OF
CLASSICAL PSYCHOANALYTIC THEORY

Inner-object functions, as delineated here, appear foreshadowed in Freud's conceptualization of the role and nature of objects in psychoanalytic theory.

Freud's interest in the concepts of object and object relationships originated with his theory of drives, since he conceived these drives to have sources, aims, and *objects*. To the degree that he developed and modified his drive theory over the years, he also developed and modified his object concept. Eventually, this concept came to encompass partial and whole, internal and external, real and hallucinated objects.

Freud redefined (partly by implication) the role and nature of the drives—and hence those of the object—when he introduced his structural theory (10). The crucial paper was the one on "The Ego and the Id." At this point in Freud's development, psychoanalytic theory not only reached a new level of complexity; but also the position of its searching telescope shifted. Through this shift in position, new clinical insights—particularly about the dynamics of depression—came into focus as new data unfolded and new perspectives opened up.

Along with these new perspectives, a "structural" psychoanalytic object concept emerged. The term *"Besetzung"* (which in English was rendered "cathexis") seemed well fitted to express this structural dimension in the object concept, as it denotes "sitting on," "occupying," "taking possession." Therefore, while the term "drive discharge," as used in a prestructural context, implied a volatile, "coming and going" quality of libidinal investment in the object, the structural viewpoint now emphasized the subject's permanent hold on the latter.[7]

Freud's structural theory, in other words, created the conceptual base which allowed the object to be viewed as being permanently tied to the subject. This structural relationship between object and subject implies that the individual needs not only drive-discharges but also to supply these drive-discharges with objects. And this supply of objects must be reliable. To a degree, the objects must become enduring and predictable. This, in turn, will affect the quality of the drive-discharges. They will have to become more modulated and, in a sense, more disciplined and toned down.

But Freud's structural theory—and this seems most important—in viewing the subject as orienting himself to structured and predictable objects, also tried to conceptualize those inner psychic schemata which made possible enduring and structured object relations. By focusing on these correlates or schemata, he came to adumbrate the concepts of inner object, object image and object-representations, as these have come to be used in psychoanalytic theory.

This implied a further shift in the position of the searching telescope: whereas the structural theory initially seemed to illuminate how inner schemata represented external objects and how the former accounted for the latter's enduringness within the psyche, these schemata, or inner objects, came also to be seen as intrapsychic forces in their own right. Hence their intrapsychic vicissitudes and their relationships to one another became matters of interest—while their relationship to external objects at times seemed to lose in significance. It is in this sense that Freud's structural theory prepared the ground for viewing inner objects as central features of a complex inner drama.

The existence of these two conceptual dimensions of inner objects—their tie-up with external objects (which they are supposed to represent) and their importance as intrapsychic forces in their own right—has subsequently created confusion and controversy about the use of the terms *inner object, object image,* and *object-representation.* Such authors as Sandler (23, 24), Hartmann (14), and Jacobson (16) have criticized the use of the term *inner object* at places where the term *object-representation* would have been more appropriate. They pointed to the elements of anthropomorphization and reification inherent in such uncritical and seemingly metaphorical usage. But they could sometimes not live up to their own critical admonitions, as Jacobson (16, p. 6, footnote), for one, is willing to admit. This is understandable because they could not disregard the power and intricacy of an intrapsychic drama which, in order to be adequately portrayed, seemed to require some recourse to anthropomorphization and metaphor.

Freud, of course, has set the precedent here as well. After he had conceptualized the structural theory, he depicted the relationship between the agencies id, ego, and superego—all of which, in the sense intended here, can be viewed as analogues or even prototypes of inner objects—in a dramatizing, anthropomorphizing manner.

We read of the ego "offering itself as a love object to the id" (8), of the ego's "erotic attachment to a sadistic superego" (12), or of the ego "acting in obedience to the superego" (11). Clearly, id, ego, and superego appear here as the chief actors, personalized and active, in a vividly depicted intrapsychic drama. The sense of inner drama was maintained when these agencies were viewed as having their own psychic organization, their own vested interests, and—although this is still a controversial issue—their own energy resources, and when conflicts and reconciliations between them came to be seen as constant and necessary occurrences.

Inner objects, it therefore follows, can be defined both with respect to external objects which they are supposed to represent *and* with respect to the intrapsychic drama in which they figure as potent forces. (It is from this latter vantage point that the agencies id, ego and superego can be considered the—admittedly often hypostatized—analogues or prototypes of inner objects.) This conclusion suggests that we use the concept "inner objects" as a broad, explanatory term.

This broadening of the term, however, in order not to result in a loss of explanatory leverage, must be balanced by an attempt to sharpen it by defining the *functions* of inner objects in their relations with external objects and/or the role they play in the intrapsychic drama. These functions I have tried to describe in the foregoing.

In thus focusing on the functions of inner objects, we deliberately bypass many of the issues relating to the genesis and nature of internalizations and identifications as these have been taken up by Jacobson, Sandler, Schafer, Modell, Loewald, Novey, and others. However, I believe we thus make it possible to approach these issues from a somewhat different vantage point and thus to work further toward an encompassing analytic theory of human relations.

INNER-OBJECT FUNCTIONS AND THE OBJECT CONCEPTS OF KLEIN AND FAIRBAIRN

I shall finally try to cast into clearer relief some features of the object-functions approach presented here by comparing it with some propositions inherent in the object concepts of Melanie Klein and Fairbairn. In so doing, I shall only touch on Klein and deal at greater length with Fairbairn. For one thing, Fairbairn's ideas appear more systematically conceptualized than those of Klein. Also, it is Fairbairn who has come to be known as a proponent of an analytic object-relations theory which differs from that of Freud. Further, he has incorporated Klein's basic ideas, which for brevity's sake I shall take up here.

Melanie Klein gave a central meaning to the concepts "inner object" and "inner world." Freud had known and used the concept "inner object," but it was Klein who made this a key concept beside which all other analytic concepts appeared to fade. The individual's inner world, his fantasies, the inner drama of envy, hate, and persecution became, in a sense, more important than his relationships with outer objects. This inner relational drama Klein (17) saw unfolding at a very early period. She was led to these conclusions by her insights into the fantasy life of children, elicited mainly during analytic play therapy. Thus, she came to assume complex, intrapsychic processes to be operating as early as in the first months of life. Of these, splitting and projective identification she considered the most important.[8]

Fairbairn has accepted Klein's basic propositions. He appears to share her belief in the primacy of inner objects and the inner world, and, also, he seems convinced that the stage for the inner relational drama is set at a very early age.

Essentially, Fairbairn's object-relations theory appears to take off from Freud's structural theory of 1923. This structural theory, I mentioned earlier, posed problems of conceptual integration in that the focus of interest shifted: Freud's theory of drives and his topographic model of the psyche needed to be reconceptualized and integrated with his new theory of psychic structures and objects (cf. Arlow and Brenner, 1). Thus there existed for Freud a conceptual and theoretical backlog which prevented him from pushing to their logical conclusion some propositions inherent in his structural theory.

Fairbairn (4), after a period of questioning and wavering, decided to disregard this theoretical backlog which handicapped Freud and set out to elaborate an object-relations theory in its own right. In so doing, he proposed to simplify analytic theory. Guntrip (13) has described the development of Fairbairn's thoughts. Fairbairn did away with the theory of drives as conceived by Freud. Thus he pursued a theoretical path radically different from Hartmann's. Fairbairn upheld the notion that the individual seeks libidinal investments, but these investments are now no longer aimed at pleasure; they are directed at objects. The libido is primarily no longer pleasure-seeking; it is object-seeking. As a consequence, Fairbairn abandoned Freud's concept of the id. Impulses, for him, thus became coupled to objects: "Impulses become bad if they are directed toward bad objects. If such bad objects are internalized, then the impulses directed toward them are internalized" (4, p. 63). We find internalized relationship systems and subsystems which are hierarchically organized.

By thus modifying analytic theory, Fairbairn could more easily focus on the inner relational drama which Freud had unveiled in his structural theory. It was mainly schizoid and hysterical patients who provided Fairbairn with insights into the nature of this drama. Fairbairn made plausible how these patients, afraid of real relationships, sought refuge and solace in inner objects. He peopled the stage of the inner drama with actors (inner objects) both more numerous and, in a sense, more alive than Freud's three main intrapsychic agents: id, ego, and superego. Finally, Fairbairn distinguished between three pairs of such inner actors: the central ego and the ideal object, the antilibidinal ego and the rejecting object, and the libidinal ego and the exciting object. Fairbairn traced the performances and pairings of these inner actors in various psychic disturbances. Depending on the pairings, the inner struggle gave rise to different kinds of psychopathology.[9]

Fairbairn, like Freud, was concerned with the question of how inner objects originate and change; and, like Freud and others, he recognized the crucial role of early internalizations.

There is, however, this difference: While Freud emphasized that identification with the good object, besides having defensive aspects, is a normal developmental process—a notion that has been accepted and elaborated by others such as Winnicott (30), Fenichel (5), Balint (2), and Schafer (26)—Fairbairn considers the early internalization of objects *only* as a defensive maneuver. Guntrip has described these differing positions. Good object relations, according to Fairbairn, provide no occasion for internalization. For good objects simply influence and promote good ego development. In becoming material for a healthy self, they disappear qua inner objects. The unsatisfying object, however, is internalized in an effort to master it. The good object plays a role in the internal drama only insofar as it serves as a defense against the internalized bad object. Fairbairn has later modified this position. According to this later stand, it is not the bad but the preambivalent object that is internalized first. The split between good and bad objects occurs later. But also this preambivalent object is internalized only because it is unsatisfactory.

In brief, internalization of objects, according to Fairbairn, is essentially a defensive maneuver and as such leads to an early ego splitting which, in turn, has a lasting impact on the developing psyche.

The inner objects of which Fairbairn conceived are thus, in general, bad objects. Bad in this sense is, for example, the "rejecting object" which the paranoid person externalizes, and bad is the "exciting object" which keeps the hysterical patient restless. This notion that the ego is struggling essentially with bad objects tends to simplify further Fairbairn's position.

Let us now ask how Fairbairn's theory of object relationships might reflect on the three main functions of inner objects as outlined earlier—the referent function, the gyroscopic function and the autonomy-furthering function.

As regards the referent function, we find that this remains very much outside the scope of Fairbairn's interests and conceptualizations.

Fairbairn does some justice to the second—the gyroscopic— function, but his treatment of it is slanted. This cannot be otherwise because of Fairbairn's almost exclusive preoccupation with bad inner objects. He thus lacks the conceptual tools for assessing the gyroscopic potential of good inner objects,[10] i.e., he fails to understand how good inner objects may direct a person to seek those real-life outer objects whose good prototypes he has internalized. In brief, Fairbairn's object-relations theory leaves little or no room to view inner objects as positive, guiding anticipatory sets. Hence, he seems unable to assess properly the disturbances of the gyroscopic function. (At the same time, he lacks the conceptual tools to grasp central aspects of the process of delegation, to be presented in later chapters—particularly Chapters 10, 11, 12, and 15.)

Fairbairn's contributions deal essentially with the autonomy-furthering function. He describes insightfully how the inner relational drama can become all-absorbing and self-defeating. This he has done mainly in regard to schizophrenic, hysteric, and phobic patients in whom—each time in a different manner—inner objects appear locked into their shadow-boxing while outer objects remain ephemeral. These latter are used merely as exchangeable props for externalizations as momentarily needed.

Fairbairn, in other words, enlarges our understanding of a pathologic (secondary) narcissism in Freud's sense of the term. But by mainly focusing on this aspect of relational pathology, he loses sight of wider issues and interconnections.

In summary, we can assess Freud's, Melanie Klein's, and Fairbairn's object-relations theories as follows: Freud's theory appears broader in scope than Fairbairn's. It allots, implicitly at least, a place to all three functions of inner objects. It allows for a wide developmental perspective, and it suggests a complex dialectic between inner and outer objects—thus paving the way for an encompassing theory of human relationships. Fairbairn and Melanie Klein illuminated mainly one aspect of this dialectic. Primarily, they brought to light disturbances in the autonomy-furthering function of inner objects. This they did by thoroughly exploiting a conceptual potential inherent in Freud's later structural theory. But, paradoxically, in thus enlarging and even transcending some of Freud's ideas, they limited the potential of others. They paid the price of conceptual foreclosure (and hence observational foreclosure) with respect to important functions of inner objects.

Notes

[1] This emphasis on the dynamic, directing moment of inner objects goes beyond what Schafer seems to have in mind. He writes: "Object representations are not in themselves motivating and regulatory psychic structures, but they do serve as guideposts of behavior, and the subject needs to maintain some clarity, consistency and organization of his

representation of other persons" (25, p. 29). However, Schafer comes close to the position presented here when he elaborates on the functions of his "inner presences". In writing about a given patient, Schafer states that "the ... presence is *serving as a net to catch suitable current objects*—such as, in this case, the analyst—to be used for externalization or actualization" (25, p. 133).

² This overlap appears even more marked in the light of Schafer's (26) formulation of the ego as a hierarchical system of regulatory aims and motives.

³ Although the former functions may later be affected by conflict, and vice versa.

⁴ Freud (8) has deepened our understanding of this dialectic by suggesting that under certain conditions inner-object change might be intensified or accelerated. As the most important condition to effect inner-object change, he singled out outer-object loss, thus offering a thesis with wide-ranging implications. The individual, according to this thesis, changes and rebuilds inner objects when he loses cathected outer objects. Loss of these outer objects can therefore be a potent force behind the change of inner objects. Freud has illuminated this in his investigation of grief and melancholia. The work of grief and mourning, among other things, serves the task of erecting the lost outer object, e.g., the values and attitudes of a lost person, within the ego. The ego, in incorporating essential aspects of the lost outer object, becomes modified and as a rule strengthened. Ego growth thus proceeds via abandoned outer-object cathexis. At one point Freud defined the ego as the precipitate of lost object cathexes.

⁵ Such voices may "perform all the functions attributed to objects in the environment ... the voices can be companions, critics, advisers, and the source of direct sexual gratification, leading in many instances to orgasm" (Modell, 20, p. 138).

⁶ Freud was aware that the secondary narcissism of the hysteric and obsessive-compulsive implied an ongoing complex relational dialectic with external things and persons. "This patient turns away from reality," Freud noted, "but analysis shows that he has by no means broken off his erotic relations to people and things. He still retains them in phantasy, i.e. he has, on the one hand, substituted for real objects imaginary ones from his memory, or has mixed the latter with the former; and on the other hand, he has renounced the initiation of motor activities for the attainment of his aims in connection with those objects.... It is otherwise with the paraphrenic. He seems really to have withdrawn his libido from people and things in the external world, without replacing them by others in phantasy" (7). But even the latter patient, I believe, while caught up in his intrapsychic relational drama, has not completely withdrawn his libido from things and people in the external world. Such a withdrawal, as this discussion suggests, seems always a matter of degree. Cf. Stierlin (28).

⁷ When Spitz (27) described the "libidinal object" of psychoanalysis, he evidently had the prestructural object concept in mind. Spitz contrasted the libidinal object with the permanent object of Piaget, which remains constant and identical over time, whereas, according to Spitz, the (libidinal) object of psychoanalysis does not. For this libidinal object changes with the affective and libidinal state of the subject, reflecting thus a tie-up with a theory of drives wherein the phenomena of drive-discharge and tension reduction, of the rise and fall of libidinal and affective investment, were crucial.

⁸ Melanie Klein's ideas suffer sometimes from being presented in a global, often

metaphorical language. Also, her assumptions and theoretical constructs, though often facilitating an imaginative clinical intervention, conflict with well-founded current notions and observations concerning the nature and pace of human development.

⁹ This picture is still incomplete. For one thing, the term actor does not do justice to important systemic properties of Fairbairn's inner objects. Also, when speaking of an intrapsychic stage, we must remain aware of the stages within the stage—the repressed, but still powerful inner-object subsystems—which determine a person's relational fate. Guntrip (13) and Sutherland (29) have emphasized these latter aspects in Fairbairn's theory.

¹⁰ Freud provided the basic argument for postulating the good inner object when he wrote: "There are thus good reasons why a child sucking at his mother's breast has become the prototype of every relation of love. The finding of an object is in fact a refinding of it" (6, p. 222).

References

1. Arlow, J. A., and Brenner, C. *Psychoanalytic concepts and the structural theory.* New York: International Universities Press, 1964.

2. Balint, M. *Primary love and psychoanalytic technique.* London: Hogarth Press, 1952.

3. Boszormenyi-Nagy, I. A theory of relationships: experiences and transactions. In *Intensive family therapy,* ed. I. Boszormenyi-Nagy and J. L. Framo. New York: Hoeber, 1965.

4. Fairbairn, W. R. D. *An object-relations theory of the personality.* New York: Basic Books, 1952.

5. Fenichel, O. *The psychoanalytic theory of neurosis.* New York: Norton, 1945.

6. Freud, S. Three essays on the theory of sexuality. (1905). *SE* VII.

7. ———. On narcissism: an introduction. (1914). *SE* XIV.

8. ———. Mourning and melancholia. (1917). *SE* XIV.

9. ———. Beyond the pleasure principle. (1920). *SE* XVIII.

10. ———. The ego and the id. (1923). *SE* XIX.

11. ———. Inhibitions, symptoms and anxiety. (1926). *SE* XX.

12. ———. Civilization and its discontents. (1930). *SE* XXI.

13. Guntrip, H. *Personality structure and human interaction.* New York: International Universities Press, 1961.

14. Hartmann, H. Comments on the psychoanalytic theory of the ego. *Psychoanalytic Study of the Child* 5, 1950.

15. ———, and Loewenstein, R. M. Notes on the superego. *Psychoanalytic Study of the Child* 17, 1962.
16. Jacobson, E. *The self and the object world.* New York: International Universities Press, 1964.
17. Klein, M. *Envy and gratitude.* New York: Basic Books, 1957.
18. Lidz, T. Family studies and a theory of schizophrenia. In *Schizophrenia and the family,* ed. T. Lidz, S. Fleck, and A. R. Cornelison. New York: International Universities Press, 1965.
19. Loewald, H. Internalization, separation, mourning and the superego. *Psychoanalytic Quarterly* 31: 483-504, 1960.
20. Modell, A. H. *Object love and reality.* New York: International Universities Press, 1968.
21. Novey, S. Further considerations on affect theory in psychoanalysis. *International Journal of Psycho-Analysis* 42: 21-31, 1961.
22. Riesman, D. *The lonely crowd: a study of the changing American character.* New Haven: Yale University Press, 1950.
23. Sandler, J., Holder, A., and Meers, D. The ego ideal and the ideal self. *Psychoanalytic Study of the Child* 18, 1963.
24. ———, and Nagera, H. Aspects of the metapsychology of fantasy. *Psychoanalytic Study of the Child* 18, 1963.
25. Schafer, R. *Aspects of internalization.* New York: International Universities Press, 1968.
26. ———. The mechanisms of defence. *International Journal of Psycho-Analysis* 49: 49-62, 1968.
27. Spitz, R. A. *The first year of life.* New York: International Universities Press, 1965.
28. Stierlin, H. *Conflict and reconciliation.* New York: Doubleday Anchor and Jason Aronson, 1969.
29. Sutherland, J. D. Object-relations theory and the conceptual model of psychoanalysis. *British Journal of Medical Psychology* 36: 109-124, 1963.
30. Winnicott, D. W. *Collected papers.* New York: Basic Books, 1958.

Part II

Family Dynamics and the Separation Process

Chapter 7

The Development and
Transmission of Delusions

DELUSIONS AND CULTURE

We customarily call delusions those ideas wrongly held to be true. But this common definition entails a problem. It seems to presuppose that in the world of the imagination and ideas there does in fact exist a generally valid and accepted truth. This is so only to a limited extent, however. Our culture shapes and defines the frame of reference in which delusions and non-delusions are distinguished from one another. What is regarded as true and unquestionable by an influential majority within one culture, or sub-culture (e.g., that witches exist and have to be burnt, that the Jews of the world are engaged in a malicious conspiracy, or that Jesus was born of a virgin) may appear delusional outside this majority and culture. Individuals can be at odds with their own time (various thinkers come to mind) without being thought deluded or mentally ill. But they have to keep one foot in their time: they must participate in the worldview of their cultural setting. Before beginning to call it into question they have to have seen "reality" through the eyes of that culture.

THE FAMILY AS A SUBCULTURE

The family is largely responsible for communicating to the growing child the definition of reality expressed in a given culture. It has to educate and socialize the child accordingly. It has to familiarize him or her with the world of language and values that has been shaped through that culture. If the family falls down in this task, the child will find orientation within this culture difficult or impossible. He will overlook or misinterpret the signs and symbols enabling participation in its frame of reference. His own culture will, consequently, become a jungle to him and his definition of reality a delusion, at least in the eyes of those who are culturally attuned.

The family's relationship to the surrounding culture is not, as a rule, simple. In one way, the family may be considered a subculture within society whose members share the same language, world of values, and definition of reality. Only on this joint basis can the family fulfill its socializing function. In another way, however, the family constitutes a private sphere offering plenty of scope for idiosyncratic values and varied educational and communicative practice. If the private sphere becomes dominant, it may be that what is considered intelligible reality within the family becomes unreal when seen from outside, or vice versa. In this case, the family appears as fostering delusion.

Most insights into the development of delusions have been given us by the families of schizophrenic patients. The private sphere of these families became accessible to scientific research through countless interviews with family members, through participatory observation of family therapy (conducted over a period of years, during which the entire family generally met with the psychiatrist for an hour once or twice a week), and also through the evaluation of films and tape-recordings made during these family sessions. This research has been going on at the National Institute for Mental Health for over twenty years. Here also, for the first time, whole families were hospitalized for observation and therapy. The writings of M. Bowen (4), L. Wynne (16, 17), T. Lidz (7), I. Boszormenyi-Nagy (3), G. Bateson (1) and their fellow workers, to name only a few, shed light on this development.

FORMS OF DELUSION

In order to understand the significance of the family in the development of delusion, we must consider several aspects of it more closely.

Delusions, in our sense of the term, do not only appear as symptoms of, or concomitant with, schizophrenic disturbances. They can also occur in apparently healthy people when they are under the influence of febrile illnesses, drugs, or extreme strain (e.g. sensory deprivation). We come across it (generally in milder forms) in many persons of seemingly little interest to the psychiatrist.

Nevertheless, schizophrenic delusions can serve as prototypes for studies of the essential features and mechanisms of delusions. Two characteristic varieties are distinguishable here, each of which, although tending to merge with the other, still reveals elements typical of the phenomenon as such.

In the first variety, a schizophrenic disturbance is recognizable quite early—during adolescence or late-adolescence. It is not unusual here for delusional ideas to take on a dramatic character. They appear suddenly. The individual seems to be possessed by them, in their power. Inge, a seventeen-year-old girl, believed, for instance, that the Virgin Mary—the guardian of feminine purity— had given her special permission to indulge in sexual intercourse. Therefore, she was apprehensive and excited. The excitement fragmented and confused her thinking; the delusions revealed her inner tension, torn state of mind, and over-stimulated imagination. In the family circle, she had the effect of a bombshell. She accused her father of wanting to rape her and tearfully sought protection in her mother's arms. A few moments later, however, she called her mother a witch wishing to suck her daughter's blood.

In the second variety, the delusions usually appear later—often not until middle-age—and much less dramatically. They seem to take root in seemingly inconspicuous and intellectually well-organized personalities. For instance, a hospitalized female patient, thirty-five years of age and a newcomer in a therapy group, delivered a well-ordered and concise series of arguments in which the role of the hospital—a small private sanatorium—was made to appear as the classical example of exploitation by a capitalistic enterprise. The other members of the group only showed astonishment and irritation when she began to talk about poisoned hospital food. After that, the patient (let's call her Sabine) stayed away from the group sessions. She was polite in dealings with the other patients, but at the same time remained sceptical and aloof. The same polite distance was preserved at first towards her doctor, who saw her four times a week for several years in individual and group therapy. Only with time did she confide to him her complex delusions and concerns about her relations.

The two types of delusions sketched here—one an expression of a fragmented, over-stimulated imagination, the other the distortion of a sensitive intelligence—are frequently met with in milder forms, e.g., the former in many passing crises of adolescence, the latter in many people combining a quarrelsome scepticism with a "one-track mind."

Despite the variety of forms taken by delusions, it is possible to bring out a few typical and recurrent psychological features. Two of these seem to me to be particularly important: first, a kind of personal alienation that cuts the personality prone to delusion off from much of the data essential for effective communication and orientation to reality; and, second, in conjunction with this, a disturbance of what I would like to call the dialectic of doing and undergoing, i.e., of our sense of owning our impulses and motives.

Alienation from oneself, the first feature, as opposed to the feeling of being owned and directed by others and outside forces, relates above all to the understanding of one's own feelings, needs, and motives. When a person misunderstands, or does not perceive, these feelings, needs, and motives, he lacks the data enabling him to situate, compare, and define those of others. Delusions then serve as a kind of stop-gap, filling in for the lack of data. The projection of personal feelings and intentions upon others, which Freud was first to describe as the central mechanism for the development of delusions, is a special case of such gap-filling. Although one may be blind to one's own needs and intentions—as Schreber was of his own homosexual needs, in Freud's description—such needs are, to a large extent, grasped correctly. They are, however, wrongly located in the other rather than in the experiencing subject and thus receive a false positional value in the whole orientation to reality (as this is evaluated by a culture-attuned outsider). In most cases of delusions, we find, in addition to or instead of projections, other gap-filling and distorting factors. These include, e.g., a kind of over-alert yet rigid selectivity which prompts the delusion-prone personality to search for grains of truth or the evidence required to back up prejudices. This was so in the case of Sabine. She could point to being served undercooked mushrooms, overlooking thereby the fact that the hospital food was generally carefully prepared and tasty. Through such concentration upon what fits into the preconceived picture, the systematized delusions of many paranoids become practically unassailable.

Disturbance of the dialectic of doing and undergoing, the second feature of delusions, emerges in both under- and over-estimation of one's personal influence and importance. A healthy feeling for one's personal value generally entails a balanced knowledge of one's own influence and agency—its extent and its limits. On the basis of such a realistic sense of importance, the individual knows that he constitutes a center of personal responsibility, initiative, and action. At the same time, however, he knows that there exists an objective causality independent of his own wishes, actions, and decisions. He is likewise aware that other people have to live their own lives, in which he himself is a mere onlooker.

This balanced knowledge is disturbed in delusion-prone people who see themselves as both powerless and omnipotent. They are the helpless victims of all sorts of conspiracies, sometimes of cosmic dimensions: hence the many variations of paranoia and distorted relational experiences. At the same time, they feel themselves to be extraordinary beings. Their thoughts alone can decide the future of mankind, war or peace. Each word they speak is a gem. (One of my paranoid patients with money troubles did not doubt for a moment that a brief treatise containing wild ideas about the earth's magnetism would bring her in a million dollars.) Hence the many forms of grandiosity.

The disturbance in the dialectic of doing and undergoing (which confronts us in an extreme form in the delusions of such patients) is shown in many attitudes and reactions to life. These include the tendency to avoid taking on personal responsibility and constantly to suspect the influence of subversive external forces. The Rorschach interpretations of many of these people bring out this tendency clearly: behind every test sheet they see a definite influence or intention which has them in its power. From this there also follows the tendency every time to hand out blame. It is always "the other guy" who is responsible for or at the bottom of something. All that the other person does is evaluated and seen from an egocentric standpoint.

THE EMERGENCE OF A DISPOSITION TO DELUSION

The formation of delusions is a two-stage process. First, the disposition to delusions arises. We can here also speak of latent delusions. Second, the delusions become manifest. They place the individual in conflict with his culture-bound surroundings and sometimes entail his becoming labeled a mental patient.

The family is involved in both of these stages. In the first stage, it promotes the development of those features we recognize as typical of all varieties of delusion: personal alienation and disturbance in the dialectic of doing and undergoing. In the second stage, it seems to affect when and how the pre-disposed individual goes astray in the conceptual world of his culture. Let us first look at the initial stage.

A lot remains unclear here. Nevertheless, the research done in many fields, often independently, enables us to gain insight into the factors at work when a delusional disposition emerges. Studies by Piaget (9) and psychoanalytic ego- and child-psychology are particularly important in this connection.

Piaget has shown us that reality—or what we call reality—is not a kind of given pattern into which the child just "grows." Instead, this reality is the outcome of many interdependent developmental steps and achievements. In a way that is reminiscent of Hegel's phenomenology, the child is called upon to create for himself the categories of time and space. He must learn to formalize and condense his originally rough and groping movements and actions into actions of his intelligence operating with symbols and minimal amounts of energy. This "building up of reality" extends into adolescence, and disturbances of psychic differentiation and integration may develop at any stage in the process, thus interfering with his orientation to reality.

Psychoanalytic ego- and child-psychology has revealed how important in building up the child's sense of reality is the quality of human relations he experiences all along. However, we still lack a set of concepts for a relations theory allowing the systematic analysis and comparison of different types of disturbed relations. (In my *Separating Parents and Adolescents*, New York: Quadrangle, 1974, I tried to develop such concepts, and I shall comment on them here in chapters 10, 11, and 14.)

This is not the place to outline the psychic development of the child as he goes about building up reality. I shall confine myself to examining three aspects of this development that are relevant to the emergence of a delusional disposition and the question of why certain persons suffer personal alienation and disturbance in the dialectic of doing and undergoing. These three aspects are interdependent and may be headed self-definition, early autonomy, and early language development.

SELF-DEFINITION

Perhaps the greatest and most important developmental achievement of a child consists in creating reliable and stable relations to his inner and outer worlds. The first kind of stable relation I propose to call "self-polarization" and the second "self-demarcation." *Self-polarization* is above all a matter of the child developing a reliable repressive or dissociative barrier which nonetheless has a certain permeability. This enables him to structure a conscious and unconscious part of his personality. Excessive permeability of this barrier can lead to just as much personal alienation, i.e., lack of data in the sense described above, as the reverse. In the case of excessive permeability, the individual is exposed to a great flood of data—feelings, vague memories, associations, etc.—and is no longer able to distinguish between wishes and reality, memories and perceptions, his own and extraneous psychic material. The confusion which results when the repressive barrier is opened too wide seems primarily to prepare the ground for a fragmented variety of delusions, as typified by Inge's case. Too narrow an opening, however, would seem to favor the type of simple projection mentioned above. In neither case are personal feelings, drives, recollections, etc. available as reliable data, and the person remains estranged from them.

Self-demarcation, the second important aspect of self-definition, is the childs' attempt to delimit his body from the outside world and thus provide a reliable basis for self-definition. The child's very first tries at playing seem largely to serve such self-demarcation. One of the first interpersonal games of my one-year-old daughter, for example, was to repeatedly take her finger out of her own mouth and put it in mine or her mother's. The later experience of a clear-cut and emotionally sustained separation from one's own excretory products is another important step in self-demarcation.

In my experience, all patients suffering from delusions demonstrate the consequences of an unsuccessful attempt at self-demarcation. They are not completely and safely "at home" in their body, i.e., they are not truly "embodied". Many delusions are known to relate to bodily sensations experienced as foreign, "made," or otherwise inflicted from the outside.

EARLY AUTONOMY

Every child has to realize that he is the locus of a causality emanating from himself, that he is a center of initiative and responsibility, and that his own wishes and actions have weight and "count." Only when this feeling of personal importance has come to be taken for granted can the child be expected to live with the limitations which follow from accepted extraneous causality—including the fact that we must one day die. This drive to be autonomous may be observed early in children, despite their dependence. Psychoanalytic literature emphasizes the vicissitudes of the anal period as being conducive to an autonomy, as we are using the term. Yet this is only partly correct. A healthy, growing child will give energetic evidence of personal intentions and preferences (such as knocking back food he dislikes) at even earlier stages.

Early disturbances in the development towards autonomy would seem to prepare the ground for those serious disturbances in the dialectic of doing and undergoing cited above as predisposing to delusions. The feeling of powerlessness and personal

insignificance is here paramount. Grandiosity and the overt or
covert egocentricity of paranoid patients are secondary, compen-
satory developments.

EARLY LANGUAGE DEVELOPMENT

"Without language", said Hegel, "there would only be the
unconscious night, which cannot distinguish within itself nor
attain clarity of self-knowledge." Language is to be understood
here in its broadest sense as the language of words, concepts,
symbols, and gestures. This language helps us to consolidate and
deepen our self-definition and autonomy as described above. It
supplies us with categories through which we can distinguish the
internal from the external, feeling from perception, the speaker
from the spoken and what is past from what is to come. Language
enables us to communicate with others of the same culture, to
learn from them and thus correct those misconceptions and rigid
stances which threaten to make us strangers within our own
culture.

There is an extensive literature now on linguistic phenomena in
delusional individuals. The evidence suggests that in almost all the
aspects indicated their language is limited or idiosyncratic. Such
limitations or idiosyncrasies often go unnoticed for long periods of
clinical observation, sometimes striking the psychotherapist only
after years of contact. It is not uncommon for paranoid individuals
to appear articulate and witty on casual acquaintance. I recall, for
example, a philosophy student whose astute and subtle logical
deductions, remarkable for their clarity of presentation, amazed
both doctors and fellow patients. Closer acquaintance with this
patient showed, however, that precisely this crystal-clear, logical
language was at the service of an alienation from self and helped
him to keep his distance from others. It had an idiosyncratic
quality and seemed unsuited to truly defining or communicating
innermost feelings.

In order to understand the limitations and deviations of language which predispose one to delusions, we need to turn to early language development. What factors are crucial here? This question leads us on to consider those people and relations who stake out the child's most important scenario for learning.

THE PROMOTION OF A DELUSIONAL DISPOSITION IN THE FAMILY

First we need to distinguish between the influence individual family members have on a child and that exerted by the family as a field or system. The relationships here are complex. In early life, children seem mostly dependent on their mothers as individuals. But more is involved here than the relation between two persons, for the way the mother relates to her child depends, in turn, on how she fits into the whole family and, in particular, how she relates to her husband. If, for instance, she feels sexually unsatisfied by her husband, or insufficiently accepted or understood, she might be inclined to seek in the child a substitute for the missing satisfaction and thus overtax the child and disturb his normal development. Such cases are frequent in clinical experience.

In order to understand the complex relationships prevailing in this context, we need to remember that children, if they are not to be exposed to self-alienation or disturbances in their autonomy and language development, must participate directly and indirectly in the most varied relations within the family. These relations must change and be adapted to the age-appropriate capacities and needs of the children. Elsewhere (14, 15) I have elaborated the basic features of these relations. At this point, I must confine myself to a few aspects of disturbed relations which shed light on the origin of a delusional disposition. My chief concern here is with the consequences of too great a distance or closeness on the growing child's relations with his parents, particularly his mother.

Investigations by R. Spitz (13) and others have taught us by now that children in foster homes, taken away from their mothers soon after birth, develop psychic disturbances, suffer impoverishment, and frequently go to pieces physically, too. Here we can talk of extremes in the early separation from the mother. An extreme emotional separation exists also in cases where the child still lives at home but is exposed to (often unwitting) coolness and rejection on the part of the mother. In some of these children, who can be unusually sensitive and intelligent, we find what looks like an early stage, as well as consolidation, of delusion and personal alienation. I have in mind certain forms of childhood autism. Such children experience all human contact as so threatening and potentially destructive that they seem to be prisoners behind an impenetrable paranoid wall. At the same time, they seem to be extremely cut off from their own feelings and bodily needs. Bettelheim (2), to whom we owe one of the most thorough studies of autism in young children, quotes the case of a child who evinced no sign of pain when suffering from acute appendicitis and who, like many other such children, was absolutely insensitive to extremes of heat and cold. Eating and excretion take place in often impassive, mechanical fashion. These children are never seen to laugh, though often they are given to periodic intensive and destructive fits. Many of Bettelheim's children came out of their autistic shells after years of devoted treatment. It has been mainly thanks to what these children did and said during their psychotherapy that we have gained insight into the role of the mother-child relationship in the emergence of a disposition to delusion.

Bettelheim interprets the extreme self-alienation observable in autistic children as being the consequence of an attempt at total defense: the child tries to defend himself against a mother he feels to be dangerous, concentrating all his energies onto a few exaggerated protective functions, which may strike the observer as odd rituals. His own bodily needs, entailing dependence on others, are thus contested or neglected. When contact with other people has been reduced to a minimum, the personal alienation is, as it were, endorsed from outside. Emotional dialogue, that complex give-and-take in which children experience themselves anew as partners, as reacting as well as initiating subjects aware of and setting boundaries, is entirely lacking. Such dialogue is needed for a proper development of self-polarization, self-demarcation, and an early autonomy. We need only think of the many spontaneous games that arise in a good mother-child relationship, like feeding each other, exchanging caresses, pushing building-blocks, etc., all of which in some way serve to demarcate one person from the others and to confirm his importance and autonomy. In so deeply disturbed a relation as autism, these dialogic processes come almost to a stop.

My experiences with paranoid patients and their families have taught me that the formative relations of the patients may be disturbed by too great a distance, by an oppressive closeness, or by abrupt switches from one to the other. All these disturbances in the balance of closeness and distance seem then to lead to a massive and precocious over-specialization of defensive structures, as autistic children seem to illustrate in extreme form. A number of these patients seem, when still children, to have channelled much of their defensive efforts into the sensitive registering of hostile movements and mood changes in their mothers. Living in too great and prolonged an empathic closeness with their mothers, they may have had special difficulties in properly developing a repressive barrier. They turned into experts at sensing hostile stirrings in other people. At the same time, they remained insensitive to much of the data and aspects of reality which normally are essential to balance our judgment and shape our over-all orientation to reality. Observations of this type help us to understand why we find dispositions to delusions or delusional developments in a number of particularly sensitive and original observers of the human psyche—for instance, in Strindberg, Rousseau, Baudelaire, and de Sade.

Families of schizophrenic patients have taught us in what

manifold and frequently drastic fashion the self-definition, early autonomy, and culture-attuned language development of the growing child may be derailed. Theodore Lidz and his collaborators (7) described a mother of identical twins who, when she was constipated, would give her two sons an enema or laxative too—an extreme but not unusual example of lack of respect for the needs and autonomy of dependent children. (Both sons later developed extensive delusional ideas.) Or a father comes to mind who used to watch his attractive eighteen-year-old daughter getting dressed every day and often touched and stroked her, while denying any sexual interest in her. This same father was constantly tortured by the idea that his daughter might fall into the clutches of an unscrupulous rake. The daughter later developed complicated delusional ideas in which red-haired men (her father had red hair) tried to hand her over to a band of gangsters, before whom she was to perform certain exhibitionist acts. Hilde Bruch (5) has provided us, as another example, with observations and comments on how children who later became either obese or anorectic (and thus seemed alienated from, and unable to regulate, hunger and other vegetative needs) had been treated like insensitive feeding and excreting machines by their parents. (These children, we may say, were in part delusionally related to their bodies.)

These observations and reflections suggest that a large number of parents of children who subsequently develop delusions need to be seen as people who are themselves paranoid and whose relations are disturbed. Usually their paranoia remains sub-clinical and (within limits) culture-syntonic, concealing those intrapsychic and interpersonal conflicts and peculiarities their children often so blatantly reveal. The clinical family researcher, however, soon discovers the sub-clinical paranoia and disturbed relationships of these parents. They shine forth in many of their statements, as well as in a number of tests developed at the National Institute of Mental Health by, in particular, Margaret Singer (10-12), in collaboration with Lyman Wynne (18, 19) and Nathene Loveland

(8), who used modified Rorschach and TAT-procedures and the so-called family Rorschach. These tests show up the parents—in their communication with the testers, their children, and each other—as (sometimes very skillful) saboteurs of any communication that aims at clarity and a progressing dialogue. In their communications we often come across the same veiled allusions, the same scotomas, the same almost imperceptible invalidations of previous statements, etc. that their "deluded" children reveal as under a magnifying glass.

Observation of these families over long periods of time often gives the impression that certain members of the family communicate in ways in which two (or more) delusional dispositions seem to complement each other. Lyman Wynne (16) has proposed the term "trading of dissociations" for this phenomenon. For example, a father spotted homosexuality in his son, and viewed it in a glaring, hostile light, while the son repeatedly wounded his father by stressing the latter's failure in his job, primarily caused by a tendency to speculate irresponsibly and to (unconsciously) destroy himself. Father and son thus hurt each other, as if acting under an ominous, reciprocal compulsion. Each attacked the other in his most sensitive area—one which the attacker himself was most estranged from. Each obviously needed the other person in order to come to grips with this area in himself in such a way as not to let it get under his own skin—that is, to keep the problem at a "working distance" from his observing ego. The family provided a suitable relational scene for this to be played out.

DELUSIONS EMERGING IN THE ATTEMPT TO SEPARATE FROM THE FAMILY

Here we deal with the second stage in the emergence of delusions. It may be discerned in a child who seemingly has succeeded in adapting to his family. But, in adapting, he developed his disposition to delusions: his self-definition, early autonomy, and language development remained shaky or became idiosyncratic.

In order to find his place in the surrounding culture, this child has eventually to leave his family behind. At the same time, he has to develop and try out sources of self-esteem and relationships not confined to the short-circuited field of the primary family. He senses pressure from all sides to move out of the family orbit, but this pressure cannot but mobilize conflicts which, in turn, may trigger delusions in a person so disposed.

In order to understand these conflicts a little better, let us return to Inge, who seemed at age seventeen to be plunging dramatically into delusions.

Inge was an unusually attractive girl, in many ways like her mother. The mother had had a particularly ambivalent attitude to her from the beginning, which caused her frequently to swing from excessive closeness to hostile distance and back. She experienced and fostered in Inge, through an uncritical, direct identification with her, the realization of her own artistic and romantic ambitions (this is one aspect of the delegating process, to be elaborated later, particularly in chapters 10, 11, and 14), but at the same time competed with her as a rival. The latter aspect had a basis in reality: Inge had a quasi-incestuous relationship with her father, who treated her like a mistress and took her with him on business trips. Inge's delusions emerged in full force when, at almost the same moment, her best friend got engaged and her elder sister had a baby. Inge now went through an inferno (like the "Inferno" described by Strindberg, which is perhaps the best account of an acute delusional experience) and was more and more impelled to get away from her family circle, while only getting more deeply involved. In her "delusions" she saw important "truths" about her family—e.g., that her mother was a "bloodsucking witch" and her father a "rapist"—but had lost the ability to weigh and qualify these "truths" within an overall culture-attuned perspective.

This is not the place to trace in detail how what the observer, from the standpoint of his culture, considers delusions can in fact be understood as an adaptation to, as well as reflection of, a given family's interpersonal reality. The book by Laing and Esterson, *Sanity, Madness and the Family* (6), provides numerous examples documenting this point of view.

One thing is certain: the observations and ideas outlined above are only a first step on the way to understanding how delusions emerge in the family.

References

1. Bateson, G., Jackson, D. D., Haley, J., and Weakland, J. Toward a theory of schizophrenia. *Behavioral Science* 1: 251-264, 1956.
2. Bettelheim, B. *The empty fortress. infantile autism and the birth of the self.* New York: The Free Press, 1967.
3. Boszormenyi-Nagy, I. A theory of relationships: experience and transaction. In *Intensive family therapy,* ed. I. Boszormenyi-Nagy and J. Framo. New York: Hoeber, 1965.
4. Bowen, M. Family relations in schizophrenia. In *Schizophrenia,* ed. A. Auerbach. New York: Ronald Press, 1959: pp. 147-178.
5. Bruch, H. Falsification of bodily needs and body concept in schizophrenia. *Archives of General Psychiatry* 1: 18-24, 1962.
6. Laing, R. D., and Esterson, A. *Sanity, madness and the family. I. Families of schizophrenics.* London: Tavistock Publications, 1964.
7. Lidz, T., Cornelison, A., and Fleck, S. *Schizophrenia and the family.* New York: International Universities Press, 1965.
8. Loveland, N., and Wynne, L. The family Rorschach: a new method for studying family interaction. *Family Process* 2: 187-215, 1963.
9. Piaget, J. *The construction of reality in the child.* Translated by M. Cook. New York: Basic Books, 1954.
10. Singer, M., and Wynne, L. Principles for scoring communication defects and deviances in parents of schizophrenics: Rorschach and TAT scoring manuals. *Psychiatry* 29: 260-288, 1966.
11. ———. Thought disorder and family relations of schizophrenics. III. Methodology using projective techniques. *Archives of General Psychiatry* 12: 187-200, 1965.

12. ———. Thought disorder and family relations of schizophrenics. IV. Results and implications. *Archives of General Psychiatry* 12: 201-212, 1965.
13. Spitz, R. "Hospitalism": an inquiry into the genesis of psychiatric conditions in early childhood. In *Psychoanalytic Study of the Child* 2: 313-420, 1946.
14. Stierlin, H. Aspects of relatedness in the psychotherapy of schizophrenia. *Psychoanalytic Review* 51: 19-28, 1964.
15. ———. *Conflict and reconciliation*. New York: Doubleday Anchor and Jason Aronson, 1968.
16. Wynne, L. Some indications and contraindications for exploratory family therapy. In *Intensive family therapy*, ed. I. Boszormenyi-Nagy and J. Framo. New York: Hoeber, 1965.
17. Wynne, L., Ryckoff, I., Day, J., and Hirsch, S. Pseudo-mutuality in the family relations of schizophrenics. *Psychiatry* 21: 205-220, 1958.
18. Wynne, L., and Singer, M. Thought disorder and family relations of schizophrenics. I. A research strategy. *Archives of General Psychiatry* 9: 191-198, 1963.
19. ———. Thought disorder and family relations of schizophrenics. II. A classification of forms of thinking. *Archives of General Psychiatry* 9: 199-206, 1963.

Chapter 8

Parental Perceptions
of Separating Children

PERCEPTIONS AS MOLDING FORCES

In this chapter* we shall ask: How do parents' perceptions influence their child's separation? This question arises from a growing literature on interactional psychology that has by now established the parents' perceptions as molding forces in their children's lives. This implies a shift in focus away from traditional lines of psychoanalytic theory, which held that the primary locus of influence was the child, who was conceived as internalizing his parents in part or whole (through imitation, introjection, or identification). The parents' own active contributions to such internalization were left largely unspecified. Various authors have subsequently corrected this imbalance. For example, the concept of "projective identification," as outlined by Klein (12) and Bion (5), implies (but does not specify) a mode of parental perception and action that causes children to become and remain captive to the parents' projections. Bateson et al. (2, 3) and Wynne (22) have emphasized the binding as well as confusing elements in certain parental attitudes. Most important in this context are the classical

---

* L. D. Levi and R. J. Savard are co-authors of this chapter.

contributions of Johnson and Szurek (8, 9) as they bear directly on problems of adolescents. Johnson (8) presents the thesis that "antisocial acting out in a child is unconsciously fostered and sanctioned by the parents, who vicariously achieve gratification of their own poorly integrated impulses through a child's acting out. In turn, the child's behavior stimulates the parents to added need for this gratification. One or both parents, in addition, unconsciously experience gratification for their own hostile wishes toward the child, who is repeatedly destroyed by his behavior." Searles' observations on "The Effort to Drive the Other Person Crazy" (20) and Laing's description of "attributions" (13, 14) clarify the transactional modes by which the parents mold the child. Laing, with Philipson and Lee (16), spoke later specifically of "interpersonal perceptions"; and Shapiro (21) elaborated the same and related phenomena under the term "delineation."

All these concepts imply that one person's perceptions of another—e.g., that this other person is lazy, weak, or shady,—may "take," becoming part of the other's self-image and motivational system. They are often distorted, because it is the dissociated or unacceptable aspects of the perceiver that are attributed to the other. Since these perceptions fulfill a defensive purpose for the perceiver, Shapiro has labeled them "defensive delineations" (21).

In order for perceptions, projections, or attributions to "take," a dependent emotional tie seems required; and the closer the tie and the fewer the alternatives for identification the child possesses, the greater the chances. For example, according to Bettelheim (4), in the presence of negative, dependent ties, Jews in concentration camps absorbed into their self-image their SS tormentors' views of themselves as dirty, inferior, and cunning.

PARENTAL PERCEPTIONS AFFECTING SEPARATION

Here we are concerned with a special group of parental perceptions—those that refer to the adolescent's capacity to separate. This group of perceptions has been implied but not systematically explored in the transactional literature. From our observations, this group appears uniquely important because at stake is the adolescent's tie to *all* parental perceptions and expectations. The adolescent remains vulnerable to parental expectations and perceptions to the degree that he still lacks a core of autonomy and remains dependently entangled with his parents. Only such children can act out the unconscious wishes of a parent, as this has been described by Johnson (8); for such acting out, as Blos (6) has pointed out, "can only take place when the emotional separation between parent and child is pathologically incomplete." The child's dependent entanglement, and hence vulnerability, are bound to decrease to the extent that he responds positively to those parental perceptions and expectations that foster his capacity to separate successfully. Perceptions and expectations bearing on separation, therefore, carry the greatest leverage because they determine his susceptibility to all other parental perceptions and expectations. They entail a meta-message or meta-perception about these other perceptions. They convey to the adolescent how his parents perceive and judge his confidence and capacity either to heed or turn away from these parents themselves! They contain a message about his ability to liberate himself from his parents and thereby to immunize himself against what they—his parents— think, say, and want that might conflict with that message.

We conceive of separation in adolescence as part of a continuous movement toward relative mutual individuation in which parents *and* children participate. The ultimate aim is mature *interdependence* of the parties. In this process, the parents bring their perceptions and expectations to bear on their children but also ordinarily open themselves to the perceptions and expectations directed at them by the children. Although the two parties in this interplay— parents on the one side, children on the other—are equally important, we shall, in this paper, focus on the parents' contribu- tions—that is, on their expectations for, and perceptions of, their children.

Parents'—and particularly the mother's—perceptions of, and expectations for, a child in his early years seem to have a particularly fateful impact because of the child's malleability and extreme dependence. The parents expose their (in this phase) totally dependent child to their "stronger reality" (see Chapter 3).[1] In adolescence not only are many earlier parental perceptions and expectations confirmed or disconfirmed, but the previously mentioned interplay between parents and children enters a crucial phase. The child at adolescence is becoming less dependent on his parents; through school and peer contacts he makes available to himself alternative models for forming his self-image and identity. He can now more effectively bring his own perceptions of his parents to bear on the latter. With new cognitive tools at his disposal and increasing claims for the merit of his judgments, he can now play powerfully on his parents' vulnerabilities by labeling them as bad parents or failures in life. He can thus shape their own image of themselves. Most importantly, due to the psychophysiological momentum of adolescence, he moves away from his parents toward new relationships outside the family orbit, whereas his parents—often mired in a crisis of middle age (c.f. Levi et al., 17), depressed and apprehensive about their future—may be confronted with unbearable loss. The power situation in the family as to who needs whom and who can hurt whom has drastically changed.

In short, as the adolescent becomes more autonomous, he tends to immunize himself against his parents' expectations and perceptions of him. Nevertheless, he remains vulnerable to these expectations and perceptions to the degree that, lacking a mature autonomy, he remains dependently entangled with them.

SOURCES OF DATA

In this project twelve families with troubled adolescents were seen in short-term family therapy and were then followed up with intensive interviews over the next several years. The adolescent index patients covered a diagnostic spectrum from strongly schizoid patients who seemed headed toward schizophrenia to various types of acting-out delinquents. Beyond that, this study drew on approximately twenty families that either were recently treated or are still in treatment. In addition to the recorded and sometimes videotaped family sessions, we made use of individual interviews with early family member and of research procedures such as Family Rorschachs and family art evaluations. These family sessions, individual interviews, and research procedures allowed us to gain a fairly consistent picture of how each family member perceived other members and how he felt he was perceived by them. In particular, we learned about the parents' perceptions of, and expectations for, their adolescent children.

VARIETIES OF PARENTAL PERCEPTIONS AND EXPECTATIONS AFFECTING THE ADOLESCENT'S SEPARATION

Three areas of parental perceptions seemed saliently to influence the adolescent's capacity to liberate himself from his parents. There are, first, parental perceptions and expectations that convey to the child a self-image of potential autonomy or lack of such autonomy. A parent can perceive his offspring either as strong and able to stand on his own feet, or as sick, weak, infantile, or innately dependent.

There are, second, perceptions and expectations pertaining to the adolescent's capacity to make shifts in his object relations (to achieve "object removal," as described by Katan, 11) away from his family of origin. They perceive him to be either successful or unsuccessful in finding friends and sexual or marital partners.

Third, parental perceptions and expectations are concerned with the adolescent's loyalty toward them, with his badness and destructiveness should he leave them.

While the first two types of perceptions and expectations imply a direct and active "delineating" attitude by the parents, those of the third group operate more indirectly: the parents convey how they themselves would be affected by the anticipated or unanticipated separation of the children. In the subsequent exposition, we shall consider this group separately.

All three types of parental perceptions and expectations—and this seems crucially important—must be inferred from a total transactional gestalt. They are complex and ambiguous and not necessarily identical with what parents say or believe at any given moment.

SEPARATION-INDUCING VERSUS SEPARATION-INHIBITING
PARENTAL PERCEPTIONS AND EXPECTATIONS

Separation-inducing perceptions convey parental confidence in the adolescent's capacity to grow and become autonomous; separation-inhibiting perceptions convey a lack of such confidence. This vision of the child's autonomous future must, of course, be made congruent with the child's actual capacities and needs as these arise in specific life phases.

Murphey et al. (18) have reported on expectations in parents of successfully separating college students. These parents, wrote the authors, "regarded the separation and the college experience as a normal expectation and a necessary experience for growth. One father said of his daughter: 'I felt she would do well in her studies. I felt she could take care of herself. I knew that, if she had a problem, she would let us know and we would work it out and, above all, she had a good mind, quick and alert and retentive.' "

In a group of students who rated low in autonomy and relatedness, however, Murphey et al. found different parental expectations. These parents "were not sure that the students would be successful in college or that they would be able to get along without them [the parents]. . . . Although these students also had experience with jobs as well as opportunities to live away from home, their parents had not been able to respond to their children's growth by a shift in their own image of the student from dependent child to young adult."

Separation-inhibiting parental perceptions and expectations abounded in our families, conveying distrust and disbelief in the adolescent's capacity to become autonomous. For example, one mother repeatedly defined her son in a family session as a "born loser," bound to make a mess of his life. The father of another truant adolescent insisted his son was now a failure and would remain a failure. Vindictively he announced that his son would not finish high school and would never hold a job. At the time of the follow-up interview approximately two years later, this son had indeed dropped out of school and appeared an inveterate drifter. Typical also were statements in which parents doubted their adolescent sons' capacities to find female partners. One mother, clearly motivated by oedipal jealousy, insisted that her son was too immature to date According to her, any girl who took an interest in him must have psychological problems. Another mother addressed her fifteen-year-old son in almost the same vein: "Any girl who goes out with you should have her head examined." In addition these parents frequently doubted their adolescent children's capacity to have satisfying friendships with members of the same sex. One mother said repeatedly: "You are a bum and the only friends you can have are bum friends. A decent, worthwhile boy would not look at you. Wait, soon your bum friends will be fed up with you." This mother subsequently provided evidence that she projected onto her son aspects of her own negative self-image and apprehension about his finding only worthless friends once he had left the house.

The parental perceptions and expectations here reported were not merely hostile to the adolescent; in one way or the other they conveyed to him that he was unable to separate successfully. The parents typically tended to focus not so much on a specific lack of skills or experiences that could be corrected through effort or training. Instead, they aimed at what they perceived as deep-rooted and incorrigible character defects.

To those cases where a parent held inhibiting expectations could be added those in which he or she had no expectations, or only fuzzy ones. This was true for several parents in our sample. One mother, for example, seemed amazingly unperturbed when her sixteen-year-old son failed in school and then had no future plans. She enjoyed and encouraged in her son a carefree, latency state that was incongruent with his actual age. This boy, with his mother's covert approval, preferred playing with toads in the cellar to doing his homework. She seemed to convey, "As long as you are not thinking about the future, neither will I. I, for my part, will not remind us of a future that separates us." Two other normally cooperative parents were, upon repeated questioning, unable to visualize their sixteen-year-old son in any job situation whatsoever. Neither could they visualize him having a relationship with a girl. Three years later this son was a patient in an expensive private psychiatric hospital, where he appeared blissfully unconcerned about his future. He seemed to operate under the assumption that his parents would always support him regardless of what happened.

AMBIGUOUS OR CONFLICTING
PARENTAL PERCEPTIONS AND EXPECTATIONS

Because parental perceptions must be inferred from an often inconsistent behavioral gestalt, we frequently deal with an ambiguous situation. What on the surface looks like a separation-inducing expectation may have a covert inhibiting dimension, and what appears as an inhibiting perception may, in effect, promote an adolescent's autonomy. In order to do justice to this complexity, we must further differentiate between *overt* and *concealed* perceptions and expectations.

For example, one father in our sample, after suffering a hemorrhage from an ulcer, told his truant and drifting son, in a seemingly determined manner, that he would no longer rescue him should he get into trouble. On the surface this seemed to indicate the father's positive resolve. It appeared to imply that he deemed his son ready and able to take responsibility for himself. The concealed expectation, however, was that the son would eventually get into trouble and then would find out how much he needed his father. At this later point the father would be able to vindictively tell his son that he could not manage for himself—that is, the father would then convey his basic, underlying inhibiting expectations.[2]

Two other parents provided a further example of how overt separation-inducing perceptions may conceal negative, inhibiting ones. During the family sessions these parents constantly pointed to the creative qualities of their fifteen-year-old daughter Evelyn. They told Evelyn, an attractive, mostly silent girl, again and again that she was highly artistic, that she had grace, and that she therefore would easily find a job as a model, if not as an actress. In individual interviews, however, these parents told the therapists that they had no faith in the girl's creative ability, that they never believed she could make it as a model or an actress, and that they were praising her only to bolster her ego. The mother revealed, in addition, that the girl resembled her (the mother's) schizophrenic brother. She (the mother) feared therefore that Evelyn might become schizophrenic like him. In the family sessions, this girl distrusted what her parents said about her. She seemed able to pick up the covert message inherent in her parents' exaggerated praise of her (that she could *not* become autonomous), yet she appeared at a loss as to how to verify her perceptions of her parents and of herself. After shouting some sarcastic and rebuffing remarks, Evelyn tended to withdraw to her room, where she would spin herself into a fantasy world, removing herself from all contacts with family as well as peers.

Not only, as in this instance, may a seemingly separation-inducing expectation conceal an inhibiting one, but also a seemingly inhibiting expectation may hide a positive intent. For example, one may see the maneuver reminiscent of that of the late football coach Vince Lombardi, who heaped invective and abuse on a player and thereby provoked him into disproving through his actions the dismal perceptions the coach seemed to have of him. Some parents in our sample seemed to trigger their son's abrupt separation from the family by categorically disparaging or questioning his ability to make it on his own. One mother, for example, repeatedly told her son he would never find a girl who would consent to marry him. According to the mother, he just was not the kind of boy a girl could find interesting. This son, then not quite eighteen, told his mother all of a sudden that he had married and moved out of the house. He soon became the father of a child and made himself and his wife financially independent.

Not infrequently an adolescent seems at a loss as to how to react to a parent's ambiguous expectations as these relate to his separation. In such a case, he or she might simply wait until the parent's expectations and intentions become clearer. This seemed to happen with Clara, the sister of the fifteen-year-old Evelyn mentioned earlier. Like Evelyn, Clara received constant ambiguous messages from her father and, like Evelyn, seemed in danger of becoming schizophrenic. Clara was a college student, who used to spend her summer vacations at home. On these occasions the father would typically berate her for being lazy, for being a financial drain, and for ruining her parents' vacation. While denouncing her in this manner, he derived evident pleasure from having her around him, particularly when she was scantily dressed and served his breakfast. The girl, unsure as to whether the father wanted her at home or not, continued to spend her vacations uneasily in the parental house. The father finally seemed to have decided that he wanted her out of the house (this was at a time when another attractive daughter had reached adolescence) and subsequently threw her bodily down the steps and out of the door. He forbade her expressly to come back home unless she had secured a job. The girl complained bitterly about the father's brutality, but, with the door shut behind her and the message clear, she was now in a position to move away and did so, living on her own as a teacher.

Some contradictions stem from different appraisals of an adolescent by his two parents, as when one parent anticipates a successful separation, while the other does not. Such differing parental perceptions are common in family life. But the same parent may hold and transmit overt yet contradictory perceptions and expectations with respect to his or her adolescent. One father typically vacillated from one session to the next in his evaluation of his boy's future. In one session he saw his son headed for a brilliant career in television, and in the next headed for chronic handouts, in lifelong dependence on the parents.

HOW PARENTS ANTICIPATE BEING AFFECTED BY THEIR CHILDREN'S SEPARATION

Optimally, in letting their children go, parents do not break all ties but prepare the ground for new and more mature relations with them. Whatever they do, parents send out anticipatory messages to the children, which the children, in turn, respond to. Depending on the parents' messages about how they will live without their children, these children can be expected to separate either relatively freely and easily or to be burdened by guilt over abandoning and hurting their parents. Laing and Esterson, in particular, have described such guilt-inducing parental messages (15). In our sample, we could distinguish three ways in which parents appeared affected by their children's anticipated separation.

First, in some instances the parents appeared to block any such anticipation out of their awareness. These parents avoided at all cost talking or thinking about their children's forthcoming separation. When asked by us specifically what their lives would be like when their children left home, they tended to dismiss such questions as irrelevant. They would say, "His (or her) going away will be no problem to us; life will go on as usual." In several cases of such denial, however, the parent appeared intrusively worried about the adolescent. One mother, for example, depicted herself to us as an independent, mature woman who was able to lead a rich life of her own, now and later. However, she could not help being constantly preoccupied with what her son was doing and tried to keep tabs on all his friends, teachers, and psychiatrists. She rationalized this activity as love for her son. Another mother spent many sleepless nights thinking about her fifteen-year-old son, who had run away from home and had lost interest in school. She was constantly struggling with the question of why he was unhappy, why he had changed, and what would happen to him. Only after nine months of family therapy did she gradually begin to consider her own excessive dependence on her son. She began to face the implications for her own life and marriage of her son's approaching separation. In these and similar cases, the parents' own fears of being made lonely and of having to restructure their own lives were buried under a flurry of intrusive activities and worries.

Similar denial was evident in a father who talked glowingly about a future without his son in the house when he would be free to do what he had always wanted. However, he appeared over-identified with his son in a highly ambivalent manner. He would dote on him, cheer his attacks on the establishment, and condone almost any scheme and whim; but he also would get into fights with him and then trivialize or totally dissociate the conflict. This father, who had lost his own father at the age of five, appeared to parentify his son to an unusual degree. He expected the son to be the father he did not have, but he also took him to task for what his actual father had done to him, namely, abandon him. This father's manic-like denial of the importance to his own life of his son's

separation seemed commensurate with the depth of his investment in this son.

Such denial of the impact of the child's separation contrasted
with an attitude of deep, depressive gloom presented by some
other parents. Indeed the wife of the father just mentioned
provided a striking contrast. This woman anticipated an empty
and meaningless life without her son. In reflecting on her son's
separation, she looked depressed and appeared to burden her son
with her depression. A similar, paralyzing depression seemed to
take hold of one father mentioned earlier when the youngest of his
four daughters reached mid-adolescence.

On the other hand, some parents anticipated being lonely and
depressed once the child left but also conveyed that they could
cope with it. This seemed to be the most desirable attitude. Here
the adolescent did not need to cope with his parents' denial, nor did
he face undue guilt for abandoning his parents and condemning
them to misery and loneliness. For example, one mother who
appeared deeply entangled with her only son seemed nonetheless
to realize that she must emotionally separate from him. She
dreaded such separation but prepared herself to grieve his loss and
to restructure her life. At the age of fifty she decided to learn to
drive a car and to look for a job. Her active, coping attitude, which
neither denied the pain of separation nor burdened her son with
her depression, may have been a factor in preventing her son from
developing a crippling breakdown.

FACTORS THAT CAUSE
PARENTAL PERCEPTIONS AND EXPECTATIONS
TO INDUCE OR INHIBIT SEPARATION

In line with the conceptual scheme here outlined, these factors
can be understood as the contributions of the two principal
parties, parents and adolescent child, to the interplay of
perceptions and expectations described above. The most critical
factor in this interplay appears to be the autonomy the adolescent

has achieved at any given point. This autonomy, reflecting the differentiation-integration of his ego, ensures that he can selectively respond to, and if necessary refute, his parents' perceptions of himself. Equipped with a solid core of autonomy, he can struggle successfully with any potentially inhibiting perceptions and expectations his parents may direct toward him. If he lacks such autonomy, he will fall easy prey to these perceptions and expectations.

Given such a core of autonomy, the adolescent can be expected to respond positively to any stratagem of the Vince Lombardi type. He can more readily be expected to cope successfully with the contradictions in parental perceptions to which he is exposed. Bateson (2), Kafka (10), and Wynne (22) have written about how a child may cope creatively with the very parental ambiguities and contradictions that, under slightly different circumstances, may contribute to his schizophrenic development.

However, against the adolescent's core autonomy and ego strength must be weighed the parents' contributions—contributions that may affect either a relatively autonomous or relatively entangled adolescent. When we try to pinpoint the critical factors in these parental contributions, we must consider two interrelated aspects. First, in any given interaction we must try to recognize the separation and autonomy-furthering intent that may exist in seemingly inhibiting perceptions and expectations. Second, we must evaluate the ambiguity and contradictions inherent in parental perceptions and expectations. As a rule, an adolescent appears to fare best when he is exposed to *interparental, as against intraparental, contradictions.* His chances to assert himself seem best when at least one parent perceives him as being able to separate and relates to him actively and energetically. The inhibiting perceptions and expectations of the other parent can thus be counteracted and neutralized. The adolescent's chances for immunizing himself against his parents appears to diminish, however, when he is exposed to inhibiting perceptions and expectations mainly from one intrusive parent, while the other parent withdraws.

This negative outcome appears even more likely when the parental perceptions and expectations are of the "sick" rather than "bad" variety, and when they are rigidly entrenched. When an adolescent, either overtly or covertly, is perceived as sick, incompetent, too weak for life, immaturely dependent, too insecure, etc., he will become more easily paralyzed and deterred from separating himself than when he is seen as bad, mischievous, and trouble-making. Perceptions of "badness," although implying dire anticipations of future failure, give the adolescent leeway for separating himself from his parents via rebellion and defiance. Perceptions of "sickness" and weakness, in contrast, tend to squelch such rebellion and defiance. However, though parental perceptions of "badness" in the child may facilitate this child's abrupt separation, they may exact the price of a negative identity. The internalization of "badness" in the child may presage the child's eventual downfall through guilt-induced self-destruction.

FIXED VERSUS CHANGEABLE
PARENTAL PERCEPTIONS AND EXPECTATIONS

To the extent that parents uphold inhibiting perceptions rigidly, these perceptions seem to insidiously numb the child into identifying with them. They will become persistently absorbed into his self-system and, as a result, will resist the child's attempts at immunization.

In our sample, we dealt frequently with perceptions and expectations the parents appeared to have formed during their children's early years. These never seem to have changed with the passage of time. For example, one mother said about her son, "Almost from birth on George was a sneaky liar. I have never experienced him otherwise. He will never change and will therefore always get into trouble." Another mother reported of her adolescent daughter, "When I saw her as a baby I knew she was the one child who would always worry me. She was always a dreamer, the impractical one. I doubted she would make it in life." It was this girl, then fifteen years old, one of four daughters, who, at the time of the family therapy and at the time of the follow-up interview, seemed headed for a schizophrenic disturbance.

SOME IMPLICATIONS FOR FAMILY THERAPY

To the extent that parental perceptions and expectations become potent forces in the separation process of adolescence, they are bound to become foci for therapeutic intervention. Family therapy reveals most clearly the significance of these perceptions and expectations and affords the best chance to deal with them. The family therapist must help the adolescent and the parents to clarify these perceptions and expectations when they are concealed, ambiguous, and contradictory. This will help all participants in the separation drama to understand better where they stand with one another. Particularly, it will help the separating adolescent to differentiate his own self-image, his own motivations and aspirations, from those held for him by his parents. Furthermore, he can now challenge and refute his parents' perceptions and expectations of him. One can say that in this manner the conflict of generations is transformed from guerrilla to open, conventional warfare.

In the effort to clarify what is concealed, ambiguous, and contradictory in the parental perceptions and expectations, the therapist, first, must be alert to what a parent expresses directly about his child's future but contradicts by other behavior—for example, when a parent declares an adolescent ready to take on a job but disparages all active attempts at job-seeking.

Second, he must pay attention to any discrepancy between what is conveyed about a given child to the interviewer or therapist and what is conveyed to the child in private or in family sessions. Note, for example, the case of Evelyn, mentioned earlier, whom the parents in her presence described as a potential actress and model and whom they devalued in the interview with the therapist.

Third, he must note what is said when the parental couple is together as opposed to what is said by each parent singly to the interviewer or therapist. Repeatedly, in our sample, parents could reveal their dire expectations about their child only when they could talk alone to a given therapist.

Fourth, he must, in line with the above, pay attention to possible discrepancies between seemingly shared family and quasi-public parental perceptions and expectations and the parents' concealed perceptions and expectations.

And, finally, he must try to deal with the anticipations described above about the impact of the separation on the parents themselves, anticipations that may be harmful to the adolescent because of either the parents' denial or their excessive, depressive gloom.

Clarification of parental expectations and perceptions, however, is not enough. Together with the task of clarification must go that of *liberation*. By liberation we mean the adolescent's freeing himself from the thwarting impact of his parents' perceptions of, and expectations for, him which by now have taken hold of him and are seriously threatening his separation and limiting his life's choices.

In order to understand what is involved in such liberation, we must consider first what these parental perceptions and expectations mean in the parents' own psychic economy. Here we focus on the defensive aspects of their perceptions and expectations, as described by Roger Shapiro (21). For example, by perceiving and labeling her adolescent son as fragile and dependent, a mother can try to come to grips with her own sense of being fragile and precariously dependent on this son. Instead of acknowledging and working through her own painful feelings, apprehensions, and conflicts relating to the approaching separation, this mother disowns and externalizes them onto her child. She recruits her child as an ever-available living receptacle for these apprehensions and conflicts. She unburdens herself by burdening her child. Such parental perceptions and expectations used defensively are, therefore, exploitative. As an adjunct to his parents' defensive system, a child is inevitably thwarted in his own growth and separation. Parental perceptions and expectations that seem designed to interfere with an adolescent's move toward autonomy bring to light most clearly the exploitative features of such parental perceptions and expectations.

The separation drama of adolescence, however, not only reveals the defensive and exploitative nature of parental perceptions and expectations but also triggers and reveals the adolescent's revengeful fury at his dawning realization of his parents' exploitation of him. Paradoxically, however, as Boszormenyi-Nagy has suggested (7), his strongest weapon for making his parents suffer now is his willingness seemingly to live up to his parents' inhibiting perceptions and delineations of him. The adolescent negatively counter-delineates his parents by delivering himself as the living proof of their own sickness or badness. Exactly in this manner he can play on his parents' guilt for having exploited him and for holding on to him. He can show up his parents as failures and prevent their own growth and liberation. The family therapy must expose the exploited and bound victim's masochism and enjoyment of power over his parents; they are inherent in his living up to his parents' defeating, separation-inhibiting perceptions and expectations of him.

Liberation, in the final analysis, must be mutual. To the extent that parents, through psychotherapeutic intervention, become able to correct their perceptions of, and expectations for, their children in the light of the adolescents' true needs and capacities for autonomy, they will promote their own growth. Instead of miring themselves and their children in a vicious circle of exploitation and counter-exploitation, they will work toward true separation and liberation.

Notes

[1] An instructive example is provided by the Genain quadruplets, who were at one time all schizophrenic. They have been described and followed up by David Rosenthal (19) and his collaborators. These quadruplets, particularly from the account given by B. W. Basamania (1), were perceived by their mother in a characteristically differentiated, yet rigid and distorted way, almost from the moment of birth. The perceptual distortions reflected the mother's own unresolved childhood conflicts. One girl, who was born only a few minutes ahead of the others, was designated for life as the responsible one, the leader; a second one as pleasant and helpful; a third one as basically inept and incorrigible; the fourth one as oversexed, hostile, and trouble-making. These early character designations, here massively condensed and simplified, did "take" to an amazing extent, as I, who had a chance to treat one of the quadruplets during her thirties, could confirm. (See Chapter 5).

[2] This example makes clear that careful clinical observation over time seems best suited to clarify the interpersonal perceptions and expectations under discussion, as against a step-by-step analysis of a single recorded interaction. Psychotherapeutic observations allow one to take in the total Gestalt, the temporal dimension, and the different levels of overtness or covertness that come into play in interpersonal perceptions and expectations.

References

1. Basamania, B. The development of schizophrenia in the child in relation to unresolved childhood conflicts in the mother. In *The Genain quadruplets*, ed. D. Rosenthal. New York: Basic Books, 1963, pp. 449-466.
2. Bateson, G. Double bind, 1969. Paper presented at the Symposium on the Double Bind, Annual Meeting of the American Psychological Association, Washington, D. C., September 2, 1969.
3. ———, Jackson, D. C., Haley, J., and Weakland, J. H. A note on the double bind. *Family Process* 2: 154-161, 1963.
4. Bettelheim, B. *The informed heart*. Glencoe: Free Press, 1960.
5. Bion, W. Differentiation of the psychotic from the non-psychotic personalities. *International Journal of Psycho-Analysis* 38: 266-275, 1957.

6.   Blos, P. Three typical constellations in female delinquency. In *Family dynamics and female sexual delinquency*, ed. O. Pollack and A. S. Friedman. Palo Alto: Science and Behavior Books, 1969.

7.   Boszormenyi-Nagy, I. Implications of the phenomenon of parentification. Paper presented at an Adult Psychiatry Branch Seminar, National Institute of Mental Health, Bethesda, Maryland, June 27, 1969.

8.   Johnson, A. M. Juvenile delinquency. In *American handbook of psychiatry*, ed. S. Arieti. New York: Basic Books, 1959, pp. 840-856.

9.   Johnson, A. M., and Szurek, S. A. The genesis of antisocial acting out in children and adults. *Psychoanalytic Quarterly* 21: 323-343, 1952.

10. Kafka, J. S. Critique of double bind theory and its logical foundation. Paper presented at the Symposium on the Double Bind, Annual Meeting of the American Psychological Association, Washington, D. C., September 2, 1969.

11. Katan, A. The role of displacement in agarophobia. *International Journal of Psycho-Analysis* 32: 41-50, 1951.

12. Klein, M. Notes on some schizoid mechanisms. *International Journal of Psycho-Analysis* 27: 34-46, 1946.

13. Laing, R. D. *The divided self—an existential study in sanity and madness.* London: Tavistock, 1960.

14. ———. *The politics of the family.* Toronto: CBC Publications, 1969.

15. Laing, R. D., and Esterson, A. *Sanity, madness and the family.* London: Tavistock Publications, 1964.

16. Laing, R. D., Philipson, H., and Lee, A. R. *Interpersonal perception.* London: Tavistock Publications, 1966.

17. Levi, L. D., Stierlin, H., and Savard, R. J. Fathers and sons: the interlocking crises of integrity and identity. *Psychiatry* 1971.

18. Murphey, E. B., et al. Development of autonomy and parent-child interaction in late adolescence. *American Journal of Orthopsychiatry* 33: 643-652, 1963.

19. Rosenthal, D. *The Genain quadruplets.* New York: Basic Books, 1963.

20. Searles, H. F. The effort to drive the other person crazy—an element in the aetiology and psychotherapy of schizophrenia (1959). In *Collected papers on schizophrenia and related subjects.* New York, International Universities Press, 1965, pp. 254-283.

21. Shapiro, R. L. The origins of adolescent disturbances in the family: some considerations in theory and implications for therapy. In *Family Therapy and Disturbed Families*, ed. G. Zuk and I. Boszormenyi-Nagy. Palo Alto: Science and Behavior Books, 1967.

22. Wynne, L. C. On the anguish, and creative passions, of not escaping double binds: a reformulation. Paper presented at the Symposium on the Double Bind, Annual Meeting of the American Psychological Association, Washington, D. C., September 2, 1969.

Chapter 9

Group Fantasies and Family Myths

Fantasies, when shared in groups, have special meanings and functions. These meanings and functions vary with the types of groups under study. In this chapter, I consider families to be groups in which fantasies are typically shared and utilized. These family groups can be compared with other groups. Such comparison, I shall try to show, casts into relief the differing theoretical and therapeutic implications of different types of shared group fantasies.

A COMPARISON OF THREE TYPES OF GROUPS

In order to trace these implications, I shall briefly compare three types of groups: *(a)* So-called *Bion groups*, containing up to twelve members, as studied on the Tavistock model. Such groups, with their characteristic dynamics and features, have been discussed by Bion (5), Rioch (9), Turquet (15, 16), and others. In the United States these groups form part of the "Group Relations Conferences," sponsored by the Washington School of Psychiatry and other institutions. Chiefly, they serve here as laboratories for the participatory study of small-group behaviors. In Europe, small Bion groups are increasingly used for therapeutic purposes. Argelander (1), in particular, has described the way in which small therapy groups of the Bion type operate over longer periods of time. *(b)* So-called *Balint groups,* i.e., small groups composed of members of the helping professions (such as medical practitioners, clergy, counselors, etc.) who, through the group experience, learn to apply psychoanalytic principles to practice-related problems. These groups are named after their initiator, the late M. Balint. Balint groups have been formed in many parts of the world. Their nature and function is described in Balint's seminal book *The Doctor, his Patient, and the Illness* (2), as well as in other writings (3, 4). *(c) Family groups,* i.e., actual families that seek counseling or therapy. These groups will be the main focus of this study.

I choose these three types of groups because they are significantly similar *and* dissimilar. They are similar in terms of their size and their members' capacity to function, for we deal in each instance with relatively small groups whose members ordinarily represent an average range of normal to neurotic difficulties. But—and this highlights what is important in this study—they are also characteristically dissimilar. These dissimilarities relate to *(a)* different group tasks and *(b)* different types of their members' involvement with one another. Briefly, these differences are as follows. Bion groups mobilize certain typical group processes which are held to reflect and, when analyzed, resolve (or at least to improve) their various members' neurotic problems. These problems, thus, find their way into the group's life, although they originated outside the group. This contrasts with what we find in families. Their members also seek therapy, but for problems which, to a large extent, originated and developed within the family itself. This, then, brings into view the central difference between small therapy groups and families. Bion groups are transient, ad hoc aggregates of people who lack a common history and, apart from the immediate group relationship, are not mutually involved. Families, in contrast, share such history, and their members have been and will be fatefully and enduringly enmeshed with one another.

Balint groups differ from both of the above groups with respect to their avowed task. For their task is not to provide therapy to their members. Rather, it is to help these members become better therapists for others. With respect to these members' "real-life" involvements with one another, however, these groups seem intermediate between small therapy groups and families. For they are not pure ad hoc groups, as are typical Bion groups. All those Balint groups that I came to know reflected numerous ties of acquaintance or even friendship among members. For example, all members of one Balint group in New Zealand knew one another well. As private practitioners in the same small community, they met frequently in professional meetings, shared many of their patients, had developed mutual loyalties and obligations, and had formed definite opinions and expectations of one another. Yet these real-life bonds were still incomparably less intense and intricate than those we find in natural families.

FANTASIES IN SMALL THERAPY GROUPS

It is these differences in the groups' tasks and their members' involvements with one another that set the stage for the development of different types of group fantasies.

Their nature and dynamics in small groups were originally examined by Bion (5), and later described by Turquet (15, 16), Shapiro and Zinner (10), Stierlin (11), Argelander (1), and others.

These group fantasies are enacted, and hence made transparent, through certain types of recurrent group behavior. This behavior mirrors characteristic "basic assumptions" shared by the whole group. Essentially, these are the basic assumptions of "dependence," "fight-flight," and "pairing," as originally described by Bion. They derive from a group climate that exerts a strong regressive pull. The members' shared sense of omnipotence, yet lack of a sense of responsibility, temporal sequence and realistic constraints are here the most striking features. They color all fantasies that evolve. Often these have a volatile, primary process quality.

These fantasies are assumed to be dormant in all small groups, but particularly in ad hoc groups. However, whether and how they gain strength and become visible depends in no small part on the group leader. Therefore, we must briefly consider his contributions.

In the small ad hoc group, the therapist's contributions seem particularly instrumental. Argelander (1) has described what is involved. In order to facilitate group fantasies, the therapist (or leader) must here weaken those nodal points for real-life involvements of members that even ad hoc groups present. For example, he must de-emphasize professional identities and status hierarchies. In addition, he must structure and maintain an asymmetry between himself and the group that has a depriving, tension- and anxiety-inducing edge. To achieve this end, he strictly abstains from acting out with the group and gives interpretations on the group level only. Thus, he deliberately aims at letting the group stew in its anxiety, as such stewing will make virulent the dormant group fantasies.

FANTASIES IN BALINT GROUPS

Balint groups, too, according to available descriptions, are no strangers to such group fantasies. But here the group leader must look at them with a wary eye. Although, within limits, he tolerates or even encourages these fantasies (because they can provide the members with useful insights about themselves and their transactions with clients), on the whole he tries to de-emphasize them. For mostly they distract from the group's primary task—to assist with the members' practice-related problems.

A closer look at these problems shows that group fantasies, as just described, become indeed less important to the extent that real-life involvements (in contrast to merely transitory entanglements) become the dominant concern of a group. Typically, real-life involvements concern a Balint group on two levels: first, on the level of those practice-related problems that stake out these groups' primary task; second, on the level of the participants' relations with one another. Although these levels imply different frames of reference, we find in each case basic orientations that diminish the significance of group fantasies as encountered in small therapy groups.

In order to make this clearer, let us turn to the first level—that of professional practice—and consider perhaps the most frequent problem with which a Balint group practitioner must deal, i.e., the problem of who is, or should be, the proper patient within a multi-person field. To illustrate this problem, we may think of a tired practitioner who makes a late house call in response to a wife's distressed telephone plea.[1] Her sense of urgency makes him believe her husband has suffered heart failure. When he arrives, he finds himself greeted by a young woman who is seductively clad in a "baby doll" night gown. He realizes at once that the whole affair has been overdramatized. The husband, who is in his early fifties, has no more than mild anginal pains of long standing. He looks sheepish and embarrassed, while groaning dutifully. The "child bride" babbles excitedly. Does this now mean—and this is a typical Balint group problem—that the practitioner (provided he can control his anger and maintain a diagnostic and therapeutic stance) must consider the alarmist wife the primary patient? Yet, in order even to think about such a switch in patient status, with all its implications, the practitioner needs to consider the tangled skein of these two people's past and present relationship. He must ask himself questions such as: What prompts the husband to let himself be recruited for the role of designated patient? Does such recruitment perhaps serve the purpose of averting a psychotic disintegration in his immature wife, who desperately tries to cover up and "disown" *her* sickness? Or does the husband masochistically acquiesce to patient status mainly because he needs to bind to him his young bride who otherwise would desert him and leave him stranded in a middle-aged depression (which, if true, would make him again the primary patient, although in a different sense than seemed to apply earlier)? Many more such questions can be asked. They all lead the questioner to examine ever more deeply these spouses' real-life involvements and to take note of those actions, obligations, expectations, merits, and debits that accrued to them during the course of their involvements.

When we now turn to the second level—that of the group members' relations with one another—we find that similar lines of inquiry are opening up. Only this time it is not the multi-person relations of their patients, but those of the participants themselves that are the issue. For while the practitioners struggle to be helpful to one another, they must also confront such unpleasant facts as a certain physician's having a rather low reputation among his peers, or his having referred a patient too late to a specialist, or his having "dumped" an unattractive, chronically complaining patient into a colleague's lap. Such facts inevitably crop up where real-life involvements exist. And it is in an attempt to cope with these facts—i.e., to prevent them from making the group's life and work unbearably difficult—that the group members resort to certain myths or fictions. For example, they resort to the myth that theirs is a particularly harmonious, well-matched group—just as the spouses in the earlier example, in their attempt to survive with each other, may overtly share and express the myth that they are a particularly well-matched and loving couple.

Because these group myths—and this is now central—are at odds with that group's reality, we may properly call them fantasies. But when we do so, we need to distinguish these fantasies from those which we found to dominate small groups of the Bion type. This, then, requires us to contrast myths, in the above-intended meaning, with the latter type of fantasies.

When we do so, we realize that both are instances of a shared group experience and, as such, have certain features in common. Both, we can say, serve as defensive mechanisms against an unpleasant reality on the group level. As such, both promise to spare their members painful confrontations, which, they fear, could unleash deep anxieties, disintegration, and chaos. But here the similarity ends, for different features of reality, different qualities of the group experience, and different implications for theory and therapy follow from the presence or absence of the members' real-life involvements, be these overt or hidden.

Group fantasies of the Bion type are essentially an outgrowth of, and a defense against, the ambivalence and conflicts that arise, as well as the primitive needs and drives that the group process itself in such ad hoc groups unleashes, yet cannot fulfill—except in fantasy.[2] Myths, in contrast, serve to obscure or deny the painful and complex reality of what the members actually did and still do to, and thought and still think of, each other. This we might call the painful reality of their factual involvement.

FAMILY MYTHS

In all groups we can expect a blend of Bion-type fantasies and myths as defined above. For even pure ad hoc groups germinate real-life involvements, which, in turn, create the need for myths; on the other side, even closely enmeshed families can be expected to drift, on and off, into "primary assumption land." Yet such drift, I submit, is minimally significant compared to what we find in Bion or even in Balint groups because family relations epitomize enduring real-life involvements. This, in particular, holds true for children's involvements with their parents. (Here we must remind ourselves that even as parents we always remain children to our own parents.) For the children's style of thinking, acting, and loving, their capacity for enjoyment, their hopes, their readiness to trust and be trusted, and many more features are linked to what they experienced or did not experience in their family. By the same token, the parents' most basic satisfactions, as well as their deepest despairs, derive to a large extent from what did and does, or did not and does not, occur in their relations with their children. It is then this *factuality* of family relations that makes family myths so important.[3]

Family myths, as here intended, have been extensively described and illustrated by Ferreira (8), who emphasized their homeostatic function. He maintained that "the family myth is to the relationship what the defense is to the individual." In the following, I want to offer a framework for the systematic analysis of such myths that derives from the above comparisons and considerations.

"TIGHT" MYTHS VERSUS "LOOSE" MYTHS

Family myths can be more or less articulate and internally consistent. They may be presented as tightly reasoned stories, as explicit family creeds, or may evolve as vaguely formulated assumptions. In the latter case, they may have a regressive, volatile, "basic-assumption" quality that calls to mind the Bion-type fantasies mentioned earlier. Such overt resemblances notwithstanding, I believe most of these assumptions to be family myths in the above-described sense—i.e., to be collaborative formulations that serve to dilute or deny the formidable realness of past and present family involvements. The vagueness of these formulations may reflect a low level of ego integration and articulation in individual family members and the family system as a whole—and/or may be a joint strategy for obscuring and bypassing painful conflicts and confrontations between members. In brief, these loosely formulated myths, no less than those that are tightly knit, serve defensive family functions; and, in order to understand them, we must take into account the members' past and present real involvements with one another.

THE FUNCTIONS OF FAMILY MYTHS

Family myths are over-determined; they share this feature with other mental and transactional phenomena. Essentially, they fulfill simultaneously two major interrelated types of functions: *defensive functions* proper and *protective functions*. *Defensive functions* come into play when the family members collusively distort their shared family reality—i.e., when, in an attempt to ward off pain and conflict, they obscure, deny, or rationalize what they do or do not do, and did or did not do, to one another. These defensive functions operate chiefly on an intra-family level. *Protective functions* of myths, in contrast, operate on the level of the family's relations with outsiders. They serve here as smoke screens that keep outsiders confused and/or ignorant about the family's real involvements. To an extent, these two types of functions always complement each other. For in order that they may help family members to defend themselves successfully against an awareness of what they do and did to each other, myths often need to be "sold" to the outside world. They must stake out the basic framework within which the outside world is to see and judge this particular family.

A CLASSIFICATION OF FAMILY MYTHS

We can classify family myths according to their major defensive function as follows: *(a) myths of harmony, (b) myths of exculpation and redemption,* and *(c) myths of salvation.* In each case, myths serve to blot out or selectively distort certain aspects and implications of the members' real past and present involvements with each other. They differ in their overall defensive thrust and chosen theme or themes. Over time these themes may shift or interweave, for myths can change, evolve, or fade away with changing defensive needs.

A. MYTHS OF FAMILY HARMONY

These myths paint a rosy picture of past and present family togetherness, harmony, and happiness—in contrast to what a perceptive observer often notes within his first minutes of contact with such families. These are families who appear miserable, conflicted, depressed, or bored, yet expressly believe—and try to make others believe—that they are the happiest and most harmonious families on earth. Here we find some of those pseudo-mutual families whom Wynne et al. (17) have described. Their eager and "loving" friendliness with one another serves to blot out and dissociate past and present disagreements and hostilities. By employing myths of harmony, they cement the dissociation and throw unpleasant facts into the "memory hole," as described in Orwell's 1984.

Jointly they rewrite the family history, just as Stalin's and Hitler's textbooks rewrote the histories of Russia and Germany. The distortions of historical facts can be similarly blatant. In one family, for example, the parents had on one occasion battered a child so severely that he needed surgical treatment. This was some fifteen years before the family entered treatment. By this later time, the members had created a myth of harmony that made such intra-family brutality appear unreal and incomprehensible. The incident was unearthed only during the course of lengthy family therapy. Typically, the battered victim, no less than his victimizing parents, had shared in the construction and maintenance of this myth—i.e., had made it into a true myth of harmony.

B. MYTHS OF EXCULPATION AND REDEMPTION

These myths have a more complicated structure than the myths of harmony. In myths of harmony, the family members primarily employ the shared defenses of denial and idealization; in myths of exculpation and redemption, they resort also to projective identification. A certain person (or persons), either inside or outside the family, either dead or alive, is jointly perceived to perpetrate (or have perpetrated) the family's badness, bad fortune, or misery. Hence he must exculpate the rest of the family, as well as himself. He must serve as his family's delegate in the sense in which I have elsewhere defined this term (12-14). As such delegate, he must above all allow the other members to observe *in him* their disowned badness or madness and to redeem themselves, *through him,* from their disowned guilt. Myths give a seeming coherence and rationality to this delegating process. This is partly analogous to the way in which the Jesus myth has served to redeem and exculpate by proxy millions of Christian believers.

These myths, we note, differ from myths of harmony in that they take more seriously the factuality of the members' enduring involvements. For they imply an assessment of what the members did or did not do to one another. Through these myths, accounts are drawn up, and blame is assigned. But such accounting becomes here prematurely closed and slanted, as it were. The difficult and painful work of probing each member's merits and faults on ever deeper levels of interpersonal complexity and of facilitating exploration, confrontation, and final reconciliation on the family level, remains undone.

Again we note that such myths, in order to be believable and effective, require the cooperation of all family members, including that of the victim-delegate. As Boszormenyi-Nagy (6) has shown, this delegate may win as well as lose. By allowing himself to become victimized, he can control the guilt lever on his parents— i.e., wield psychological power over them.

Myths of exculpation and redemption do not necessarily involve an immediately available victim-delegate. They may implicate someone absent or dead, for example, a "bad" alcoholic father who no longer is in sight. This father, so the myth goes, deserted his faithful wife and loving children. Therefore, he needs to be shunned and castigated. It takes much probing often before such notions can be recognized for what they are, namely, myths, the more so as the alleged perpetrator (and implied redeemer) of the family's plight cannot account for himself in person. Nonetheless, such myths can be corrected. Here I think particularly of one family in which a "deserting" father was, indeed, perceived as the cause of all family troubles. All family members shared in the belief that he was innately bad, corrupt, irresponsible—in brief, the scum of the earth. This father's "desertion" occurred approximately ten years before the family entered therapy. Meanwhile, the mother had remarried. Her new husband, the children's stepfather, had also come to believe that the family's current difficulties—such as the mother's depression, the oldest girl's promiscuity, the boy's school difficulties—were essentially due to this father's desertion. Gradually, though, this myth was punctured as it became known that the father's "desertion" was in part engineered by the mother, who at that time was having a love affair with her boss. More and more this father came to be seen not so much as an irresponsible runaway, but as a pathetic evictee, who again and again clamored to re-enter the family yet each time was rebuffed.

C. MYTHS OF SALVATION

Myths of salvation extend the myths of exculpation and redemption. Jesus, who took upon himself the sins of others, promised not only redemption but also salvation. This required, in turn, the additional myth of a paradisical state after death, to be found in some heavenly Beyond where all-loving and giving parents (God and the Virgin Mother Mary) would provide a happiness and approbation precluding painful strivings, conflicts, and sufferings. Salvation myths on the family level are similar in essence. Also, here we find the shared belief that somehow the pains, conflicts, injustices, and sufferings inherent in family life, and inherent in the process of individuation and separation, can somehow be avoided or undone through the benign intervention of some strong, if not omnipotent, figure or agency. Naturally, a family therapist, particularly when presenting himself with charismatic verve, may become and remain such a mythical person, the more so when his contacts with the family are brief and hence not subject to sobering disillusionments. In other cases, family members may jointly believe in the power and benevolence of some relative or friend (such as an uncle or senator) who can lift them into a life in which painful conflicts and efforts are not required.

These myths, like the others, thus serve to distort aspects and implications of the members' real past and present involvements with one another.

THE PROTECTIVE FUNCTIONS OF MYTHS

Apart from defending the members against painful confrontations (which for them spell family disintegration and chaos), myths must protect the family from outsiders. When we focus on such protective functions of myths, the comparison with Bion groups yields further insights. Bion groups, being ad hoc groups, have nothing to hide, as it were—except, that is, for those unpleasant, embarrassing, or conflictual primitive cravings and attitudes (e.g., envy, greed, voyeurism, vindictiveness, or a sense of omnipotence) that the immediate group process releases. Families, in contrast, have much, if not everything, to hide. They fear, rightly, that public exposure will recall unsettled accounts and thereby open up old and new wounds and experiences of guilt and shame. As matters stand, they cannot but see outsiders, particularly so-called family therapists, as intruders who want to afflict them with pain and embarrassment. The more they fear such intrusion and accounting, the more they cling to myths.

THERAPY IMPLICATIONS

Such awareness of the defensive and protective functions of myths has therapeutic implications. The family therapist must realize that myths are clung to as long as they are needed. He cannot afford to be fooled by these myths, but neither can he afford to challenge them unless he can provide the family members with a model and framework for the safe exploration of their interpersonal accounts. Boszormenyi-Nagy (7) has perhaps best described what this involves. Essentially, fairness, integrity, and an empathic curiosity are required from the therapist.

As an impartial explorer and arbiter, he investigates the various facets of these members' involvements with one another. As such, he may observe within minutes how the members' transactions belie the myths they proffer. For example, he may note how veiled hostilities undercut a professed myth of harmony. But instead of pinpointing such discrepancies, he may more profitably foster a climate of exploration, which allows these myths to "die a natural death." This requires, among other things, that he adopt a multi-generational perspective, which widens the scope within which accounts are assessed. For how can he possibly do justice to a schizophrenogenic mother who dumps onto her child her own dissociated badness or madness unless he also takes into account how this mother was bound and psychologically exploited by *her* mother?

Also, the therapist of Bion groups, while stirring up manageable amounts of anxiety, helps the members to explore their attitudes to one another. In so doing, he too shows fairness and integrity. But such fairness and integrity have dimensions different from those found in natural families, where real-life involvements and accounts are at issue.

These differing dimensions come into view when we consider briefly how differing transference phenomena evolve within these two types of groups. The concept of transference derives from a dyadic analytic relationship and therefore becomes problematic when applied to groups, be they Bion-type groups or small families. Still, it appears useful when differing qualities in the relations between leaders (or therapists) and their groups are considered. In Bion groups we can speak of a "group transference" that reflects the earlier-mentioned asymmetry between group and leader. Such group transference, as fostered by the leader's depriving abstinence, somehow channels and transforms into one "transference amalgam" what each member contributes.

With families, the term *transference*, when at all applicable, means something different. Here also certain amalgams of expectations and attitudes affect the relation between therapist and family and these, too, can be called transference (or countertransference as the case may be). But these phenomena, whatever their specific content and source, reflect, foremost, one fact—that transferences originate within families. It is family transactions that give rise to those relational patterns later transferred, inappropriately and repetitively, to non-family contexts. Myths, I submit, serve as a sort of strait-jacket that keeps these relational patterns locked up within the family system, i.e., prevents them from being pried loose and from being experienced and recognized as transferences. This contrasts again with what small Bion groups present, where transference processes, as we saw, can rather easily be mobilized.

Myths, in brief, appear to safeguard the family members' entrenchment and involvement with one another. Instead of being windows through which a therapist may look into a family's interior, they are rather like painted walls of ghetto buildings distracting and/or amusing while keeping the onlooker safely outside.

SUMMARY

Family myths can be compared with shared fantasies that evolve in small groups such as Bion and Balint groups. Depending upon their dominant theme, we can distinguish family myths of harmony, myths of exculpation and redemption, and myths of salvation. These myths fulfill defensive and protective functions. On the intra-family level, they defend the members against painful confrontations with aspects of their real past and present involvements with each other. In relations with the outside world, they bar intrusions and unsettling judgments. Their therapeutic implications are cast into relief through a comparison with other types of group fantasies.

Notes

[1] Argelander (1) has described in detail the prototype of the above situation.

[2] In various "encounter" and psychodrama groups, this process is carried one step further. Instead of being stirred up in order to be contained and analyzed, many of these fantasies are acted out with the encouragement and participation of the group leader. Such acting out ranges from various forms of touching to actual sexual intercourse. This implies processes of denial and dissociation that are rather different from those found in Bion and Balint groups.

[3] Such "factuality" does not exclude certain fantasies from playing important roles in these members' involvements with one another. In fact, such involvements often imply that other members are exploitatively recruited by projective identification and other processes. These others must here "embody" those "bad" fantasies the recruiter needs to disown, yet also needs to keep in a close "working distance" to himself. These "fantasy phenomena," as occurring on the intra-family level, are part of the reality of exploitation that I subsume under the term "factuality of family relations."

References

1. Argelander, H. *Gruppenprozesse/Wege zur Anwendung der Psychoanalyse in Behandlung, Lehre und Forschung.* Reinbeck: Rowohlt, 1972.
2. Balint, M. *The doctor, his patient, and the illness.* London: Pitman Medical Publishing, 1964.
3. Balint, M., and Balint, E. *Psychotherapeutic techniques in medicine.* London: Tavistock, 1961.
4. Balint, M., Gosling, R., and Hildebrand, P. *A study of doctors.* London: Tavistock, 1966.
5. Bion, W. *Experience in groups.* London: Tavistock, 1961.

6. Boszormenyi-Nagy, I. Loyalty implications of the transference model in psychotherapy. *Archives of General Psychiatry* 27: 374-380, 1972.

7. ———, et al., eds. *Invisible loyalties.* New York: Hoeber-Harper, 1973.

8. Ferreira, A. Family myths and homeostasis. *Archives of General Psychiatry* 9: 457-463, 1963.

9. Rioch, M. "All we like sheep—" (Isaiah 53:6): followers and leaders. *Psychiatry* 34: 258-273, 1971.

10. Shapiro, R., and Zinner, J. Family organization and adolescent development. In *Task and organization*, ed. E. Miller. London: Tavistock, 1972-1973.

11. Stierlin, H. Gruppendynamische Prozesse: Übertragung und Widerstand. In *Analytische Gruppenpsychotherapie*, ed. H. G. Preuss. München/Berlin/Wien: Urban & Schwarzenberg, 1966.

12. ———. Family dynamics and separation patterns of potential schizophrenics. In *Proceedings of the Fourth International Symposium on Psychotherapy of Schizophrenia*, ed. Y. Alanen. Amsterdam: Excerpta Medica, 1972, pp. 169-179.

13. ———. Interpersonal aspects of internalizations. *International Journal of Psycho-Analysis* 54: 203-213, 1973.

14. Stierlin, H., and Ravenscroft, K. Varieties of adolescent "separation conflict." *British Journal of Medical Psychology* 45: 299-313, 1972.

15. Turquet, P. Bion's theory of small groups. Lectures presented at the National Institute of Mental Health, Bethesda, Maryland, June 8 and 9, 1965.

16. ———. Four lectures: the Bion hypothesis: the work group and the basic assumption group. Presented at the National Institute of Mental Health, Bethesda, Maryland, May 26, May 28, June 2, and June 6, 1971.

17. Wynne, L. C., Ryckoff, I. M., Day, J., and Hirsch, S. I. Pseudomutuality in the family relations of schizophrenics. *Psychiatry* 21: 205-220, 1958.

Chapter 10

Psychoanalytic Approaches to Schizophrenia within a Family Model

So far, no generally accepted family theory of schizophrenia seems in sight. Rather, we find competing viewpoints whose therapeutic implications differ. In this chapter, I shall take up one of these viewpoints, trace some of its therapeutic implications, and compare it with psychoanalytic approaches to schizophrenia.[1]

This family viewpoint, more than other such viewpoints, is shaped by psychoanalytic considerations but, in a strict sense, is not psychoanalytic. For psychoanalytic theory and practice grow out of the special analytic situation, delineated by Freud, which obtains between analyst and analysand. Family theory and practice grow out of a different situation—that obtaining between therapist(s) and family.[2] This situation, like any other, reveals certain data while it conceals others. For example, it reveals typically recurrent multi-person transactions, while it conceals— or at least makes less visible—certain offshoots from the unconscious (e.g., dreams, fantasies, and subtle perceptual transference distortions) on which psychoanalysis focuses. Out of these different situations, each with its own observational framework and primary data, evolve the different concepts and theories of the psychoanalytic and family approaches.

Despite—and even, to some extent, because of—these differences, each approach can throw some light on issues that are central
to both. The nature and treatment of schizophrenia is one such
issue. To illuminate it, I shall now present a family viewpoint on
schizophrenia.

TRANSACTIONAL MODE DISTURBANCES

My chosen viewpoint, supported by the work of the Washington Study Group on the Psychotherapy of Schizophrenia[3] and my
own therapeutic and research experiences with approximately
forty families, involves a rather elaborate concept which I have
described and illustrated elsewhere (34, 36, and, with Ravenscroft,
37). Here I can present it only in briefest outline, at the risk of
massive over-simplification and distortion. This is the concept of
transactional modes.

These modes try to grasp and reflect the interplay and/or
relative dominance of pushes and pulls into and out of families
throughout all stages of the individuation and separation process.
In this interplay, the transactional modes operate as the covert
organizing background to the more overt and specific child-parent
(or therapist-patient) interactions. When age-appropriate transactional modes are too intense, out of phase, or are inappropriately
blended with other modes, the negotiation of a mutual individuation and separation between parent and child (or therapist and
patient) will be impeded. We may therefore speak of *transactional
mode disturbances.*

The transactional modes bring into view salient contributions of
the parents *and* of the children to the ongoing interpersonal
process, but also reveal systemic properties of the evolving
relationship. These modes can be considered both *transitive* and
reciprocal. They are transitive in that they denote the parents' active
molding of an offspring who is still immature, dependent, and
hence captive to parental influences. They thus reflect the fact

that parents, from the beginning, impress on their child their "stronger reality" (see Chapter 3), often unconsciously by covert and subtle signals and sanctions. The child must adapt to this "stronger reality" or suffer. But also, these modes are reciprocal: the children mold and influence their parents as much as the latter mold and influence them.

Elsewhere (34) I have delineated and illustrated the three major modes of *binding, delegating,* and *expelling* which bring into view the transactional fates of binder and bindee, delegator and delegate, expeller and expellee. In briefest summary, these modes operate as follows:

When the *binding mode*[4] prevails, the parents interact with their offspring in ways that seem designed to keep the latter tied to them and locked in the family orbit. Such binding can operate on three major levels.

First, it can operate primarily on a dependency level where primitive drives and affects are strong. The child there appears bound by the exploitation of his dependency needs, as he is offered undue regressive gratification. We are inclined to speak in this context of "id-binding."

Second, binding can operate on a more cognitive level. Drives and affects contribute to this level also, but chiefly as forces that fuel and shape cognitive processes. Here we find that the binding parent interferes with his child's differentiated self-awareness and self-determination by mystifying the child about what he feels, needs, and wants. He "misdefines the child to himself," as it were. Bateson (3, and et al. 4, 5), H. Bruch (9), Searles (30), Wynne and Singer (31, 32, 39, 40), Lidz et al. (22), Haley (15), and Laing (19), among others, have illuminated various aspects of this interactional process. It implies often idiosyncratic language and patterns of communication. We can call cognitive binding "ego-binding," as the parent forces the child to rely on the parent's distorted and distorting ego instead of developing and using his own discriminating ego.

The binding mode can, finally, operate on a third level where an intense archaic loyalty and guilt come into play. Loyalty needs, like those for dependency and cognitive guidance, can be seen as legitimate needs of children. And, as happened in id- and ego-level binding, such legitimate needs are now, at one and the same time, fostered, thwarted, and exploited. Children who are bound chiefly on this level are thus likely to experience any thought, not to mention attempt, of separation as a crime which demands the harshest punishment. These children, whom we may call "superego bound," are prone to suffer intense primitive "breakaway guilt" that operates often unconsciously and gives rise to acts of either massive self-destruction or heroic atonement.

Where the *expelling mode* prevails we find an enduring neglect and rejection of children, who tend to be considered nuisances and hindrances by their parents. A strong centrifugal force pushes many of these children into premature separations. These children appear not so much exploited, as they appear neglected and abandoned.

Where, finally, the *delegating mode* is predominant, it is blended with binding and expelling elements. The child is allowed and encouraged to move out of the parental orbit—up to a point! He is held on a long leash, as it were. Such qualified "sending out" is implied in the original Latin word "*de-legare,*" which means both to send out and to entrust with a mission. The latter meaning implies that the delegate, although sent out, remains beholden to the sender. Here too loyalty to the parents must be strong, but unlike the more primitive and archaic loyalty mentioned in the binding mode proper, this loyalty must allow for selectivity and differentiation. Otherwise, the delegate could not fulfill his missions. Such missions may be to become a famous artist or scientist in fulfillment of the parents' unrealized ego-ideal, or it may be to enact the parents' disowned delinquent impulses. Whatever the mission, the delegate is encouraged to differentiate and to separate to the extent that his mission requires. (An overview of various types of missions is given elsewhere. Cf. Stierlin, 37.)

The above transactional modes of binding, delegating, and expelling imply a long-term view of the process of individuation-separation, in which it is evident that parents who bind, delegate, and/or expel their children do not necessarily act in a pathogenic manner. These modes become exploitative and damaging to the child only when they are inappropriately timed or mixed, or are excessively intense.

Extremes of binding in schizophrenia. In many of the most severe cases of schizophrenia, the child appears intensely bound on all three levels—the affective, cognitive, and loyalty. This results in the mutual thralldom of parents and child. Frequently such state is termed *symbiosis* or *symbiotic union.* This symbiotic union distorts, by exaggeration and prolongation, the normal symbiotic phase of development which M. Mahler (23) described. It is difficult to convey the oppressive strength of such a pathologic union. Ricks and Nameche (26) have written:

A parent and a child form an inseparable unit, prolonged over a long period beyond the usual end of symbiosis (as described by M. Mahler). The child is not considered a separate person and boundaries between the parent and child are not recognized. The parent may therefore bathe the child well into adolescence, be so intrusive as to deny the child any privacy in action or thought, and be impervious to any desires that the child expresses in his own right. The child is expected to comply to parental distortions of the environment, physical restraint, and socialized relations . . . the child must remain functionally helpless, have no other close relationships, and not attempt to escape. The record contains no evidence that the child has ever been permitted outside the walls of the home to visit relatives or friends or has ever attended overnight camp.

Of the three levels of binding, the cognitive has been given most attention, as we have been alerted to "the double bind" (Bateson et al., 4), to "the transmission of irrationality (Lidz et al., 22), and to "attempts to drive the other person crazy" (Searles, 30). In all these dynamics or stratagems which play a role in the cognitive binding of schizophrenics, mystification appears as a central element.

R. D. Laing (19) introduced this concept into family theory. He borrowed it from Karl Marx, who employed it in a socioeconomic context. Capitalist exploiters, according to Marx, mystified their workers with the help of religion when they made them believe that suffering and lowly work were tickets to a blessed after-life. Similarly, parents were seen to mystify their children about what these children really needed, wanted, or believed. Three major dynamics, according to Laing, are to be found in mystification: attribution, invalidation, and induction.

In *attribution,* parents may, as Laing noted, attribute to their children such traits as insecurity, stubbornness, sickness, meanness, recklessness, which, in one way or the other, implant a negative self-image. Such negative attributions can be classified either as "attributions of weakness" or as "attributions of badness" as was shown in Chapter 8. As a rule, attributions of weakness damage a child more severely than attributions of badness because the latter, when internalized, often leave room for a separation via a "negative identity," whereas attributions of weakness keep the child captive to parental "protectors."

Invalidation, another term of Laing, denotes a coercive disqualification of a dependent person's statements, as when parents invalidate those views of their children which threaten parental authority and positive self-image. Laing refers here to the first schizophrenic patient in the psychiatric literature whose major "feature" was his hate of his father. The psychiatrist, Dr. Morel, serving as the father's agent (and becoming the inventor of the term *dementia praecox*, which preceded schizophrenia), managed to invalidate this hate by declaring it to be a symptom of mental illness.

The term *induction*, also used by Laing, refers to the active molding and recruitment of another person. While the mystifier attributes badness or weakness and invalidates the other's meanings, he also tries to enlist the other's cooperation. Thus, he induces his victim to embrace and become a partner in his own mystification. Attribution, invalidation, and induction, according to Laing, are "transpersonal defenses, whereby self attempts to regulate the inner life of the other in order to preserve his own" (21). Such transpersonal defenses interweave with, but also differ from, the intrapsychic defenses of classical psychoanalysis.

Mystification, as here defined, is common in human relations and family life. Families with schizophrenic offspring give us a prime example of how it works. Here the contributions of L. Wynne and M. Singer stand out. These researchers illuminated the many ways in which family members may confuse, unsettle, leave stranded—in brief, mystify—one another. They do this by failing to structure and share with one another a common focus of attention, as when they frame as a question a seeming assertion, or insidiously shift the topic under discussion, or leave the partner in doubt as to whether closure has been achieved. By an innovative use of Rorschach tests, these authors identified approximately forty "communication deviances" which occurred massively, yet not exclusively in families with schizophrenic offspring. We can therefore say that Wynne and Singer developed a phenomenology of mystification which, at one and the same time, is rich, detailed, clinically relevant, and subject to verification and scoring.

I myself became particularly impressed with the archaic loyalty-boundness of many of these patients—a boundness which caused them to suffer from deep (largely unconscious) "breakaway guilt." Out of such guilt they then strove for heroic atonement and/or cruel self-punishment. For example, in our longitudinal study on adolescents of high risk for schizophrenia and their families, conducted at the National Institute of Mental Health, I counted two schizophrenic youngsters who courted death at a time when they most seriously seemed to break away from their parents. Both happened to be runaways, but, typically, had no peers to run to and could only resort to their idiosyncratic introjects. I have called these adolescents lonely schizoid runaways (35). They appeared to roam aimlessly, stumbling into one potentially dangerous situation after the other. One was finally killed when he bedded down in a sleeping bag at the edge of a country road and was hit by a speeding car, the other when he foolishly waved a knife in front of a policeman. From my knowledge of these schizophrenic adolescents and their families, I had no doubts that their thinly veiled suicides reflected attempts to appease their excruciating "breakaway guilt."

Extremes of parental delegating leading to schizophrenia. Extreme delegating, often interwoven with maximal binding, may also give rise to schizophrenic disturbances, although these can be expected to differ in phenomenology, prognosis, and treatment implications from those resulting from excessive binding. Delegated patients who become schizophrenic are torn asunder by conflicts of missions and loyalties. Yet they can be expected to have a better long-term prognosis than more pervasively bound patients. For these delegated schizophrenic patients, even though gripped by conflicting loyalties and missions, can get a foothold in the world of peers and alternate adults and can thus promote their final liberation. We can expect them to become acutely, rather than chronically, disturbed, and to be released—at least occasionally— from psychiatric institutions. My own, mainly psychotherapeutic, experiences with schizophrenic patients and their families bear this out, as does the research which Nameche et al. (24), Scott and Montanez (29), and others report.

In order to fathom the intensity of the conflicts and stresses to which such delegates can be subjected, we must reflect on the missions they are expected to fulfill. Many of these missions imply extreme demands on the delegate and his reconciling capacity incompatible with his age and ordinary adaptational requirements.

Several "missions impossible" particularly stand out here, such as, first of all, the mission to destroy one parent out of loyalty to the other—the mission for which Hamlet, hovering on the brink of a schizophrenic breakdown, provides the classic paradigm.

We must, second, mention the mission to embody and actualize a parent's grandiose ego-ideal. The more such a parent senses that he or she cannot realize this ideal alone, the more desperately he or she turns to the child. This child, even if of only average endowment, must try to reach dizzying heights of achievement and fame and must share these efforts willingly with the delegating parent. In other cases, he might have to embody all the beauty and vitality which this parent feels wanting in himself or herself.

Third—and this is the perhaps most fateful mission—such a delegate might be recruited to embody the badness and craziness which a parent, in his innermost self, fears to be his fate. This child must then serve his parent's self-observation, which Freud defined as one of the three functions of the superego (besides ego-ideal and conscience; cf. Freud, 13). Living under the (disowned) threat and spell of madness, such a parent seems often impelled to search for—and, in the process, induce—madness in the child. This behavior is understandable in parents who are haunted by the shadows of mad relatives or ancestors (see Scott and Ashworth, 28). They have grown up with the notion and expectation, frightening beyond comprehension, that madness again will strike their tainted family. It is in an attempt to control, contain, and neutralize this feared and ever-threatening madness that a child becomes delegated to enact it—i.e., becomes the mad family member.

SOME THERAPEUTIC IMPLICATIONS

Given the above model, the therapeutic task depends on how the various modes dominate and/or blend with one another.

First, let us consider some therapeutic implications of extreme binding. Where such extreme binding prevails, the therapist has a short-term and a long-term task to fulfill. The short-term task is to prevent what Scott and Ashworth (27) have called "closure," and the long-term task is to help the parents and schizophrenic offspring to *un-bind.*"

"Closure," according to Scott and Ashworth, threatens when a patient (ordinarily an adolescent offspring) comes to be perceived as " 'ill,' mad, beyond human influence or concern. . . ." In fact, he seems condemned to a living death—a shadow existence in a mental hospital. But—and this highlights the paradox of extreme boundness—this "dead" patient, condemned to live in a shadowy Hades, retains the power to fill his parents' lives with never-ending terror, concern, and guilt. The patient's "dead" body, although removed from the house, remains available for continuous ritualistic observances. Thus, unlike the dead heroes described by Virgil and Dante, who feared (or perhaps relished) being forgotten, many "living dead"—called chronic schizophrenics—are refused Lethe's drink: although completely alienated, they stay intensely bound to their parents.

Scott and Ashworth have perceptively traced how closure comes about. "When the 'child' first breaks down," we learn, "he becomes as a rule the center of a peculiarly intense parental awareness. He becomes the object of parental scrutiny, usually silent and oblique," while "conflict between the parents, often deep and unresolvable, now invariably takes place through the patient to a greater extent than before." At this point many psychiatrists become agents in sealing such closure enduringly. They spell out a "diagnosis" and hence officially sanction a sentence of "mental illness." It is here that a psychiatrist's short-term intervention may become crucial. For this psychiatrist is typically brought into the picture when parents, after a period of agony and ambivalence, are about to dramatically evict their child. These parents then try to enlist his help to resolve their ambivalence. They recruit him as a surgeon who is expected to diagnose and cut off the bad, gangrenous "family flesh," to effect its radical sequestration and expulsion. They expect this psychiatrist to label the patient as sick and in need of institutionalization. By giving official medical approval, it is hoped, he will sanction the rejecting side of the parents' ambivalence and relieve their guilt about expelling their child.

Thus, this psychiatrist is placed at a critical juncture in the patient's and family's lives. He can use his influence to keep the potential expellee within the family orbit and, in so doing, can try to redistribute to the family the patient's badness and symptoms—that is, he can try to keep alive and "workable" the parents' ambivalence; or he can, by the power of his authority, provide the definitive, expelling push—which, as we saw, does not imply real separation, but a tragic boundness in which all parties forfeit their chances for growth and happiness.

But such prevention of closure is only the beginning of what is therpeutically required. The immensely difficult job of loosening the multi-person binding is still to begin. Above everything, the therapist must now be sensitive to the dilemma that every prospect of the patient's making progress in his individuation and separation will inevitably trigger a systemic backlash of renewed binding. This affects, among other things, many a bound patient's evolving "positive" transference to his individual therapist, as Boszormenyi-Nagy (7) has shown. By developing such a positive transference, the patient commits the number-one crime of betraying his loyalty to his parents. Hence, he is increasingly driven to atone by presenting himself as sicker and more unworthy of a fulfilled life than every before—in brief, he suffers or engineers a "setback" by acting out or becoming more crazy.

Through such a "setback"—and this opens up another therapeutic angle—the patient-victim punishes himself while, at the same time, he gains leverage for making his parents guilty: he delivers himself as living proof of their failure and badness as parents. While masochistically surrendering himself to craziness and self-restriction, he becomes—to his parents——an all-powerful sadistic torturer. When this happens, it is important that the therapist be able empathically to share the plight of the victimized victimizers (the parents) while also appreciating the victimizing victim's (the child's) power inherent in his suffering.

Where we find extremes of delegating, similar backlash phenomena and power ploys need to be dealt with. In addition, the delegate's conflicts of missions and conflicts of loyalties, as mentioned above, need to be analyzed and redistributed. For example, all family members may have to realize that one adolescent delegate cannot very well serve, at the same time, the mission of being his mother's vicarious thrill-provider (e.g., become a precocious sex athlete) and that of realizing her virtuous ego-ideal (e.g., study for the ministry). Such insights may then cause parents to "re-own" (own up to) traits, needs, and conflicts which they "disowned" by exploiting their delegate—a process which family therapy may facilitate. At the same time, they may cause this delegate to "own" the anguish of his grief and loneliness—experiences which await him once he plans and executes those goals and missions in life which are truly "his."

THE DEFICIENCY VS. CONFLICT
DISPUTE IN THE LIGHT OF A FAMILY MODEL

Let us, with the above model in mind, take a new look at the roles and therapeutic implications of a conflict versus a deficiency model in schizophrenia.

The deficiency model. G. Aronson (2), representing the Los Angeles study group, summarized the deficiency-versus-conflict controversy in his contribution to the above workshop.

The deficiency model, according to Aronson, rests on Freud's seminal formulations of 1915. Later Federn (10), Pious (25), Wexler (38), and others elaborated this model. At its center is the notion of an ego so fragile that it easily collapses under the "stress of disappointment, frustration, uncertainties about how to proceed in life, requirements and desires for intimacy, etc." While collapsing, this ego becomes unable to hold on to its unconscious representations of outer objects. When "these object-representations are decathected, the mute phase of schizophrenia is ushered in. Experiences of world-destruction, disappearance, emptiness, and death are the correlates of the process. So intolerable are these experiences that a second phase follows quickly: restitutional hallucinations, delusions, bizarre actions— the enormously varied picture of the schizophrenic psychosis noisily eclipses the terrifying first phase."

Such assumed ego deficiency, then, favors a treatment approach that advances the "real relationship" between patient and therapist (i.e., fosters face-to-face contacts, aims at the control of instinctual outbursts, educates, assists with reality adaptations, etc.), while it de-emphasizes—at least during the disturbed phase—conflict and transference interpretations.

Holzman, in his contribution to the panel, also favored such a deficiency model. "No data," he stated, "support a conflict theory as the common etiology of both schizophrenia and neurosis, while much can be cited to support a special psychoanalytic theory of schizophrenic restitution." For, "any theory of schizophrenia must account not only for the apparent 'withdrawal' from personal contacts, but must account for strange and awkward body movements, unusual sensitivities, thought slippage such as dereistic thinking or autistic logic, confusion and uncertainty in personal identity, body image distortions, extraordinary dependency, pleasurelessness, characteristically poor competence, the flat and spotty modulation of affect, disproportionate rage reactions, hypochondriasis, sensory input compulsions, panics when alone, and many other behavioral symptoms not seen in neurotic conditions" (16, pp. 3-4).

The conflict model. The conflict model of schizophrenia contrasts with the above deficiency model. This conflict model derives from the Freud of 1895 and 1911 (11, 12), Klein and her co-workers (17, 18), and Arlow and Brenner (1). Here the loss of internal representations and the deformation of the ego reflect active defensive processes designed to ward off intolerable affects, impulses, and painful reality. These processes are shaped by the infant's immature cognitive structures and are intense and primitive, but in principle do not differ from those found in neurotic conflicts.

This model favors a therapeutic approach which is more classically psychoanalytic and therefore sanctions or encourages the interpretation of conflicts, transference, and countertransference.

THE DIALECTIC OF INTRAPSYCHIC AND
INTERPERSONAL CONFLICT IN THE FAMILY MODEL

We are now in a position to draw some conclusions from the earlier-described family model. For this model, which conceptualizes transactional mode disturbances, opens up a perspective in which the terms "conflict" and "deficiency" in schizophrenia both take on new meaning.

Let us, first, consider the new meaning it gives to "schizophrenic conflicts." Essentially, it widens our view of such conflicts and alerts us to interpersonal, rather than to intrapsychic, conflicts. Depending on which transactional modes are dominant, the nature and intensity of these interpersonal conflicts vary. Under the binding mode, for example, parent-child conflicts tend to become ambivalent, intense, and protracted, as the child finds here no other objects than his parents. Under the delegating mode, in contrast, the child may dilute or displace his conflicts with parents by turning to peers (cf. Stierlin and Ravenscroft, 37). Whatever their specific nature and intensity, such interpersonal conflicts, then, affect and interweave with the intrapsychic conflicts on which Arlow and Brenner (1), Klein (17, 18), Bion (6), and other analysts have focused.

Intrapsychic and interpersonal conflicts imply differing conceptualizations and vantage points. In the one case, we focus on a "divided self" whose drives or needs work at cross purposes (e.g., oral or destructive drives versus the need to be loved), in the other, on a (more or less) unified self seen as pitted against other selves—chiefly those of his parent(s).

Notwithstanding these differing conceptual axes, we can relate the two types of conflicts to each other. For we can examine and conceptualize how a "divided self"—i.e., a self conflicted from within—generates interpersonal conflict which, in a negative spiral, triggers and amplifies further intrapsychic conflict. This accords with the position taken by M. Klein. In her view, the child, unable to "own" his envy and destructiveness, disowns them by splitting them off and projecting them into the mother (or the maternal breast). But since he depends on his mother (or her breast), these disowned elements return to him with a vengeance. They turn the mother and her breast into frightening, persecutory forces which embroil him in deep interpersonal conflict. Such interpersonal conflict then divides the self even further—i.e., aggravates his intrapsychic conflict.

When we apply the above family model, the main focus is on early parental transitivity, as defined above. As a result of such transitivity, interpersonal conflict is seen as generating intrapsychic conflict, and the flow of the disowning process appears reversed. It now moves from the parent—the possessor of the stronger reality—to the child. In order to spare himself (or herself) painful self-assessment, self-change, and inner conflict, the parent recruits the child under the binding or delegating modes, as

226   PSYCHOANALYSIS AND FAMILY THERAPY

described. This implies interpersonal conflict inasmuch as vital
needs of parents and child clash—e.g., the parents' need to disown
pain and badness with the child's need to be free of pain and
badness and yet retain a loving and supportive parent. The child
then tries to resolve this interpersonal conflict by submitting to
intrapsychic conflict, but it is a conflict of such magnitude that it
shakes his nuclear ego and distorts his perceptions of his inner and
outer worlds.

Such intrapsychic conflict then reflects, as well as shapes, the
child's efforts to adapt to a stronger (binding or delegating)
parent's reality. Thus, a severely bound child becomes "cognitively
violated" and stirred up, and must turn himself into a "specialist in
symbiotic survival," as I have described this elsewhere (34). This
implies for him, during the most formative stages of his
development, an uneven psychic, and possibly physiologic,
differentiation and integration. He must specialize his talents and
skills for detoxifying and yet retaining (as far as possible) the
dangerous, over-demanding and intrusive parent, chiefly the
mother. In so doing, he must sacrifice, or leave underdeveloped,
other skills and capacities needed for his healthy overall growth
and for his progressive individuation and separation.

In this way the family model can account, I believe, for many
(maybe all) of the deficiencies of the schizophrenic ego, particularly its excessive "fragility"—deficiencies which appeared juxta-
posed to conflicts as long as they were viewed exclusively from
within one of the above psychoanalytic perspectives.

While thus accounting for schizophrenic deficiencies in part or
whole, the family model also allows for a re-evaluation of some of
their functional significance. In being bound or delegated, the
"deficient"—i.e., "sick," "crazy," non-functioning, etc.—schizophrenic family member often reveals a paradoxical strength, as I.
Boszormenyi-Nagy in particular has shown. Indeed, this deficiency may turn out to be an asset once we focus on the whole family's
therapeutic needs. For while in one sense he is the weakest,

because most openly disturbed member, in another he is now the strongest: he "owns" the disturbance which the others must disown, and through such "owning" can become the focus of the whole family's treatment and the promoter of its growth.

TREATMENT PERSPECTIVES

This family view of schizophrenia thus leaves room for a conflict *and* a deficiency model. At the same time, it seems—at least at first sight—compatible with the therapeutic approaches which derive from these contrasting models.

On the one hand, it seems compatible with a non-analytic approach, as advocated by Greenson and Wexler (14) and others. This approach, we saw, tries to support the patient's fragile ego while it "anchors" him in reality. To this purpose, the therapist offers himself as a human reality different from that which the patient found—and often still finds—in his parents. Unlike the binding or delegating parents who exploited him, subjected him to unbearable conflict, and forced him into an uneven development, this therapist tries to be present and real without inducing such disturbances. Thus, he offers the patient a corrective emotional, as well as cognitive, experience.

On the other hand, the above family model seems also compatible with an analytic approach, which Searles (30), among others, has advocated. This approach rests on the premise that all emotional and cognitive experience, in order to be truly corrective for the schizophrenic, requires a re-living, on a deep symbiotic level, of those early parent-child interactions that forced him into unbearable, disruptive intrapsychic conflict and uneven growth. In the therapeutic process, the patient then cannot but cast the therapist in the role of binding and/or delegating parent. The therapist, in turn, struggles with this role—becoming himself bound and delegated—until he finally extricates himself from it. This type of "corrective experience" then demands that the therapist share, as well as contain, the patient's anxieties, conflicts, frustrations, and distortions in an unfolding transference-countertransference relationship.

However, while seemingly compatible with the above approaches, the family model also casts doubt on them. It makes us aware that a corrective emotional and cognitive experience, whether it be provided by a stable, clear-cut, anti-exploitative human environment or by a shared, long transference-countertransference journey, may not be enough for schizophrenic patients—and may even be harmful to them.

To understand this paradox, we must finally consider that dimension in schizophrenia which, I believe, only a family model highlights. I would like to call this the dimension of "interpersonal justice."

Central to it is the notion that the above processes of "owning" and "disowning" pain and conflict, of victimization and sacrifice, of exploitation and counter-exploitation make all family members participants in a system of "invisible accounts." I. Boszormenyi-Nagy (7, and, with G. Spark, 8) has developed this perspective in a deep and original manner.

Massive guilt, an immense though thwarted need for repair work as well as for revenge, a deeply felt sense of justice or injustice,[5] and of loyalty confirmed or betrayed—all operating largely outside of awareness—become here formidable dynamic forces, influencing the members' every move. And the stakes in this "morality play" are high. On the one side, we find parents who, exploited and crippled by their own parents, attempt to survive by living through their children, crippling them in turn; and, on the other side, we find children who, as self-sacrificing, lifelong victims, gain the power to devastate their parents by inducing deep guilt. This power of loyalty-bound victims presents perhaps the most difficult single problem in the treatment of schizophrenia.

With its focus on the power of the self-sacrificing schizophrenic victim, the conflict model also gains new therapeutic relevance. We may see in a new light the "sadism" of schizophrenic sufferers, which Searles and others have emphasized—of patients seemingly determined to torture their parents, as well as therapists, by stubbornly staying "sick." Also, we may better understand why Kleinian analysts can be successful with certain of these patients, as their interpretations (whatever their theoretical justification) seem aimed at making the patients "own," in the sense of own up to or take responsibility for, their destructive wishes and actions, thereby decreasing not only their guilt and fear over their destructiveness but also their power over their parents. For this may well trigger a positive circle of liberating repair work in which both parties—parents and children—can be the contributors as well as beneficiaries.

Notes

[1] This discussion owes much to the stimulating responses and remarks received from members of a workshop on "The Influence of Theoretical Models on Practice in Treating Schizophrenia," at the 1972 Annual Meeting of the American Psychoanalytic Association in New York City. Its participants, including this author, were: Drs. C. J. Aronson, D. L. Burnham, S. E. Eldred, J. C. Gunderson, P. S. Holzman, H. S. Searles, and R. S. Wallerstein. Drs. L. Mosher and J. C. Gunderson of the Center for Studies of Schizophrenia, National Institute of Mental Health, arranged the panel at which the paper that forms the basis for this chapter was presented.

[2] Also, they grow out of a broad theory of human relationships.

[3] It includes Drs. M. Adland, J. C. Cameron, D. Finesilver, J. Fort, J. C. Gunderson, L. Mosher, C. G. Schulz, L. C. Wynne, and this author. This group is one of four study groups in the United States which, during 1972 and 1973, have operated under the sponsorship of the Center for Studies of Schizophrenia at the National Institute of Mental Health.

[4] Such transactional meaning of binding differs from psychoanalytic meanings, as found, for example, in the "binding of libido or cathexis."

[5] We may here recall that many a terrorist is ready to blow up the world out of a deeply felt sense of injustice.

References

1. Arlow, J. A., and Brenner, C. *Psychoanalytic concepts and the structural theory.* New York: International Universities Press, 1964.
2. Aronson, G. The influence of theoretical models on practice in treating schizophrenia: defense and deficit models/their influence on therapy. Paper presented at the Annual Meeting of the American Psychoanalytic Association, New York City, December, 1972.
3. Bateson, G. Double bind. Paper presented at the Symposium on the Double Bind, Annual Meeting of the American Psychological Association, Washington, D. C., September 2, 1969.
4. Bateson, G., Jackson, D., Haley, J., and Weakland, J. Toward a theory of schizophrenia. *Behavioral Science* 1: 251-264, 1956.
5. ———. A note on the double bind. *Family Process* 2: 154-161, 1963.
6. Bion, W. Differentiation of the psychotic from the non-psychotic personalities. *International Journal of Psycho-Analysis* 38: 266-275, 1957.
7. Boszormenyi-Nagy, I. Loyalty implications of the transference model in psychotherapy. *Archives of General Psychiatry* 27: 374-380, 1972.
8. Boszormenyi-Nagy, I., and Spark, G. *Invisible loyalties.* New York: Hoeber-Harper, 1973.
9. Bruch, H. Falsification of bodily needs and body concepts in schizophrenia. *Archives of General Psychiatry* 6: 18-24, 1962.
10. Federn, P. *Ego psychology and the psychoses.* New York: Basic Books, 1952.
11. Freud, S. Paranoia (1895). Draft H. *S.E.* I.
12. ———. Psycho-analytic notes on an autobiographical account of a case of paranoia (1911). *S.E.* XII.
13. ———. The ego and the id (1923). *S.E.* XIX.
14. Greenson, R. R., and Wexler, M. The non-transference relationship in the psychoanalytic situation. *International Journal of Psycho-Analysis* 50: 27-39, 1969.
15. Haley, J. The family of the schizophrenic. A model system. *Journal of Nervous and Mental Disease.* 129: 357-374, 1959.
16. Holzman, P. The influence of theoretical models on the treatment of the schizophrenias. Paper presented at the Annual Meeting of

the American Psychoanalytic Association, New York City, December, 1972.

17. Klein, M. *Contributions to psychoanalysis, 1921-45.* London: Hogarth Press, 1948.

18. ———. *Developments in psycho-analysis.* London: Hogarth Press, 1952.

19. Laing, R. D. Mystification, confusion, and conflict. In *Intensive family therapy,* ed. I. Boszormenyi-Nagy and J. L. Framo. New York: Harper & Row, 1965.

20. ———. *The self and others: further studies in sanity and madness.* London: Tavistock, 1961.

21. ———. *The politics of the family.* Toronto: CBC Publications, 1969.

22. Lidz, T., Fleck, S., and Cornelison, A. R. The transmission of irrationality. In *Schizophrenia and the family,* ed. T. Lidz, S. Fleck, and A. R. Cornelison. New York: International Universities Press, 1965.

23. Mahler, M. *On human symbiosis and the vicissitudes of individuation.* Vol. 1: *Infantile psychosis.* New York: International Universities Press, 1968.

24. Nameche, G, Waring, M., and Ricks, D. Early indicators of outcome in schizophrenia. *Journal of Nervous and Mental Diseases.* 139: 232-240, 1964.

25. Pious, W. A hypothesis about the nature of schizophrenic behavior. In *Psychotherapy of the psychoses,* ed. A. Burton. New York: Basic Books, 1961.

26. Ricks, D., and Nameche, G. Symbiosis, sacrifice, and schizophrenia. *Mental Hygiene* 50: 541-551, 1966.

27. Scott, R. D., and Ashworth, P. L. "Closure" at the first schizophrenic breakdown: a family study. *British Journal of Medical Psychology* 40: 109-145, 1967.

28. ———. The shadow of the ancestor: a historical factor in the transmission of schizophrenia. *British Journal of Medical Psychology* 42: 13-32, 1969.

29. Scott, R. D., Ashworth, P. L., and Montanez, A. (1971). The nature of tenable and untenable patient-parent relationships and their connexion with hospital outcome. Unpublished manuscript, 1971.

30. Searles, H. The effort to drive the other person crazy—an element in the aetiology and psychotherapy of schizophrenia. In *Collected Papers on Schizophrenia and Related Subjects.* New York: International Universities Press, 1959.

31. Singer, M. T., and Wynne, L. C. Thought disorder and family relations of schizophrenics. III: Methodology using projective techniques. *Archives of General Psychiatry* 12: 187-200, 1965a.

32. ———. Thought disorder and family relations of schizophrenics. IV: Results and implications. *Archives of General Psychiatry* 12: 201-212, 1965b.

33. Stierlin, H. *Conflict and reconciliation*. New York: Doubleday Anchor and Jason Aronson, 1969.

34. ———. Family dynamics and separation patterns of potential schizophrenics. In *Proceedings of the Fourth International Symposium on the Psychotherapy of Schizophrenia*. Amsterdam: Excerpta Medica, pp. 156-166, 1972a.

35. ———. A perspective on adolescent runaways. Unpublished manuscript, 1972b.

36. ———. Interpersonal aspects of internalizations. *International Journal of Psycho-Analysis*, 1973.

37. Stierlin, H., and Ravenscroft, K. Varieties of adolescent "separation conflict." *British Journal of Medical Psychology* 45: 299-313, 1972.

38. Wexler, M. Schizophrenia: Conflict and deficiency. *Psychoanalytic Quarterly* 40: 83-99, 1971.

39. Wynne, L. C., and Singer, M. T. Thought disorder and family relations of schizophrenics. I: A research strategy. *Archives of General Psychiatry* 9: 191-198, 1963a.

40. ———. Thought disorder and family relations of schizophrenics. II: A classification of forms of thinking. *Archives of General Psychiatry* 9: 199-206, 1963b.

Chapter 11

Shame and Guilt in Family Relations

Shame and guilt are central human experiences. Also, they are central elements in psychiatric theory and practice. They deeply preoccupied philosophers such as Kierkegaard, Nietzsche, Sartre, Heidegger, and Jaspers, as well as psychoanalysts such as Freud and Erikson. Both concepts denote painful and complex emotions. They interweave with each other, but have different phenomenologies and dynamics. To understand shame and guilt in family theory and practice, we must first briefly elaborate these differences.

THE DIFFERING PHENOMENOLOGIES AND DYNAMICS OF SHAME AND GUILT

F. Alexander (1)—who speaks mostly of "feelings of inferiority" where the other authors speak of "feelings of shame"—Piers and Singer (18), Lynd (15), and, recently, Lewis (14), among others, examined differences and similarities in the two phenomena. Shame and guilt, they concluded, while often appearing similar, differ with respect to common usage and ethnological roots.

Shame essentially implies painful embarrassment, humiliated fury, and a sense of devastation and mortification often so deep that one wishes to sink into the ground. This feeling of shrinkage and diminution contrasts with the uplift that pride and triumph—the opposites of shame—provide.

Shame grows mainly out of a competitive defeat, rebuff, and weakness, out of a sensed loss of self-control with accompanying loss of self-esteem. As Erikson (4) has written: "A sense of self-control without loss of self-esteem is the ontogenetic source of a sense of free will. From an unavoidable sense of loss of self-control and of parental overcontrol comes a lasting propensity for doubt and shame." Also, shame seems specific to a sense of physical and sexual deficiency. A girl might feel ashamed because of her small breasts, her (assumed or real) sexual coldness or too ready arousal (that, to her, might indicate weakness); a boy, because of impotency, the size of his penis, or exposure to sexual ineptness. The German word *Schamteile* (literally, "shame parts") for genitals reflects the close affinity between sexual function or anatomy, and shame.

Guilt, in contrast, denotes the anguish and pain over hurting or wronging others or sacrosanct institutions such as the family, church, or homeland. It seems specific to situations where we (in deed or fantasy) attack, cheat, manipulate, humiliate, defy, or envy those whom we believe or wish to love or obey. (Envy, more than other emotions, seems to have simultaneous links to guilt *and* shame, particularly in children. For a person often feels envy to be destructive to others, as well as deeply humiliating to himself.) In brief, "guilt anxiety"—to use the formula of Piers and Singer—"accompanies transgression, shame, failure" (18, p. 11).

Freud's constructs of the ego-ideal and superego (8-10) served to illuminate the differing phenomenologies and dynamics of shame and guilt. Freud found that these emotions reflect, as well as generate, the tensions that arise between ego and ego-ideal (or superego). Freud clarified the nature of these tensions when he distinguished three superego functions: *ego-ideal, conscience,* and *self-observation* (10). Of these, the ego-ideal relates primarily to the experience of shame and conscience to that of guilt, while self-observation plays a central, though differing role in shame *and* guilt.

In the superego construct we deal with shame where we fail to fulfill the demands of the ego-ideal: i.e., where we fail to be as strong, beautiful, self-possessed, competent, or sexually potent as we feel we should be.

We speak of guilt when we violate our conscience that urges us not to hurt, cheat, humiliate, or disobey those whom we should love or respect. Hence, the German notion of guilt as the "bite" of conscience (*Gewissenbiss*).

Self-observation, the third superego function, mediates how we experience either shame or guilt. In the meaning here intended, it includes self-judgment, as well as observation and judgment of others and the total situation insofar as these affect the behavior of the self. Thus, self-observation, in this extended meaning, determines how far we feel we stray from ego-ideal or conscience. Such self-observation, as is well known, varies greatly among persons in strictness and acumen. It appears strong, overfocused, and searching in some; and weak, underfocused, and lax in others. Also, most importantly, it can be unhooked, perverted, or bypassed, allowing the person to evade (more or less) the pain of shame or guilt. Such defensive use (or, better, nonuse) of self-observation accounts for characteristic dynamics and discharge routes of shame and guilt, all serving to attenuate pain.

In shame, the person typically tries to massively avoid or blot out self-observation. He may literally close his eyes to or hide from and deny (i.e., make nonexistent) what happened. In guilt, he typically tries to silence the voice of conscience by distorting perception and judgment of accountability, particularly through the use of projection. He may get rid of guilt, at least momentarily, by accusing, blaming, or punishing others, as this has been described in the analytical writings of Freud, (9), Fenichel, (5, 6) and many others. At the same time, he often unwittingly sets himself up for being blamed or punished.

SHAME-GUILT CYCLES

Shame and guilt alternate with each other, forming cycles (1, 4, 18, 27). These cycles reflect shifting transactional scenarios and shifting perceptions of meaning and accountability, reminding us of the words of Nietzsche: "There are no moral [i.e., shame- or guilt-arousing] phenomena. There is only a moral interpretation of phenomena" (*Beyond Good and Evil*, aphorism 108, 17). Dostoevski illustrated complex shame-guilt cycles in his novels; Alexander (1) found them to underlie many criminal careers:

> In the little boy the intensely ambitious and competitive hostile attitude toward brothers and father provokes guilt feelings and fear of retaliation. Under the pressure of guilt feelings and fear he abandons his competitive attitude and adopts a submissive role by means of which the inhibited and intimidated boy tries to gain the love of his dangerous and powerful competitors.
>
> This submissive attitude now creates intense inferiority feelings, hurts the male pride, and leads to aggressive criminal behavior by means of which a tough, independent, stubborn, unyielding attitude is demonstrated and every dependence denied. This attitude becomes a new source of guilt feelings that lead to new inhibitions that again cause inferiority feelings and again stimulate aggressive behavior (p. 126).

Similar cycles are known from psychoanalytic practice. The following cycle, observed in my practice, seems fairly typical. A patient believed he had seriously hurt me by bad-mouthing me to a friend. Stung by guilt, he scrutinized me for evidence that would retrospectively justify his bad-mouthing. He finally focused on my occasional drift into inattention and accused me of not caring for him. When I interpreted his attacks on me as attempts to assuage his guilt over bad-mouthing me, he became upset and cried. Yet while he cried, he was overcome by shame. He called his crying a despicable show of weakness, and blamed me for having triggered it. Out of his humiliated fury, he attacked me again, thus starting a new (albeit slightly attenuated) guilt-shame cycle.

Conceivably, he could also have felt pride over his very weakness and self-disdain. For the possibilities of subjectively juggling meaning and accountability seem endless. Nietzsche was aware of this when he wrote: "He who despises himself, still esteems himself as the despiser" (aphorism 78). And, "We may train our conscience so that it kisses at the same time that it bites" (aphorism 98) (17).

SHAME AND GUILT
IN OUR INVOLVEMENT WITH OTHERS

Further aspects of shame and guilt emerge when we focus on how these experiences involve others. Such involvement can reveal paradoxical features. Sartre, for one, elaborated these with respect to shame (19). In shame, Sartre found, we lose the other— or, more correctly—we lose (or at least believe we lose) his esteem or love while, at the same time, we court his approbation. While we try to flee him, we also install him as the judge of our worth.

A similar paradox obtains with respect to guilt, for the sense of guilt leaves us bound up with the other even when we, in trying to rid ourselves of guilt by projection (or outright attack), manage to hurt or destroy him. Our conscience then resurrects the other as an introject that may spur us to relentless, lifelong repair work or search for self-punishment. It was here also that Dostoevski revealed, more than others, the tortuous, intense bonds between those who inflict and those who suffer guilt.

Traditionally, negative aspects of shame and guilt stood out, and

analysts accordingly tended to describe these phenomena as
defenses—particularly superego defenses—that restrict growth
and are self-destructive.

But positive functions can also be found. Ward (27) has
described some of these with respect to shame. Shame, he noted,
may safeguard a person's self-esteem, foster his growth, and
stabilize his relations with others. Earlier, Winnicott (28)
emphasized similar positive aspects with respect to guilt. Guilt, he
argued, presupposes a capacity and motivation to experience
concern. It implies that we realize that our aggression hurts
others, and this realization then lays the ground for constructive
repair work. Winnicott came to view concern and guilt as vital
elements in our ongoing moves toward growth and object love.
(He noted in this context that they induce many physicians,
including psychoanalysts, to live long careers of repair work.)

Positive aspects, as here intended, are cast into clear relief
whenever normal shame and guilt appear to be missing. Recently,
the anthropologist Colin M. Turnbull (26) described an apparently
guiltless and shameless society—the Ik, a mountain people living
in East Africa. Several years ago the Ik roamed the country as
nomadic hunters. When a large game park was created, they were
resettled and forced to give up their nomadic ways and hunting.
Uprooted, their social organization shattered, their skills made
useless, and threatened by starvation, they seemed to turn into
guiltless and shameless, as well as loveless, beings. *Homo* became
homini lupus.

Consider, for example, how Turnbull describes his first
acquaintance among the Ik, a man called Atum. Atum organized
the building of Turnbull's hut—and kept much of the laborers'
wages for himself.

Frequently, Atum asked Turnbull for medicine for his sick wife.

Then Atum's wife died. Atum told me nothing about it,
but had stepped up his demands for food and medicine

and I felt that if she was really sick I should try to get her to the hospital in Kaabong. He refused the offer and said she was not that sick. Then after a while, when I still had not once seen her, his brother-in-law, the beady-eyed Lomongin, sidled up to me and said that he supposed I knew that Atum was selling the medicine I was giving him for his wife. I was not unduly surprised, and merely remarked that that was too bad for his wife. "Oh no," said Lomongin, enjoying the joke enormously, "she has been dead for weeks. He buried her inside the compound so you wouldn't know." No wonder he did not want her to go to the hospital; she was worth far more to him dead than alive.

Among the Ik, Atum turned out not to be unusual. Although the Ik shared a compound, each Ik was utterly alone in the world. Husbands and wives went separately to search for food, and they never shared what they found. Children were unloved and were driven out of their homes by their parents at the age of three. Turnbull adduces example after example supporting his thesis that loving human bonds were absent among the Ik.

Turnbull compares the Ik to the inhabitants of modern shanty towns and ghettoes who, in losing their social cohesion, turn similarly shameless and guiltless.

SHAME AND GUILT IN GROUPS

Shame and guilt reflect and shape processes that operate in small as well as large groups (including nations and cultures). Freud's concept of the superego or ego-ideal proves pivotal to our understanding these processes as well. "The ego-ideal," he wrote, "opens up an important avenue for the understanding of group psychology. In addition to its individual side, this ideal has a social side; it is also the common ideal of a family, a class, or a nation" (8, p. 101).

In a group, Freud argued, the individual gives up his ego-ideal and substitutes for it the group ideal, now embodied by the leader. At the same time, he identifies—or, better, overidentifies—with the other group members. According to Kohut (13), he is also frequently bolstered by a "grandiose group self." This results in the suspension of the ordinary, culturally conditioned workings of shame and guilt. The group individual now indulges in acts that otherwise would embarrass or pain him. Normally inconspicuous citizens can, as members of an SS unit, murder innocent women and children; and suburban businessmen and housewives can, as members of an encounter group, shout obscenities, dance in the nude, or examine each other's genitals with specula. Each time, the group dynamics—surrender of the ego-ideal to the group leader and each member's concomitant heightened identification with other members—generate apparent shamelessness or guiltlessness and can turn into a source of pride and triumph that normally would be considered abominable or shameful.

As an example of this, consider the following speech by Heinrich Himmler before a select group of SS-men:

> Among ourselves it should be mentioned quite frankly—but we will never speak of it publicly—just as we did not hesitate on 30 June 1934 to do the duty we were told to do and stand comrades who had lapsed up against the wall and shoot them, so we have never spoken about it and will never speak of this . . . I mean cleaning out the Jews, the extermination of the Jewish race. It is one of those things it's easy to talk about—"The Jewish race is being exterminated . . . its our programme, and we're doing it." And then they come, eighty million worthy Germans, and each one of them has his decent Jew. Of course the others are vermin, but this particular Jew is a first-rate man. . . . Most of *you* must know what it means when a hundred corpses are lying side by side, or five

hundred or a thousand. To have stuck it out and at the same time (apart from exceptions caused by human weakness) to have remained decent fellows, that is what has made us so hard. This is a page of glory in our history which has never been written and will never be written (16).

SHAME AND GUILT IN FAMILY GROUPS

Families, too, are groups in which group processes relating to shame and guilt can be expected to operate. This expectation seems borne out in families such as those reported by Tessman and Kaufmann (25) and frequently is observable in families whose members apparently condone and/or practice incest without shame or guilt. We might here conclude that these members, like individuals in groups, surrender their (culturally conditioned) ego-ideal to a group or family leader (or leaders), while they overidentify with one another and perhaps jointly espouse a "family self" which grandiosely dispenses with the incest taboo.

At closer inspection, however, such views appear wanting. We find rather that, as groups, families are so singular as to greatly modify or even nullify the above group processes and to introduce new complexities.

In the following I shall examine just two of these dynamics of shame and guilt in families. First, I shall consider how families employ shame and guilt as regulatory and communicational devices that affect each member's attempts at individuation and separation. Here I focus on what I shall call the *homeostatic function of shame and guilt*. Second, I shall consider how family relations affect an offspring's developing superego (including ego-ideal, conscience, and self-observation) and hence his disposition to experience (or fail to experience) shame and guilt. Here I focus on the family as the cradle of superego development. These two aspects interweave.

HOMEOSTATIC FEATURES OF SHAME AND GUILT IN FAMILIES

Jackson (12), above others, observed homeostasis in family relations, specifically in families with schizophrenic offspring. Such family homeostasis, he noted, is often coercive and restrictive: the family members tie themselves up with each other, endlessly repeat their emotional responses, and jeopardize their growth and separation. Wynne et al. (30) illuminated subsequently two homeostatic constellations that they called *pseudomutuality* and *pseudohostility*. They found the two to be structually similar in that they draw family members into restrictive and collusive binds that limit the range of their emotional experiences and make liberating moves difficult, if not impossible. In pseudomutuality, only warm, loving, supporting feelings are tolerated and expressed. The members often hold each other's hands and exude mutual concern and care. They dissociate hostile, angry, and other "negative" feelings that therefore remain unavailable for examination and integration into each member's and the family's image. In pseudohostility, the tables appear turned. The members express angry and hostile feelings, while they dissociate tender and loving ones. However, here too they jeopardize individual growth and family separation.

Pseudomutual and pseudohostile families, I observed elsewhere, imply centripetal forces (21) that impede and delay each member's individuation. This contrasts with other families where centrifugal forces, fostering premature family break-up and fragmentation, operate. The latter families are as yet insufficiently studied, although they seem numerous and increasingly important. (For example, see Bronfenbrenner's (3) studies on differing family relations and child-rearing practices in present-day Russia and the United States.)

In the following I shall consider shame and guilt—and the defenses against them—as major centripetal (i.e., binding and separation-delaying) family forces. As such they fulfill a positive, homeostatic function and serve *family* cohesion and solidarity, just as, on a social scale, shame and guilt serve *societal* cohesion and solidarity. (Shame, for example, plays a major cohesive role in Japanese and Thai societies.) But in the family, as in the larger society, this homeostatic function of shame and guilt easily exceeds what is required. Cohesion and solidarity then turn into restriction and boundness. To understand this, let us look more closely at how shame and guilt operate in some pseudomutual and pseudohostile families.

In pseudomutual families, guilt rather than shame appears to dominate as a centripetal (i.e., restrictive, over-stabilizing) force. Here, it seems, all family members try collusively to prove unfounded any notion that they might hurt each other in deed or fantasy. In sharing guilt over their (real or presumed) destructiveness, they weave the all-embracing carpet of loving, harmonious togetherness.

Pseudohostile families, in contrast, appear dominated by shame, as they seem more embarrassed over being "weak" (i.e., soft, loving, or tender) than guilty over being destructive (i.e., angry, hostile, aggressive). They must constantly prove—to themselves as well as others—that they are tough and can fight.

MARITAL SHAME-GUILT CYCLES

Closer inspection, though, reveals that guilt plays a role also in seemingly shame-dominated, pseudohostile families, and that shame is not absent in seemingly guilt-dominated pseudomutual ones. The following family, whom I shall call the Torrins, shows a typical pattern.

THE TORRINS

The Torrins consisted of Mr. and Mrs. Torrin and their son, Max, who was 15 years old when he and his parents entered our research and therapy project in the Family Studies Section of the Adult Psychiatry Branch, National Institute of Mental Health. The Torrins participated in three months of conjoint family therapy and thereafter were followed up over a five-year period. To reduce complexity, I shall at first deal with shame and guilt in the marital relationship and then in the parent-child relationship.

From the beginning to the end of our contact with them, Mr. and Mrs. Torrin appeared in a pseudohostile deadlock. In the therapeutic sessions they fought within minutes. Mrs. Torrin, her eyes astare and her cheeks flushed, would attack with fury and blister; Mr. Torrin, who was more passive and reflective, would wait for the moment when he could deliver his underhanded but well-aimed blows.

Their fights, monotonous and inconclusive, revealed recurring sequences: typically, Mrs. Torrin would accuse Mr. Torrin of acting like a spoiled child. With mounting irritation she would bemoan his temper tantrums that allegedly ruined their after-dinner hours. For any—in her opinion—minor mishap such as a spilled ash tray could sour Mr. Torrin for hours. It would then be Mr. Torrin's turn to accuse his wife. Mainly he deprecated her for being fussy and bossy. After a while, to top it all, he would call her a poor housekeeper. At this point Mrs. Torrin invariably became deeply upset; her eyes would roll and she would seem close to fainting. At one time she even dashed out of the room and intimated a heart attack. Now Mr. Torrin would relent and allow Mrs. Torrin to compose herself. When she had done so, it would again be her turn to lash out furiously at Mr. Torrin and accuse him of being a dependent baby who recruited her as his mother. Reeling under these attacks, Mr. Torrin would once more retaliate in the above-described manner, with increasing effectiveness, thus renewing the sequence.

This sequence reveals regulatory, or homeostatic, features of shame and guilt. Simplifying, we can say that each partner tried to cope with his own sense of shame by shaming the other. This involved a trading of projective identifications, or "trading of dissociations," as described by Wynne (30).

There is a large and important group of family problems for which conjoint family therapy is indicated in which the intrafamilial problems are complementary and interlocking. This significant kind of problem is so complex that the discussion of it here must take place by way of illustration. The general form of these problems is the following: Each person sees himself as having a specific limited difficulty that he feels derives from another family member and that he announces can only be alleviated by the other family member. While the claims appear to have some basis in fact, the person about whom they are made does not recognize the possibility that he himself makes any contribution to the problem. However, this other family member may be highly perceptive about corresponding difficulties that are similarly unacknowledged (dissociated) by the first, or another, family member. Thus, there is an intricate network of perceptions about others and dissociations about oneself in which each person "locates" the totality of a particular quality or feeling in another family member. Each person perceives one or more of the others in a starkly negative, pre-ambivalent light and experiences himself in a similar but reciprocal fashion, with the same abhorred quality in himself held dissociated out of his awareness. What is distinctive about this pattern, and therapeutically difficult, is the trading of dissociations: the fixed view that each person has of the other is unconsciously exchanged for a fixed view of himself held by the other (pp. 297-298).

In our case Mrs. Torrin's ego-ideal required that she be in control of herself (i.e., strong and independent) and be a perfect housekeeper. In disowning her weakness and ineptitude, she shamed her husband by projecting on him these dissociated aspects of herself. When Mr. Torrin refused to be shamed and shamed her instead, she signaled the limits of her endurance by intimating a heart attack. At this point her husband appeared guilty over what he had done to her. He relented in his attacks and, in order to atone, offered himself as the (more or less) willing target for her shaming. But when he reeled, it was her turn to feel guilty and hence to relent and offer *herself* as a target for *his* attacks. So the cycle, which we may call an *intramarital shame-guilt cycle*, continued. And, as seems typical, it fed on the partners' underlying sexual shame and frustration, as the following considerations show.

Even before their marriage in their mid-30s, shame had haunted their sex lives. Mrs. Torrin, a hysterical woman, had always feared sex. Consciously, she experienced it as dirty and repulsive; unconsciously, as a scenario for mutilation and castration. To the extent that her sexual outlets remained blocked, she was overly excitable. But while excitable, she also felt shame over being weak and captive to "worthless" men. In her 20s she had highly arousing but unconsummated "affairs" with Don Juan types who invariably ditched her. She finally married Mr. Torrin on the rebound from the last of these affairs when she was 35. At that time in her life, she decided to be "beyond the age of passion."

Mr. Torrin, similarly conflicted and inhibited, by the time of this marriage had abandoned—or been forced to abandon—sexual pursuits because of his worsening ulcerative colitis. To all practical purposes, he had then turned into a sexual, as well as somatic, cripple who primarily needed a nurse. His wife became such a nurse and finally nursed him back to precarious health and modest sexual potency. Throughout, she remained in control, submitting to sexual relations only a few times when her wish to have a child proved stronger than her neurotic conflicts and inhibitions. Still, insofar as she was deprived of sexual fulfillment, she could not help feeling bitter and angry toward the apparent source of her misery—her crippled and sexually crippling husband. Hence, her need to aggressively shame him, but hence also her collusion in the repetitive, "pseudohostile" shame-guilt cycle described above. Similar and complementary dynamics operated in Mr. Torrin.

(Marital shame-guilt cycles, as here described, can also be called shame-guilt—or guilt-shame—binds because of their restrictive and homeostatic nature. Therefore, I shall subsequently speak interchangeably of shame-guilt cycles and shame-guilt binds.)

THE FROSTS

Let us now compare the Torrins' relationship with that of "the Frosts." The Frosts' relationship impressed me as pseudomutual. For the Frosts never fought with each other and exuded unending kindness, harmony, and togetherness. But even though their relational style seemed to be the opposite of pseudohostile, they had certain characteristics in common with the Torrins. Mrs. Frost, like Mrs. Torrin, was hysterical, excitable, outgoing, and sexually inhibited; Mr. Frost, somewhat like Mr. Torrin, was retiring, reflective, and impotent. The families differed mainly insofar as guilt over (real or presumed) destructiveness was to the Frosts more painful than was shame over weakness or sexual ineptness. Therefore, the Frosts dissociated from awareness all angry and hostile feelings that would have increased their guilt and, in a reaction formation both massive and collusive, made a display of all-encompassing love and tenderness.

However, closer inspection also revealed here shame-guilt (or, more correctly, guilt-shame) cycles similar to those found with the Torrins. Mr. Frost, we learned, would throw temper tantrums resembling those thrown by Mr. Torrin, triggering countertan-trums by Mrs. Frost. It became evident that both spouses would then feel embarrassed (i.e., ashamed) about their loss of control. But such shame gave way quickly to guilt over what they experienced as their explosive, uncontrollable destructiveness. In their attempt to bypass and blot out this guilt, they instantly resumed a pseudomutual stance that could be considered this family's enduring relational phenotype.

INTERGENERATIONAL SHAME-GUILT CYCLES

A further homeostatic dimension of shame and guilt comes into view when we consider parent-child interactions. Whereas marital cycles appear to operate *horizontally*, parent-child cycles occur *vertically*, that is, *intergenerationally*. They alert us to how shame and guilt affect the generations' mutual individuation and liberation.

In practice, horizontal (marital) and vertical (intergenerational) cycles interweave and together account for what I called a family's relational phenotype (for example, pseudomutual or pseudohostile). However, before we can examine such interweaving of cycles we must first deal with the intergenerational aspects of shame and guilt and for this purpose must look at the family as the cradle of superego development.

PARENTAL CONTRIBUTIONS TO
THE CHILD'S SUPEREGO DEVELOPMENT

To conceptualize and understand a child's superego development (and hence his later bouts with shame and guilt), psychoanalytic theory focused chiefly on the vicissitudes of identification. The works of S. Freud (particularly on the Oedipus complex), A. Freud (7), and many others established this perspective. Lewis (14), summarizing the major work in this area, distinguished two prototypes of identification that can tilt superego development either toward shame or guilt proneness. In the first type, called "anaclitic identification," the child, destined to become shame prone, internalizes the parental ego-ideal primarily in the context of a dependent, submissive, and admiring relationship. In the second type, he identifies with the aggressor, as described by A. Freud (7). Here his submissiveness becomes ambivalently tainted with retaliatory, albeit subdued, aggression. Given a sufficient capacity for concern (in Winnicott's meaning of the term), such a child very likely will acutely feel the "bite" of conscience and be primarily guilt prone.

DELEGATES IN THE SERVICE OF THEIR PARENTS' SUPEREGO

However, these and similar efforts to conceptualize superego formation from the vantage point of the identifying (or internalizing) child remain limited. We must integrate them with a transactional perspective that recognizes the contributions of parents *and* children (22, 24). To conceptualize the parents' along with their children's contributions, I developed the concept of the delegating mode (22-24). The delegating mode obtains where a child (and particularly an adolescent) is allowed and encouraged to move out of the parental orbit—up to a point! He is then held on a long leash, as it were. Such qualified "sending out" is implied in the original Latin word *delegare*, which means, first, "to send out" and, second, "to entrust with a mission." The latter meaning implies that the delegate, although sent out, remains beholden to the sender. He remains bound to his sender in a special and selective manner that implies a strong yet often invisible loyalty. Crucial here is our understanding of the missions that the delegate, held on a long leash of loyalty, must fulfill. I have elsewhere listed major recurrent types of missions (22, 23). With my present focus on shame and guilt, I shall here limit myself to missions that implicate the superegos of delegator and delegate and shall, in particular, consider those adolescent missions that primarily serve the parents' ego-ideal, conscience, and self-observation.

Where a delegate must chiefly fulfill a parent's unrealized ego-ideal, he may have to become the creative artist, actor, scientist, or business tycoon that the parent failed to become. This child is typically sent out into the world so that he may feed back to his parents creative excitement, fame, or business success. In this process he becomes vital to his parents' self-esteem regulation. Embodying their extended ego-ideal, it is now up to him to save them from being crushed by their chronic and seemingly irremediable shame.

Where delegates primarily serve their parents' conscience, guilt rather than shame is at issue. Winnicott, for one, referred to children who seem weighed down and made joyless by what we may call "borrowed guilt"—guilt borrowed from their parents. He noted that a child's "reparation urge may be related less to the personal guilt-sense than to the guilt-sense or depressed mood of a parent" (29, p. 96). Such borrowing of guilt by the children implies a lending, or trading, of guilt by parents.

In taking over their parents' disowned guilt, many delegates also feel compelled to atone for it. We may think here of those German students who worked hard on Israeli *kibbutzim* in order to atone for a guilt that their parents, one-time supporters of Nazi Germany, had incurred yet disowned. Such efforts to undo parental guilt by proxy may be no less exacting than those to undo chronic parental shame.

Such delegates, in addition to doing their parents' repair work, frequently become targets for their parents' righteous wrath. They let themselves be victimized insofar as they relieve their parents' conscience by acting provocatively and so justifying their parents' attacks on them. Thus, they remind us of those loyal communists described in Koestler's *Darkness at Noon* who, even though innocent, confessed to heinous anti-Communist crimes, thereby destroying themselves while vindicating Stalin, their delegator.

Delegates who serve their parents' ego-ideal or conscience and thereby relieve them of shame or guilt also serve their parents' self-observation—or, more correctly, serve their distortive use of self-observation. Through their actions they now substantiate, at least partially, their parents' misperceptions and misjudgments regarding the sources of, and accountability for, the shame and guilt that are at issue. Thus, such self-observation is no longer distorted as, in Hegel's language, "the negation is negated." The parents can now easily shame their children for their (the parents') disowned weakness, ineptness, or messiness and can make them feel guilty for their disowned badness, rebellion, or neglect. The child is not only made to fit, but is maneuvered into fitting himself into the parents' extended self, an always available receptacle for their disowned, yet potentially most painful experiences—those involving shame and guilt.

Such delegating of children, however, designed to relieve parents of shame and guilt, easily backfires. An intergenerational dialectic (or backlash) can arise that returns with a vengeance to the parents the pain of shame and guilt they tried to disown. For parents who massively delegate their children cannot help exploiting them psychologically: they subject them to an uneven development, rob them of a fulfilled life, and interfere with their age-appropriate individuation and growth. Such exploitation inevitably increases the parents' conscious or unconscious guilt. At the same time, it makes them vulnerable to their children's retaliatory ploys. For these children, made into victims and sufferers, are now strategically placed to operate the shame and guilt lever on their parents. In the very act of carrying out self-sacrificing missions, they can deliver the living proof of their parents' ineptness (i.e., shame-worthiness) or badness (i.e., blameworthiness). Boszormenyi-Nagy and Spark (2) have well described these complex dynamics. They account for typical intergenerational "guilt and shame cycles or binds" that resemble, yet also differ from, those found in marital relations.

To illustrate these intergenerational dynamics of shame and guilt, let me return to the Torrin family and focus on the relation of Max to his mother.

INTERGENERATIONAL SHAME-GUILT CYCLE
BETWEEN MAX AND MRS. TORRIN

Mrs. Torrin's life and marital relations, we saw, were overshadowed by a shame that fed on conflicts and apprehensions relating to her weakness and sexual exploitability. To these we must now add another source of shame: her lowly social origins and deficient education that embarrassed her unendingly because she measured them against an ego-ideal valuing only social prominence, erudition, and culture.

Both areas of apprehension and embarrassment—one relating to sex, the other to social and educational status—shaped her attitudes toward Max. Her shame and fears over sex made her infantilize him and thus interfered with his growing into a sexually mature adult who might—in a renewed oedipal promise—aggravate her sexual conflicts and vulnerabilities. Therefore, she manipulated Max's dependency and smothered him with regressive gratification. Max, as a result, developed into a spoiled, obese, and uncouth youth who, with his mother's covert (and sometimes overt) approval, drank one bottle of soda after the other, overate, and became loquacious and messy. To the extent that his oral pursuits won out over genital ones, girls touched his life only marginally and, at best, figured only as parties to a short-lived, clowning camaraderie.

While keeping Max dependent and infantile, Mrs. Torrin attacked in him her disowned messiness and dependency. At the same time, she used him as an ally in her marital battles. In being messy and uncouth, Max not only served his mother's self-observation but also constantly annoyed his father and thereby gave credence to his mother's contention that the latter was just as immature and childish as Max. But Max, as his mother's delegate, had to fulfill still another mission—to realize her own unfulfilled ego-ideal of becoming a shining social and academic success. Only through this mission, it appeared, could he hope to erase her shame definitively.

Initially, Max bade fair to succeed as such a delegate. As a small child he delighted his prodding mother with his precocious charm and wit. Bolstered by his early show of promise, she made him set his goals high and saw him growing into a famous artist, bold explorer, and canny politician, all rolled into one.

When I saw Max at age 15, these early implanted goals still seemed alive; he talked about running a nuclear research laboratory, making it as a successful playwright, and becoming a U.S. senator. But, measured against his actual social and academic performance, these ambitions now seemed hollow, if not delusional. Apart from a transient triumph in his school's debating team, Max gave no inkling of impending academic, social, artistic, or political success. For his grades were low, he lacked stamina and self-discipline, and he succeeded socially mainly as a clown.

It was not only that his talents, once so promising, were not up to the dizzying tasks set out for him, but also that major missions proved incompatible. For how could he possibly, at one and the same time, remain a regressively gratified, desexualized child and, as a scientist or artist, march on unfalteringly to success against fierce competition?

But this was not all. Not only was Max destined to fail as his mother's delegate, he also turned into her unwavering tormentor, while appearing loyally committed to her. For, to the extent that Mrs. Torrin has commissioned Max to serve her self-esteem, she had also psychologically exploited him. In subjecting him to excessive and conflicting demands, she had contributed to his uneven development. In brief, in recruiting Max to allay her shame, she had incurred guilt over impeding his growth. This then gave Max leverage to devastate her by merely being what she covertly wanted him to be—infantile, asexual (or, better, presexual) and regressively dependent. In developing these traits, he also delivered the living proof of her badness as a parent, i.e., made her guilty. She, in turn, tried to discharge this guilt by blaming him anew for being lazy, demanding, messy—in short, an ill-begotten child. This process, elsewhere described as a negative mutuality (20,21), entrenched the two of them ever more deeply in a seemingly unbreakable intergenerational shame-guilt cycle.

A FURTHER EXAMPLE OF AN
INTERGENERATIONAL SHAME-GUILT CYCLE

Intergenerational shame-guilt cycles (or binds), similar to the above, operated also in a family that I have elsewhere described as "the Smith family" (24). More than most other disturbed families, this family seemed haunted by shame; yet, it took more than a year and a half of family therapy, conducted twice weekly, before some of its sources and dynamics revealed themselves. Here I shall limit myself to some aspects of Mr. and Mrs. Smith's relationship with Cindy, their youngest daughter.

Cindy, looking like a della Robbia angel turned tramp, was admitted to the National Institute of Mental Health after a lengthy runaway episode that had taken her as far away as Oregon. While on the road she had taken numerous drugs, had "freaked out" on several LSD trips, had been "gang-banged," had been jailed, and had contracted lice. When admitted to our ward, she appeared washed out, vague, depressed, and troubled by feelings that everything—and particularly her body—were unreal and "freaky." A detailed diagnostic interview revealed that many "crazy and funny things" were going on inside her mind and body; but none of these experiences seemed clearcut and blatant enough to warrant a diagnosis of actual schizophrenia. Instead, she was diagnosed as borderline, with a potential for schizophrenia. Before she had run away her schoolwork had deteriorated. Increasingly she had skipped classes and had become disorderly. This had aroused her father's ire; he had lambasted her as a slut and drifter, finally (according to Cindy) forcing her to run away together with a girl friend who seemed no less troubled and unhappy (22, p. 174).

As the therapy progressed, Mrs. Smith revealed two major areas of shame. In each she recruited Cindy as her delegate. Herself obese and ugly, she tried to retrieve through Cindy the promise of physical beauty and attractiveness she herself had despaired of realizing. To serve here as her loyal delegate—and this was her first mission—Cindy had to be radiant, beautiful, a sexual knockout. Second, Cindy had the mission to allay a secret shame that Mrs. Smith had carried since the age of eight. At that time she had started a sexual relationship with a half-brother that had lasted until she was about 13 years old. Ever since, she had experienced herself as innately bad, corrupt, and sluttish. Never analyzed or worked through, this experience had come to envelop her in a pervasive sense of primitive, all-encompassing shame that she vividly conveyed itself during our sessions. Yet, instead of "owning" this shame and coming to grips with it, Mrs. Smith delegated Cindy (i.e., recruited) as, among other things, a sinful and shameful tramp, allowing her to deal with her disowned shame by projective identification. In trying to comply with this covert need of her mother's, Cindy then acted indeed in a sinful and shameful manner.

But Cindy served as not only her mother's but also her father's delegate. (This embroiled her in deep loyalty conflicts that accounted for much of her plight yet, at this point, cannot be further pursued.) Mr. Smith was a high-school dropout, yet moved in professional circles where people flaunted (so, at least, he believed) master's degrees and doctorates. Feeling chronically embarrassed about his lack of schooling, he pushed Cindy to instant academic success. Cindy tried hard to fulfill her father's unrealized ego-ideal—no less than her mother's—but failed under signs of conflict and guilt. For how could she succeed academically as long as other delegated dilemmas drained all her energies?

Also here, as in the Torrin family, the delegating of an adolescent reinforced the parents' guilt over psychologically exploiting their child and made them vulnerable to this child's operation of the guilt lever. At the same time, it locked them and the child into an intergenerational shame-guilt bind so tight that even a long family therapy was unable to break it.

SOME THERAPEUTIC IMPLICATIONS

Where family members lock themselves into shame-guilt binds, the family therapist faces a difficult task. Theoretically, he can bring help through his clarification, enlightened judgments, or forgiving acceptance. In practice, any such efforts are likely to flounder. For to families who are wrapped up in shame-guilt binds, the outside looks forbidding rather than liberating. Caught up in shaming or blaming one another, the members also become sensitive to being shamed or blamed by strangers. Myths, we saw in Chapter 9, entrench them in their predicament, as they keep them ignorant about the nature and sources of their shame and guilt. At the same time, they keep outsiders—including family therapists—at bay.

Faced with this dilemma, a family therapist may decide to approach shame-guilt binds with a hammer, as it were. In the fashion of a charismatic group leader, he may offer to substitute his seemingly liberated, as well as liberating, ego-ideal and conscience for that of the family, dismissing their embarrassment and guilt while presenting himself as an admirably shame- and guilt-free human specimen.

Such frontal attacks on a family's shame-guilt binds, however, are not likely to succeed. For shame and guilt are not easily dislodged, particularly when their roots reach deeply into a family's shared past. Thus, even where a therapist may seem to cut back on manifest shame and guilt, these roots sprout ever-new growth. For example, while family members might eagerly identify with their therapist's seemingly more tolerant ego-ideal and conscience, they might also measure their own restriction against the therapist's seeming inner freedom and then feel shame over feeling ashamed—or guilty over secretly hating this well-meaning therapist.

This means that shame and guilt in families, to yield to constructive interpretive work, must be explored as to their intrafamilial, including intergenerational, sources and dynamics, but also must be voluntarily admitted and accepted. (Ward (27) has shown how this holds true for shame.) Where they are prematurely exposed against the family's will and without any attempt at understanding their place in the family's topology, they will most likely merely sprout new offshoots.

To avoid premature, destructive exposure and foster therapeutic exploration, the therapist must build trust. Boszormenyi-Nagy and Spark (2) have described what this involves. Here it suffices to state that, in exploring the operation of shame-guilt binds, he must be empathic and fair to all members and must be able to see their binds in a multigenerational perspective. For he can hardly trace meaningfully the family's sources of shame and guilt and establish each member's "balance of merits as related to factual events unless he includes in his vision at least several generations. (For example, in order to do justice to Mrs. Torrin's exploitative behavior toward her son—which entrenched her and him in tenacious shame-guilt binds—I had to take account of Mrs. Torrin's cruel rejection and exploitation at the hands of her own mother, here omitted.) To achieve the above objectives, the therapist will benefit from understanding how shame and guilt affected—and possibly still affect—his own family life.

References

1. Alexander, F. *Fundamentals of psychoanalysis*. New York: Norton, 1963.
2. Boszormenyi-Nagy, I., and Spark, G. *Invisible loyalties*. New York: Hoeber, 1973.
3. Bronfenbrenner, U. *Two worlds of childhood: U.S. and U.S.S.R.* New York: Russell Sage Foundation, 1970.
4. Erikson, E. H. *Identity, youth and crisis*. New York: Norton, 1968.
5. Fenichel, O. *The psychoanalytic theory of neurosis*. New York: Norton, 1945.
6. ———. Early stages of ego development. In *Collected papers of Otto Fenichel*. New York: Norton, 1954, pp. 25-48.

7. Freud, A. *The ego and the mechanisms of defence.* New York: International
    Universities Press, 1946.
8. Freud, S. On narcissism: an introduction. *SE* XIV, 67-102. London:
    Hogarth Press, 1957.
9. ———. The ego and the id. *SE* XIX, 3-66. London: Hogarth Press,
    1961.
10. ———. New introductory lectures. *SE* XXII, 57-80. London:
    Hogarth Press, 1964.
11. ———. Inhibitions, symptoms and anxiety. *SE* XX, 77-175. London:
    Hogarth Press, 1959.
12. Jackson, D. D. Family interaction, family homeostasis, and some
    implications for conjoint family psychotherapy. In *Science and
    psychoanalysis: vol. 2. Individual and family dynamics,* ed. J. H. Masserman.
    New York: Grune and Stratton, 1959.
13. Kohut, H. Thoughts on narcissism and narcissistic rage. *Psychoana-
    lytic Study of the Child* 27: 360-400, 1972.
14. Lewis, H. B. *Shame and guilt in neurosis.* New York: International
    Universities Press, 1971.
15. Lynd, H. M. *On shame and the search for identity.* New York: Science
    Editions, 1961.
16. Manvell, R., and Frankel, H. *Himmler.* New York: Paperback Library,
    1968, pp. 146-147.
17. Nietzsche, F. *Friedrich Nietzsche/Werke in drei Bänden.* Munich: Hanser,
    1954.
18. Piers, G., and Singer, M. *Shame and guilt: a psycho-analytic and a cultural
    study.* Springfield, Ill.: Charles C Thomas Publisher, 1953.
19. Sartre, J.-P. *L'Etre et le neant/Essai d'ontologie phenomenologique.* Paris:
    Gallimard, 1943.
20. Stierlin, H. *Conflict and reconciliation.* New York: Doubleday Anchor
    and Jason Aronson, 1969.
21. Stierlin, H., Levi, L. D., and Savard, R. J. Centrifugal versus
    centripetal separation in adolescence: two patterns and some of
    their implications. In *Annals of American Society for Adolescent Psychiatry:
    Vol. II. Development and Clinical Studies,* ed. S. Feinstein and P.
    Giovacchini. New York: Basic Books, 1973.
22. Stierlin, H. Family dynamics and separation patterns of potential
    schizophrenics. In *Proceedings of the IVth International Symposium on*

Psychotherapy of Schizophrenia. Amsterdam: Excerpta Medica, 1972, pp. 169-179.

23. Stierlin, H., and Ravenscroft, K. Varieties of adolescent separation conflicts. *British Journal of Medical Psychology* 45: 299-313, 1972.
24. Stierlin, H. *Separating parents and adolescents.* New York: Quadrangle, 1974.
25. Tessman, L. H., and Kaufmann, I. Variations on a theme of incest. In *Family dynamics and female sexual delinquency,* ed. O. Pollak and A. S. Friedman. Palo Alto: Science and Behavior Books, 1969, pp. 138-150.
26. Turnbull, C. M. *The mountain people.* New York: Simon and Schuster, 1972.
27. Ward, H. Shame—a necessity for growth in therapy. *American Journal of Psychotherapy* 26: 232-243, 1972.
28. Winnicott, D. W. Aggression in relation to emotional development. In *Collected papers: through paediatrics to psycho-analysis.* Basic Books, 1958, pp. 204-218.
29. ———. Reparation in respect of mother's organized defence against depression. In *Collected Papers.* New York: Basic Books, 1958, pp. 91-96.
30. Wynne L. C. et al. Pseudo-mutuality in the family relations of schizophrenics. *Psychiatry* 21: 205-220, 1958.
31. ———. Some indications and contraindications for exploratory family therapy. In *Intensive family therapy: theoretical and practical aspects,* ed. I. Boszormenyi and J. L. Framo. New York: Hoeber, 1965, pp. 289-322.

Chapter 12

Roles and Missions
in Family Theory and Therapy

As the social sciences developed, one concept—that of social roles—became ever more pivotal, if not paradigmatic, as the works of Mead (15), Weber (29), Parsons (18), Dahrendorf (5), and Spiegel (20) attest. Moreover, hardly any other concept linked social theory as strongly to psychiatric practice. And it was largely in the area of the family as an issue for study *and* treatment that theoretical and clinical concerns were articulated through this concept.

Here I shall review the concept of social roles in the light of my experience as family researcher and therapist. In so doing, I shall liken it to a telescope which, because of its focus and position, conceals as well as reveals. I shall then argue that the concept of roles, as currently employed, conceals—or, perhaps better, leaves unmapped—much that is relevant. To make this point, I shall later take up another concept—that of missions—which may widen our perspectives. To begin, let me outline some relevant features and implications of the role concept.

CLASSIFYING VS. DYNAMIC APPROACHES TO ROLES

We can distinguish two approaches to social roles: one *classifying*, the other *dynamic*. The first aims at their inventory and is comparable to the practice of Linnaeus, the naturalist, in differentiating the various plant and animal species from one another. The other approach, closer to that of Darwin, focuses on how roles evolve and how they conflict or harmonize both with one another and with the systems they subserve.

To classify social roles is not easy. As human societies evolve, they spawn more formal and informal subsystems and institutions—e.g., the family, the church, the state, the peer group, educational and professional organizations, and many more. In all of these, individuals have to assume roles. Thus, a member of our present American society may play, at one and the same time, the roles of citizen, churchgoer, male (gender role), parent, spouse, child (to his own parents), professional, school-board member, political party member, and sports enthusiast, among many others. Some roles are well defined, others not; some are central, others marginal; some are stable, others unstable; some are in his awareness, others disavowed; and so on. To cope with this complexity, roles came to be distinguished as formal or informal, ascribed or achieved, legitimate or illegitimate, implicit or explicit. All these interweave, overlap, and often conflict with one another.

If we adopt a dynamic perspective, however, we focus, first, on how certain roles—e.g., of parent and child or male and female—require and complement each other. Second, we focus on a transactional process (or relational dialectic) whereby roles come to life or fade away. The agents in this process affect each other reciprocally. On the one side are those who assign (or negate) roles by expectations, sanctions, and manipulations (or their absence): we may call these people role assigners. On the other side are those who accept (or refuse), learn (or refuse to learn), internalize (or externalize), absorb roles into (or extrude them from) their personal motivations: these we may call role assignees. Furthermore, role assigners and role assignees may change places (depending on the roles involved), thereby further complicating the relational dialectic.

Third, in approaching roles dynamically, we focus on how they become functional or dysfunctional, harmonious or deviant, for the individual role bearer, as well as for the system he subserves. The better we delineate given roles and the systems to which they are tied, the better we conceptualize their evolution, interplay, and conflicts. This becomes evident when we turn, next, to that system which is central to this chapter—the family.

THE FAMILY AND ROLES

Two reasons make the issue of roles in the family especially important. First, family relations are, by and large, the narrow funnel through which society's central roles are passed on to new members. The family is, in other words, society's main socializing—i.e., role-inducing—arm, as it stakes out, teaches, or affirms basic gender, parent, child, spouse, age, and other roles. Also, as it bears on the child's education, it shapes his choice of vital vocational roles. These are mostly so-called formal roles which fit more or less "naturally" one's anatomical gender, age, station in life, etc., yet which nonetheless require subjective preparation and compliance. It is this compliance which the family ensures. Where it is lacking—as when a man behaves and feels like a woman, or an oldster like a child—the person is threatened into anomie in reference to the social system, and insanity on the individual level.

Second, while it fulfills its socializing functions, the family also constitutes a complex system in its own right, providing its members with meaning, security, and vital gratifications. As such, it has its own intricate role structure, which may harmonize or conflict with its broader socializing functions.

Thus, the family offers a complex role panorama. Parsons and Bales (19), in particular, have charted it, advancing a classifying *and* dynamic perspective. As their work seems paradigmatic and central to my critique, I shall briefly comment on it.

Within the classifying perspective, these authors delineated those family roles which they believe constitute the American family's basic role structure and, at the same time, implement its socializing functions. Here their distinction between instrumental and expressive roles became central. Within the dynamic perspective, they conceptualized the socializing (role-inducing) process in families mainly by means of a psychoanalytic model: this process requires, on the one side, parents who, committed to the given society, act as models and use rewards and age-specific sanctions (e.g., oral gratifications given or withheld) to nudge their children into society's mold and, on the other, children who respond (e.g., by internalizing them) to such models and to parental rewards or sanctions. The socializing process, then, depends on the vicissitudes of various developmental phases (e.g., oral, anal, oedipal), on ego and superego maturations, on the availability and nature of parental models, rewards or sanctions, and others. With the help of this theoretical model, the authors then traced how role-inducing and role-maintaining processes in families may derail, resulting in various individual, family, and social pathologies. Lidz et al. (14), most notably, applied Parsons and Bales' ideas to further illuminate disturbances within families, particularly those with schizophrenic offspring. Here the socializing process was observed to be lacking, as parents failed to model or teach their children vital roles. For example, parents may turn their potentially schizophrenic children massively into their confidants, allies, and quasi-lovers, interfering in their children's appropriate age, gender, or other role development. This parental behavior leads to a characteristically skewed or under-differentiated family role panorama, one which signifies an interpersonal dialectic gone awry. Jackson (11) and others working with such families painted a seemingly opposite panorama—one with rigid and over-differentiated roles—which to them revealed a "family homeostasis." However, as I showed elsewhere (24, and see Chapter 15), these two panoramas are not mutually exclusive: the family members' very brittleness and confusion and insecurity regarding their roles may cause them to lean over backwards to ensconce themselves in constrictive, nearly immutable roles. Wynne et al. (31), described subsequently family scenarios of pseudomutuality and pseudohostility which, albeit in opposite ways, exemplified such homeostatic deadlock.

FURTHER DEVELOPMENTS IN FAMILY ROLE THEORY

As therapists and researchers saw more families, they extended their classifying and dynamic perspectives. As a result, the family role panorama grew still more complex.

Thus, covert roles were often found to contradict overt ones, as when children were treated like parents or parents treated like children. In the first case, we speak of parentification (we lack as yet an appropriate term for the opposite process). For example, parentification occurs in many families with battered children, as parents assign children the roles of parents who must emotionally nurture and comfort these parents themselves. When their children do not oblige, the parents beat them.

Further, various informal roles, such as those of clown, strongman (or strong woman), leader, delinquent, conciliator, sick member, victim or victimizer, came to be recognized. However, these roles did not necessarily adhere to one member only. Rather, over time various members could change places (roles), as in a game of musical chairs. For example, a sickness role, as shown by depressive symptoms, could pass from mother to daughter to father, back to mother, and so on. Or a father could turn delinquent—i.e., become truant, engage in shady business deals, embezzle money, etc.—the very moment his delinquent son "straightened out." These two discoveries—that covert roles may contradict overt ones, and that roles may "circulate" within families—shaped subsequent directions in family theory and practice.

SPIEGEL'S THEORY OF ROLE CONFLICTS

J. Spiegel (20) built on the first discovery, as he traced both the intrapsychic and interpersonal conflicts inherent in the co-existence of overt and covert (or, as he calls them, explicit and implicit) roles. Such conflicts, according to Spiegel, shape the interpersonal dialectic between roles assigners and role assignees. Here Spiegel highlighted the struggle that any attempt to change roles unleashes. Specifically, he distinguished between role modification, role induction, and role dislocation. When conflicts are relatively mild, we find chiefly role modification, achieved through negotiation and compromise—i.e., through a "loving struggle." Where conflicts are severe, the struggle intensifies and positions polarize, as the partners attempt now either to induce or dislodge roles in the other. Typically, each role-inducing technique (or strategy) elicits a counter-technique according to the principle "control or be controlled." Spiegel enumerates five techniques of role induction: (i) coercing ("pushing the other around") elicits the counter-technique of defying; (ii) coaxing (defined as the manipulation of present and future rewards) triggers withholding; (iii) evaluating calls forth denying; (iv) masking summons up unmasking; and (v) postponing leads to provoking. An analogous struggle ensues when partners attempt to dislodge roles either by exchanging, displacing, or attenuating them. Role displacements, for example, are "central to many of the complicated shifting and defensive processes experienced by the doctor and patient during psychotherapy" (p. 137), but clearly they are equally central to families. This holds true also for so-called role attenuations, under which Spiegel subsumes exclusion-reservation, segregation, and attrition, all of which imply an "impoverishment of the number and quality of the roles available to the participants in the role system" (p. 137).

As therapist, Spiegel favors the strategies of role modification, which involve negotiation and conciliation, over role induction and role dislocation, which lock partners into adversary positions. While the adversaries try to control and outwit each other, they often end up deadlocked and polarized. When this happens, Spiegel advocates the use of third-party mediators. If they are recognized as objective and fair, these mediators can nudge the stalemated parties toward a compromise, as do, for example, mediators in labor-management disputes. In the mental health arena, such mediators may be psychiatrists, social workers, counselors, or others.

SYSTEMATIC FEATURES OF ROLE CHANGES

The second discovery—that (informal) roles may shift around in families—caused researchers to focus on somewhat different phenomena than did Spiegel. Essentially, they inquired into the wider, systems aspects of role changes and asked: Do role shifts within families, e.g., to and from sickness or delinquent roles, signify deeper systems changes? Mostly the answer was no. While roles were here reshuffled, on inspection it appeared that little else changed, as the members remained constricted, their perceptions unmodified, and the old games—e.g., those of mutual blaming, scapegoating, mystification—went on. Changes occurred within the system without substantially affecting it. Hence the increasing concern with those role changes which implied deep, or structural, changes—changes that make for altogether new roles and an altogether different system.

To make further theoretical and practical headway, researchers then had to clarify the difference between changes within a system and changes in the system itself. Here, I believe, Watzlawick et al. (27,28) have been so far most successful as they, relying on the works of Bateson et al. (3), Erickson (6), and others, drew on the mathematical theory of groups. As a result, they distinguished first-order changes from second-order changes, and elaborated their differing phenomenology and implications.

> Group Theory gives us a framework for thinking about the kind of change that can occur within a system that itself stays invariant; the Theory of Logical Types is not concerned with what goes on inside a class, i.e. between its members, but gives us a frame for considering the relationship between member and class and the peculiar metamorphosis which is in the nature of shifts from one logical level to the next higher. If we accept this basic distinction between the two theories, it follows that there are two different types of change: one that occurs within a given system which itself remains unchanged, and one whose occurrence changes the system itself. To exemplify this distinction in more behavioral terms: a person having a nightmare can do many things *in* his dream—run, hide, fight, scream, jump off a cliff, etc.— but no change from any one of these behaviors to another would ever terminate the nightmare. *We shall henceforth refer to this kind of change as first-order change.* The one way *out* of a dream involves a change from dreaming to waking. Waking, obviously, is no longer a part of the dream, but a change to an altogether different state. *This kind of change will from now on be referred to as second-order change* (pp. 10-11).

Such second-order change, the authors proceed to show, hinges on the availability of a meta-perspective—i.e., a position or point of view outside the given system. Where therapeutic change is at issue, this meta-perspective has to provide a locus for manipulative intervention, one which offers leverage not only to reshuffle but to transform and expand existing roles in an enduring way. Bateson et al. (3), Haley (10), Minuchin (16), Watzlawick et al. (28), and Selvini-Palazzoli (17) are among those who have elaborated and illuminated the principles of such manipulative intervention. Here therapists "prescribe the symptom", redefine meaning, startle, give contradictory yet well-meaning orders—in brief, intervene to "jolt" the system. To be successful, they must emphasize the positive, be forceful, imaginative, and attuned to what a given patient and family offer—as a growing literature on strategic and structural therapies exemplifies.

If we compare these two directions in family role theory—the one represented by Spiegel, the other by strategic and structural therapists—we recognize that they have much in common. Both focus, albeit from different vantage points, on how the interpersonal dialectic between role assigner and role assignee can stalemate or derail. For Spiegel, such an eventuality signifies a power struggle polarizing and locking partners in their roles; for the strategic therapists, it implies a frozen system. To break the stalement and change the system along with the roles, a fresh look and fresh start, through an intervention from outside the system, are needed each time. These can be provided by a third-party mediator, a strategically intervening therapist, or a combination of the two.

DERAILMENTS OF THE SOCIALIZATION PROCESS

Keeping in mind the above development of family role theory, we return to the socialization process as it unfolds in families—i.e., the process whereby central gender, age, vocational, and other roles are taught and assigned. We are now in a better position to understand and conceptualize various derailments of that process. Essentially, these derailments occur whenever the family system becomes so idiosyncratic, needful in its own right, or ridden with conflicts that the assignment of various (mainly informal) family roles—particularly sickness or scapegoating roles—interferes with a child's preparation for those more formal roles which the larger society stakes out and supports.

MARVIN AND HIS FAMILY:
THE SOCIALIZATION PROCESS DERAILED

To exemplify such family-induced derailments of the socialization process, let us turn briefly to Marvin and his family, whom I saw over several years in conjoint therapy. Here I limit myself to outlining some of those features in the relationship between Marvin and his parents, particularly his mother, which are central to the issue under discussion.

Marvin's family (I shall call them the Schultz family) consisted of two parents in their mid-forties and two children, Marvin himself and his younger sister, both in their early twenties. Mrs. Schultz, slender and full-bosomed (she had had her breasts "refurbished" with silicone), was beautiful, intense, and apparently totally dedicated to her family, but especially to Marvin, as her only son. Mr. Schultz, jovial and obese (and therefore concerned with coronaries and cholesterol) worshipped his beautiful, generous wife. Mary, a college student, resembled her mother, as she too, was sexy, giving, strong. Only Marvin, by the time I saw him, had—seemingly to everyone's surprise—become a blemish and source of family worry, for his life lay then in ruin. After a promising start, he had dropped out of college, drifted, acted bizarrely and irresponsibly, and, finally, after a suicide attempt, been hospitalized as a mental patient. As such, he was given a diagnosis of schizophrenia, schizo-affective type. When he was discharged after some ten months, he tried a job as a department store clerk, but soon stopped working and withdrew with another ex-mental patient into an apartment rented with his parents' money. Here he usually slept until noon, watched television, masturbated, daydreamed, held long conversations with his roommate, and occasionally went out for a movie. He did not date or seek new employment. However, after about half a year spent in this manner, he and his parents managed to seek out psychiatric help once again. Thus it came about that I started to work with the Schultz family.

In outlining Marvin's derailed socialization, I shall focus briefly on those central social roles—gender, age, and vocational—for which the family, as society's major socializing arm, ordinarily prepares its young members. Clearly, with Marvin, much was here in disarray.

First, Marvin's male gender role was fragile and undifferentiated, if not skewed: so far, he had never dated on his own initiative. The few girls with whom he had gone out in his late high school days had been aggressive types whom he experienced (almost) as boys, while he assumed the role of girl. Throughout, he has shunned heterosexual as well as homosexual contacts, preferring masturbation. In this activity he sometimes fantasized himself as a girl succumbing to a stronger person's advances, leaving the sexual identity of this person blurred. Second, something was amiss with his age role. This had to do with how he experienced his body—now clearly that of a young adult (although flabby from lack of exercise), he continued to perceive it as handsomely adolescent—but also it had to do with his avoidance of adult responsibilities.

Third, his preparations for a feasible vocational role had gone awry. Originally, he had seemed headed for a career as a commercial artist, as he had shown promise as a painter and designer. But after a brief try at a vocational school, this promise had evaporated, and he had done little drawing thereafter. There was then talk, on his and his parents' parts, of training for a more mundane job such as bank clerk, department store manager, etc. This was no more than talk, however, since he could not bring himself to answer classified ads or to report for interviews.

MISSIONS: A SHIFT IN THE
FOCUS OF THE TELESCOPE

What caused Marvin's socialization to derail? To find an answer within current role theories, we would have to examine his family's homeostatic deadlock and its structure of informal roles, as described above. In so doing, we would have to consider the Schultzes' pseudomutuality, the mother's and father's "marital skew" (as described by Lidz et al., 14), their assigning, to a colluding Marvin, of various sickness and scapegoat roles, and other such phenomena, all well described in the family literature and borne out by what I observed in the Schultzes.

But here I shall not take that course; nor shall I elaborate on those earlier-outlined treatment principles (aimed at changing the family's role structure and thereby setting the socialization process back on track) which grow out of the above perspective. Rather, I shall now introduce a related yet differing perspective, one that delimits the applicability of the role concept. This is the concept of missions.

FEATURES OF THE DELEGATING PROCESS

While the concept of roles relates centrally to *the socializing process,* the concept of missions relates to the *delegating process.* In the two preceding chapters and elsewhere (23, 26, and see Chapter 11), I described various aspects of the delegating process. Here I shall focus on those features only that may highlight differences in the two conceptual approaches.

A delegate, we saw earlier, is allowed and encouraged to move out of the parental orbit—up to a point! He is then held on a long leash of loyalty, as it were, and his separation is made limited and conditional. He proves his loyalty through the real life in which he carries out the missions which his delegators (i.e., his parents) assigned to him.

DERAILMENTS OF THE DELEGATING PROCESS

The delegating process, I showed further, derails in typical ways. First, a delegate-son might be expected, at one and the same time, to provide the excitement of a wayward youth and the solid reassurance of a virtuous student. Here the delegating process derails under *a conflict of missions*. Or a delegate may receive the mission from one parent to undercut or destroy the other. Here the derailment results from a *conflict of loyalties* (as Hamlet, hovering on the brink of schizophrenia, exemplifies).

The delegating process may derail in another (and, from my present vantage point, more important) way. To grasp it, we must remind ourselves that the word *delegare* means, first, to send out and, second, to entrust with a mission. These components stake out the conditions under which delegates cease to be delegates: when they have missions but are not sent out or when they are sent out but have no missions. We deal then with relational extremes which negate the delegating process in opposite ways.

In the first extreme—where the delegate has missions but is not sent out—he remains locked into his parent's orbit. Psychologically, such a child may have continually to submit to his parents' infantilization, or he may have to serve his parents' unending self-observation in ways that jeopardize his own growth. Here I spoke of "bound delegates."

In the other extreme derailment of the delegating process, a child is sent out (often very early), yet has no mission to fulfill. Instead of being clung to for sheer parental survival, he is expendable, as he has little, if anything, to offer. Psychologically and economically, such child is family surplus, at best uneasily tolerated, at worst brutally rejected, but always neglected.

MISSIONS AND ROLES COMPARED

In light of the above, we can now compare more closely the role model and the missions model. We realize at once that many missions, as just defined, can also be viewed as roles. For example, the orgy-prone delegate who busily executes thrill-providing missions can also be seen as bearer of a delinquent role—a role he was assigned by his parent(s) and one which subserves the larger family system. A flamboyantly crazy (e.g., schizophrenic) member might be held to serve his parent's self-observation, yet also may be seen to play a vitally needed sickness role, and so on. Evidently, the concepts of role and mission apply here to similar, if not identical, phenomena.

Do these concepts then merely give different names to pieces of the same pie? I believe they do not. Rather, I shall argue that they conceptualize differently what is important in human relations and, at the same time, establish different treatment perspectives for individuals as well as families.

My argument takes off from the meanings of *lex* (law) and *ligare* (to bind), which are embedded in the concept of delegating (*delegare*). This concept thus includes the elements of trust, obligation, and personal meaning and loyalty—in brief, a contractual and ethical dimension which the words "role" and "socialization" fail to convey. Two aspects in this ethical dimension stand out: the personal loyalty bond in which missions are rooted and the psychological exploitation which missions often imply.

PERSONAL MEANING AND IMPORTANCE
DERIVED FROM A LOYALTY BOND

To grasp the first aspect, we need to remind ourselves of the domain where the notion of roles seems most natural—the stage. Here the actors "play their roles" (i.e., act out a design of which they are the unwitting agents). This holds true also when we view the whole world as a stage, as did, for example, Dahrendorf (5), who in his elaboration of the concept of social roles, took off from these lines of Shakespeare:

All the world's a stage,
And all the men and women merely players;
They have their exits, and their entrances;
And one man in his time plays many parts,
His acts being seven ages. At first the infant,
Mewling and puking in the nurse's arms.
And then the whining schoolboy, with his satchel
And shining morning face, creeping like snail
Unwillingly to school. And then, the lover,
Sighing like furnace, with a woeful ballad
Made to his mistress' eyebrow. Then a soldier,
Full of strange oaths and bearded like the pard,
Jealous in honor, sudden and quick in quarrel,
Seeking the bubble reputation
Even in the cannon's mouth. And then, the justice,
In fair round belly with good capon lined,
With eyes severe and beard of formal cut,
Full of wise saws and modern instances.
And so he plays his part. The sixth age shifts
Into the lean and slippered pantaloon,
With spectacles on nose and pouch on side,
His youthful hose well saved, a world too wide
For his shrunk shank; and his big manly voice,
Turning again toward childish treble, pipes
And whistles in his sound. Last scene of all,
That ends this strange eventful history,
Is second childishness and mere oblivion,
Sans teeth, sans eyes, sans taste, sans every thing.

—*As You Like It* (act 2, scene 7)

Let us, then, in light of the above, compare the two statements: "I play (or I embody) a role" and "I fulfill a mission."

The first suggests less than total commitment. As commonly understood, any role I may play remains more or less extraneous to my true self: I am merely an actor performing a part.

It is different with the second statement, as the term mission evokes obligation as well as dedication (if not zeal or even fanaticism). Here we are apt to think of crusaders, missionaries, and ideologues who, gripped by their missions, do not shrink from hardship or sacrifice, as they merge with and derive strength from what they do. Thus they are willing to try to move mountains— and sometimes succeed. "He who has sworn on the Fuhrer's banner forefeits all he owns," said those young Nazis whom Hitler, their delegator, had made to feel immensely important while they turned into his blindly obedient tools (26). Such a sense of importance and meaning, inherent in being commissioned, derives typically from a highly personal (or at least personalized) and deeply loyal relationship.

As its paradigm, we can take the feudal relationship between lord and vassal involving an intense bond of loyalty. Because this bond was intense, personal, and meaningful, it could cause deep satisfaction or distress. The latter arose whenever loyalty was betrayed, as happened typically when the delegate-vassal slackened in his missions or, worse, dared to tear himself loose from his lord and delegator. When this happened, the delegate was prone to suffer fierce breakaway guilt, a guilt which often operated unconsciously and could trigger cruel self-punishment as well as heroic atonement. The depth of such breakaway guilt thus measured the meaning and strength the loyalty bond had generated.

PSYCHOLOGICAL EXPLOITATION

To grasp the second aspect revealed through the concept of missions—that of psychological exploitation—we must reconsider the conflicts that are at issue. These conflicts, we saw, became central to Spiegel (as well as other role theorists), who viewed most role partners as being locked into adversary positions.

Conflicts between partners become crucial whenever delegating processes are recognized, but highlight now characteristic dynamics of psychological exploitation and counter-exploitation which have an ethical dimension. Essentially, these derive from the nature of the (more or less hidden) bargain or contract a delegate strikes with his delegator: while the delegate, by executing his mission (or missions), finds vital meaning and a sense of importance, he also accedes to a dependency that often limits his freedom, saps his initiative, and stunts his growth. Whether it is a good bargain depends on the mission. In some cases, it may work out well for the delegate, as when a child, commissioned to serve his parent's ego-ideal, succeeds as a creative artist and thus realizes himself in fulfilling his mission. It is different when his chief mission is to absorb his parent's disowned badness or craziness. For here he defeats rather than realizes himself—or, perhaps more correctly, realizes himself by defeating himself, as he remains now bound, forfeits his growth, and perhaps becomes schizophrenic. To all appearances, he strikes a disastrous bargain.

Still, he can try to come out on top if he manages to operate the guilt lever on his exploitative parents and becomes counter-exploitative in turn. He may achieve this by executing his mission with a vengeance—i.e., by stubbornly staying mad, delinquent, incurable, etc.—and thereby showing up his parents as inept, bad, or both.

MARVIN AND HIS FAMILY:
AN EXAMPLE FOR A DERAILED DELEGATING PROCESS

To illustrate these dynamics, let me return to Marvin and his family. Earlier I traced the derailment of Marvin's socialization process, with its negative consequence for the boy's developing gender, age, and vocational roles. I shall now trace the derailment of the delegating process, taking off from the same underlying clinical phenomena but using my present contrasting focus. Here, too, I shall be selective, and limit myself to describing a few major missions which originated with his mother—the parent with the "stronger reality" (21) who acted as Marvin's main delegator.

The first mission was to be a recipient of his mother's "generosity" and thereby to confirm her overt yet inwardly doubted self-image as an all-giving, loving, and strong parent. This mission, serving her self-observation, required Marvin (as well as the other family members) to be receiving and needful. Consequently, he had to remain the little boy whom she could shower with food and physical affection. The mother did not seem to realize that thereby she infantilized him (i.e., interfered with the development of an appropriate age role), made him fat, or sexually excited him—and in the process exploited him to serve her own self-esteem and self-image regulation.

Second, as part of such exploitation, she commissioned Marvin to fulfill her own unrealized ego-ideal of becoming a famous artist. While she idled her days away, her beauty fading, she turned to Marvin to provide her with what she craved but failed to obtain by her own efforts: excitement, glamor, and a sense of achievement. To the extent that this mission overburdened him and exposed him to conflicts, it was bound to interfere with his developing a workable vocational role.

Third, and perhaps most fatefully, she imposed upon Marvin a repair mission that derived from what had happened before he was born. At that time, she gave birth to a girl with congenital defects who died a year later. Guided (or, better, misguided) by her own binding mother, she had allowed all traces of the child, such as pictures and toys, to be at once removed. As a result, she had never mourned her loss nor faced her feelings of guilt and shame. When Marvin was born, she (more or less unwittingly) made him a substitute for the girl and interfered thereby with his developing an appropriate gender role. She anxiously watched his every step, called him by her dead daughter's name, unendingly searched him for signs of congenital defects, and overfed and overprotected him. Thus she gave Marvin the mission of relieving her of the ever-present fear of being a bad, neglectful mother. Here too she made him serve her self-observation in that she unconsciously needed Marvin's defectiveness to contrast with and highlight her own (inwardly doubted) perfection and beauty.

These missions subjected Marvin to deep inner conflicts. How could he, at one and the same time, be the passive, adoring recipient of her givingness and yet be self-assertive and strong; fulfill by proxy her own artistic aspirations and yet remain the target of her anxious, overprotective ministrations; become a man when she wished him to be a girl; develop a healthy body-image, when she, haunted by her unmourned daughter's memory, searched him constantly for hereditary defects?

Furthermore, intense conflicts of loyalties interwove with the above conflicts of missions. In remaining closely and loyally tied to his mother, Marvin came to perceive and despise his father as rival and interloper, thereby losing him as a respected masculine model.

In such conflicts of missions and loyalties, the delegating process could not but derail—the more so as Marvin's missions, by their very nature, kept him locked into his mother's orbit and thus precluded his being *sent out* as delegate.

Above all, it was such derailment of the delegating process that cast into relief the two above-mentioned aspects—the sense of personal meaning and importance a delegate derives from fulfilling even "self-destructive" missions, and the dynamics of psychological exploitation and counter-exploitation—which a focus on missions rather than roles first brought out.

There could be no doubt that Marvin derived an enormous sense of importance from being his mother's loyal, self-sacrificing (albeit derailed) delegate. Even though, in being passively bound, he seemed unlike such active delegates as Christian crusaders and

missionaries, righteous Puritans, or fanatical Nazis or Communists, he shared with many of them a willingness to trade self-
defeat and self-destruction for a gain in meaning, self-certainty
and a feeling of being loved and needed—in brief, for a sense of
importance.

PSYCHOLOGICAL EXPLOITATION AND COUNTER-EXPLOITATION IN MARVIN'S RELATIONSHIP WITH HIS MOTHER

Even though Marvin felt important to his mother, he came out
the loser in his unconscious bargain with her. In trying to execute
her missions, he had stopped growing and forfeited his life
prospects. At the same time, he had failed as her delegate, since his
overgrown body and passive existence belied his (and his
mother's) image of himself as a youthful artist destined for
success. His response to his predicament was rage—rage at his
binding, delegating, and exploitative mother. Inevitably, he had
recourse to counter-harassment and counter-exploitation. His
most effective stratagem in the counter-exploitative struggle was
to stay "sick." By simply remaining a flabby, freeloading idler, he
delivered himself as the living proof of her failure as a parent,
deepening her shame and guilt. He threw one huge, continuous
temper tantrum, as it were, and, under the guise of sickness and
helplessness, tortured her sadistically. Hence his need to thwart all
attempts—by therapists, friends, and parents—to help him, as any
improvement in his condition would have reduced his power to
torture her (that is, work the shame and guilt lever). But hence
also his need to punish *himself*, his mother's cruel torturer, by
fiercely destroying his chances for growth and happiness.

AN INTERPERSONAL DIALECTIC

A focus on the delegating process reveals thus an interpersonal
dialectic. Here the perspective repeatedly shifts depending on who

is giver and who debtor, exploiter and exploited, victimizer and victim. In the above example, we found the mother, as delegate to her own parents, initially to be generously giving, as she showered Marvin (as well as the other family members) with endearments, embraces, and gifts. Such giving, we saw, became binding and exploitative of its recipient. As a result, Marvin, the bound-up delegate, emerged as the real giver: while he sacrificed his own growth and happiness, he ensured his mother's psychological survival. In becoming giver, he also became victimizer, turning his mother into debtor and victim and thereby locking her and himself into an ever more negative mutuality.

TREATMENT IMPLICATIONS

Finally, we are now in a position to point to some of the treatment implications revealed by a focus on missions and the delegating process rather than on roles and the socialization process. (We realize that both foci imply a contrast to psychoanalytic approaches, which emphasize intrapsychic rather than interpersonal vicissitudes and shape therapeutic interventions accordingly.) Even though they share an interpersonal (or transactional) orientation, major differences exist between role and mission models. Within a role model we found it to be the therapist's main task to bring about roles and system changes, as described earlier. Manipulative techniques such as paradoxical injunctions which "jolt" the system seemed particularly indicated, as these promise to facilitate fresh starts for all role partners and to redirect the socialization process where it had gone awry.

However, this therapeutic approach downplays or disregards those deeper systems aspects (in vertical as well as horizontal human relations) which a mission and delegation model brings into view: those having to do with loyalties and obligations fulfilled or betrayed, with shame and guilt, with psychological exploitation and counter-exploitation, and with interpersonal justice—aspects that have a subjective as well as objective (or existential) dimension. It seems that, among role theorists, John Spiegel comes closest to recognizing those aspects and their therapeutic implications. He espouses therapeutic strategies of role-modification, such as negotiation and conciliation by a third-party mediator, which clearly raise issues of interpersonal justice. Still, in adhering to his role model, he fails to perceive those therapeutic implications which derive from the deeper systems aspects revealed through a missions model. Boszormenyi-Nagy and Spark (4) and this author (24-26 and Chapter 11 herein) have elaborated some of these implications. Essentially, these relate to how a therapist, aiming at a "multidirectional partiality" or "involved impartiality," analyzes all members' conflicts of missions and loyalties, considers their "ledger of merit," facilitates interpersonal justice, and engages the partners in a reconstructive dialogue that, optimally, spans several generations and aims at eventual mutual understanding, forgiveness, and reconciliation.

References

1. Ackermann, N. W. *The Psychodynamics of family life*, New York: Basic Books, 1958.
2. ———. *Treating the troubled family*. New York: Basic Books, 1966.
3. Bateson, G., Jackson, D., Haley, J., and Weakland, J. Toward a theory of schizophrenia. *Behavioral Science* 1: 251-264, 1956.
4. Boszormenyi-Nagy, I., and Spark, G. *Invisible loyalties*. New York: Hoeber & Harper, 1973/74.
5. Dahrendorf, R. *Homo sociologicus*. Aufl, Cologne and Opladen: Westdeutscher Verlag, 1964.
6. Erickson, M. *Advanced techniques of hypnosis and therapy*, ed. Jay Haley. New York: Grune & Stratton, 1967.
7. Freud, S. *Inhibitions, symptoms and anxiety* (1926). SE XX, 77-178. London: Hogarth Press, 1959.
8. ———. *The ego and the id* (1923). SE XIX, 3-68. London: Hogarth Press, 1961.

9. ———. *New introductory lectures on psycho-analysis* (1933). *SE* XXII, 3-182. London: Hogarth Press, 1964.
10. Haley, J. *Uncommon therapy.* New York: Ballantine Books, 1973.
11. Jackson, D. D. Family, interaction, family homeostasis, and some implications of conjoint family psychotherapy. In *Science and psychoanalysis: individual and familial dynamics,* Vol. 2, ed. J. H. Massermann. New York: Grune & Stratton, 1959.
12. Lidz, T. *The family and human adaptation.* New York: International Universities Press, 1963.
13. Lidz, T., Cornelison, A. R., Fleck, S., and Terry, D. The intrafamilial environment of the schizophrenic patient. II. Marital schism and marital skew, *American Journal of Psychiatry* 114: 241-248, 1957.
14. Lidz, T., Fleck, S., and Cornelison, A. R. *Schizophrenia and the family.* New York: International Universities Press, 1965.
15. Mead, G. H. *On social psychology.* Chicago: University of Chicago Press, 1956.
16. Minuchin, S. *Families and family therapy.* Cambridge: Harvard University Press, 1974.
17. Selvini-Palazolli, M. *Self-starvation.* London: Chaucer Publishing, 1974.
18. Parsons, T. *The social system.* Glencoe: The Free Press, 1951.
19. Parsons, T., and Bales, R. *Family, socialization and interaction process.* Glencoe: Free Press, 1955.
20. Spiegel, J. *Transactions.* New York: Jason Aronson, 1971.
21. Stierlin H. The adaption to the stronger person's reality. *Psychiatry* 22: 143-152, 1959.
22. ———. Family dynamics and separation patterns of potential schizophrenics. In *Proceedings of the Fourth International Symposium on Psychotherapy of Schizophrenia,* ed. Y. Alanen. Amsterdam: Excerpta Medica, 1972, pp. 169-179.
23. ———. The adolescent as delegate of his parents. *Australian and New Zealand Journal of Psychiatry* 7: 249-256, 1973.
24. ———. Family theory: an introduction. In *Operational theories of personality,* ed. A. Burton. New York: Brunner/Mazel, 1974.
25. ———. *Separating parents and adolescents: a perspective on running away, schizophrenia, and waywardness.* New York: Quadrangle, 1974.

26.   ———. *Adolf Hitler—Familienperspektiven.* Frankfurt a.M.; Suhrkamp, 1975.
27.   Watzlawick, P., Beavin, J. H., and Jackson, D. D. *Pragmatics of human communication: a study of interactional patterns, pathologics, and paradoxes.* New York: Norton, 1967.
28.   Watzlawick, P., Weakland, J., and Fisch, R. *Change, principles of problem resolution.* New York: Norton, 1974.
29.   Weber, M. *Wirtschaft und Gesellschaft.* 2. Aufl., Tubingen: Mohr, 1925.
30.   Wynne, L. C. Selection of the problems to be investigated in family interaction research. In *Family interaction: a dialogue between family researchers and family therapists,* ed. J. L. Framo. New York: Springer, 1972, pp. 86-92.
31.   Wynne, L. C., Ryckhoff, J. M., Day, J., and Hirsch, S. I. Pseudo-mutuality in the family relations of schizophrenics. *Psychiatry* 21: 205-220, 1958.

Part III

The Theory and Practice of Psychoanalytic Family Therapy

Chapter 13

Family Therapy with Adolescents

The adolescent who attempts to separate himself from his family faces three interdependent tasks, all bearing on his psychological growth. They relate to his individuation as well as to his (relative) separation. I would like to define these tasks as *tasks of reconciliation*. Various aspects of them have been described in the psychiatric and psychoanalytic literature, particularly in the works of A. Freud (8), P. Blos (1, 2), and E. H. Erikson (5-7). By emphasizing their reconciling nature we can, I believe, best study their individual, as well as family system, aspects and trace their implications for family therapy.

The first of these tasks of reconciliation refers to the psychophysiologic differentiations and integrations which are required of the adolescent. We may speak here of the *task of integrative reconciliation*. This task encompasses the differentiation of the adolescent's drives, feelings, and motivations and their integration into a viable organization of defenses and identity. This task is made difficult by the powerful, partly hormonally caused upsurges of his sexual and aggressive energies, which find few, if any, acceptable outlets. These energies, while pressuring for discharge, must be absorbed into and tamed by a structured identity as solid as it is differentiated and complex. This applies particularly to his (or her) gender identity.

The second task presupposes such a framework but also transcends it. In my book, *Conflict and Reconciliation* (12), I have tried to adumbrate this task which I would now like to call the *task of adaptive reconciliation*. This task demands that modern adolescents— more, I believe, than members of any other age group—reconcile several interrelated yet polarized action trends or "existential" attitudes. Most important here are the polarities doing/undergoing, choice/renunciation, and self-realization/self-limitation.

Doing here refers to the adolescent's needs for self-affirmation and self-determination. It stands for his ability and willingness to experience himself as the shaper of his destiny, and implies that he can say and feel: "I do, I plan for myself, I am my maker, I. am responsible for myself."

The adolescent must reconcile such doing with "undergoing," the ability and willingness to experience his actions as influenced or determined by forces outside himself. It implies that he can recognize and accept the givens of this world (and himself as one of these givens), saying and feeling: "I depend on others, I cannot totally plan myself, I am not absolutely responsible."

For today's adolescent the above dialectic has become radicalized. He must open himself up to wide-ranging sources of learning and so remain excessively dependent on those bodies which facilitate such learning—mainly the universities and the parents who pay his tuition. At the same time, he is strongly pressured into "doing" and "self-determination" in the sense that he must (in the words of Erikson) make "a series of ever-narrowing selections of personal, occupational, sexual and ideological commitments." He must choose to realize himself by establishing and accepting his limits.

This adolescent must, next, attempt to liquidate the burden he carries from his interpersonal past. This means trying to correct and outgrow those fixations, traumas, and consequences of an uneven development forced upon him by others which now threaten to hamper his growth. He must try to get rid of—or at least modify—those bad parental inner objects (or object images) that might thwart his future object relations.

The *task of reparative reconciliation*, the third interdependent task mentioned above, encompasses all these attempts. If they are to be successful, they often demand a "reintegration at the base," characterized by inner turmoil, intense anxiety, and a temporary disintegration and regressive loosening of the personality. Also, these attempts entail a painful mourning process, as described by M. Sugar (13), through which the adolescent disengages himself at least partly from his parents both as inner objects (referred to as his separation from his oedipal parents) and as real persons. Finally, I include in the task of reparative reconciliation the possible coming to grips with the burden of the past through artistic creativity. This avenue, though, seems open only to a limited number of adolescents.

RECONCILIATION ON THE FAMILY LEVEL

These three tasks of reconciliation, in order to be understood and supported by professional help, must be seen in a family context. When focusing on the family, we deal with a different system, a different order of complexity, and a different level of reconciliation. In the family the growth of one is the growth of the others, and the separation of one is the separation of others. The "others" are here, of course, chiefly the parents of the adolescent and, to some extent, his siblings.

The three tasks of reconciliation outlined above imply a reconciling effort on the family level. I shall examine each in turn and thereafter consider how the family therapist may assist such effort on this level.

In taking up the first task—that of integrative reconciliation—I shall limit myself to discussing some problems which are posed by the adolescent's awakening sexuality and need to achieve a viable gender identity.

In this regard we can state the following general rule: an adolescent can accept and master his or her budding sexuality only to the extent that his or her parents have done so with respect to their own sexuality. In order to illustrate this point (and others to be taken up later), I shall now refer to the "Allen" family, consisting of Mr. and Mrs. Allen, two respectable middle-class suburbanites, and Evelyn, their only daughter.

The Allens came for treatment at the Family Studies Section of the Adult Psychiatry Branch, National Institute of Mental Health, because Evelyn, a sweet-looking and somewhat precocious girl of sixteen and a half, had run into the kind of troubles that nowadays seem common. She had taken to drugs (acid, speed, pot, and others) and bad boys (usually two or three at a time). Also, she had become truant, and, in order to cover up her truancy, had entangled herself in a web of lies, deceptions, and forgings of passes. Getting more and more anxious, Evelyn finally ran away to New York where, after several days, she was rescued by her devastated father. Evelyn believed at that time she was pregnant and was tormented by fears that she might give birth to a LSD-deformed monster. (She was not pregnant.)

In the family sessions Evelyn found little parental understanding or even sympathy for her agonies. Instead, the parents appeared to compound Evelyn's sexual difficulties. The mother alternated between stances of righteous indignation and an (to the observer) insatiable, though covertly expressed, interest in Evelyn's unsavory company and sexual experiences. The father, through sly "come-on" smiles, encouraged Evelyn to put her dumb mother down, thereby intensifying the oedipal tangle and preventing its resolution. Evelyn responded to the father's messages and exasperated her mother by being defiant and cocksure. With almost sadistic glee, she now presented herself as a real swinger, "with it," whereas her mother—"this most pathetic example of someone over thirty"—was a stupid, hopeless square.

In the family therapy it quickly became apparent how the parents' own sexual difficulties bore on Evelyn's plight. The mother, a flamboyant yet frigid, hysterical woman, channeled into Evelyn that mixture of prurient sexual excitability and righteous moralizing which had become the chief manifestation of, as well as coping device for, her own immature and conflict-ridden sexuality. The father, an overcontrolled, obsessive type, behaved rejectingly, as well as seductively, toward Evelyn. Subjected to confusing messages, she responded by developing her confused, "hit and run" sexuality.

In order to achieve a viable and mature sexual identity of her own, Evelyn needed her parents to do likewise. She put them under pressure to work on their own growth and to make certain reconciling moves. We will better understand what this implied for the parents when we consider, now, within the family context, the second task mentioned above—the task of adaptive reconciliation. In turning to this task, we deal with a problem that encompasses an area traditionally known as the adolescent's *quest for autonomy*.

I indicated earlier that this second task of reconciliation tends to become radicalized for the modern adolescent because of the growing and conflicting social pressures he has to meet. This radicalization, I believe, is also reflected on the family level. We notice here how such radicalization affects and highlights certain areas of conflict and of needed reconciliation within the family. To make this clearer, let me again turn to the Allens.

I have already mentioned Evelyn's rebellious defiance of her mother, as when she called the latter "a hopeless square over thirty." I must now add that Evelyn had generalized this defiance into a rejection of almost everything that her parents considered good and worthwhile. In this respect Evelyn differed little from many other members of her age group. Not only did Evelyn flaunt a vocabulary of four-letter words, dress sloppily and in hippie fashion, experiment liberally with drugs, and (it seemed) sleep with every boy in sight; but she also wrote, as editor of her high school paper, articles in praise of Castro and Ho Chi Minh and plotted, with the help of some "SDS advisers," the ouster of her "reactionary" high school superintendent. In the light of such generalized radical rebellion on Evelyn's part, we can better understand why her parents found it difficult to be patient and sympathetic with her. Pushed into a corner and feeling threatened in what they believed and valued most, they could, it seemed, no longer afford understanding or sympathy. They could only experience rage and exasperation. And in experiencing these painful emotions, they sensed that all meaningful communication between them and their daughter had broken down.

Anybody who in these days has worked on an adolescent ward can probably empathize with Evelyn's parents—he knows what it feels like to be constantly shown up as wrong, "square," worthless, and impotent. And so can, in fact, many a parent, teacher, or citizen over thirty who sees modern youth espousing with seemingly devilish cunning every possible hero or value that runs counter to his or her own cherished beliefs—pitting Che Guevara and John Lennon against the "Establishment," or the hippie life in the "here and now" against the plastic, rat-race culture of suburbia.

We can speak here of the adolescent's *self-determination against his parents.* Such self-determination has always been part of the conflict of generations and of the separation drama of adolescence. And it has always tended to become fiercer the stronger the underlying emotional ties have been. I believe, however, that today many an adolescent's self-determination against his own parents has—for reasons which I cannot elaborate—tended to become more radical, as well as mandatory. It has necessitated balancing moves—on the part of the adolescent and of the parents—of corresponding strength.

Such radicalized self-determination, in order not to result in mere intergenerational warfare, must now include a self-determination *with* the parents. That is, it entails an ability and willingness in all partners to keep the dialogue going despite temporary alienations and breakdowns in communication. Doing and self-determination, this means, have to be reconciled with undergoing and receptivity. And this reconciliation must reflect a family effort. A family climate and culture must be created and maintained wherein mutual—intergenerational!—learning and growth may occur along with mutual individuation and separation.

I see it here—and this brings me to the issue of family therapy—as the main task of the family therapist to help create and improve such family climate and culture—and to do so in the face of the powerful forces which threaten to erode or overthrow the latter. In this task he can with profit reflect on the concept of a shared focus of attention, as elaborated by L. C. Wynne. Wynne, in collaboration with M. T. Singer, has made this the pivotal concept for the study and classification of relational pathology in families with schizophrenic offspring (10, 11, 14, 15). It becomes pivotal also, I believe, when applied to the study of, and psychotherapeutic intervention in, the separation drama of neurotic and relatively normal adolescents. By pointing out again and again how the parents and their adolescent offspring fail to share such a common focus, how they avoid listening to each other, and how they cannot confirm either agreement or disagreement, the therapist establishes himself as a facilitator of communication instead of the stern, guilt-inducing and partial judge he is often expected to be. He becomes the chief reconciling agent.

In the case of the Allens, our chosen example, the psychotherapists had persistently to take up the many ways in which the family members tended to talk parallel to and against, but not with, each other. In thus serving as facilitators of family communication, the therapists not only helped to de-radicalize the bitter intergenerational (and marital) war, but they also made it possible for each member to gain new perspectives, to learn from and about one another. Such learning to learn, made possible within a seemingly immobilized family, could then lead to further needed changes which, in order to be beneficial, had to occur in the area of the parents' own thwarted sexual development, as mentioned earlier. But along with and beyond that, these changes had to encompass growth on what appears to be an even deeper level. It is this level to which I turn next.

This level relates to the third reconciling task mentioned in the beginning—the task of reparative reconciliation. I described this as being aimed at correcting and outgrowing the burden of one's past. Let us now consider how it becomes a task for the whole family and how it affects needed psychotherapeutic interventions.

Again, one aspect of the Allen family may serve as an illustration. As the therapy with them got underway, I began to notice the following characteristic sequence unfolding between the mother and Evelyn. They both seemed to become repeatedly sad and grief-stricken and then doubly vituperative with each other. When I encouraged them to put their sadness and grief into words, Evelyn talked in a vague way about feeling lonely and bad, whereas the mother turned more and more to talking about her past, about her own parents and unhappy youth. In so doing, she related the following. The daughter of poor European immigrants, she had had to endure her mother's constant nagging tirades, had been overwhelmed with household chores, and had been forbidden to take part in the "frivolous" activities of her peers. Among these peers was a cousin, Erna, a beautiful, outgoing, and popular girl whom she envied and tried to emulate. This cousin Erna came to stand in Mrs. Allen's mind for all that she, as an adolescent, could not be and could not have. As Mrs. Allen talked about this cousin, she emphasized how much Evelyn resembled her, and at one point she inadvertently called her daughter Erna.

It seemed now significant that Mrs. Allen, after having told of her deprivation at the hands of her own mother, appeared to turn against Evelyn with a vengeance, victimizing her mercilessly. But it seemed no less significant that Evelyn, by some particularly defiant and provocative word or gesture, appeared to actively invite such victimization. How can we explain this?

I am, above all, indebted to Boszormenyi-Nagy (3) and Boszormenyi-Nagy and Spark (4) for understanding more fully the meaning of a transactional sequence such as the one just outlined. This sequence reveals some crucial features and problems in the mother's and Evelyn's efforts at a reparative reconciliation, as I understand this concept. Risking the danger of oversimplification, we may state these features and problems as follows.

After having learned to communicate more freely with Evelyn, the mother began to see the latter a little differently. She seemed to become more able to perceive of Evelyn as a person in her own right. Along with thus viewing Evelyn more objectively, she could, with the support of the therapists, face and experience some of the deprivation and frustration she had suffered at the hands of her own mother. This led to her becoming depressed and grief-stricken, as indicated above. But also—and this seems important—it caused an upsurge of painful guilt. Dimly the mother seemed to grow aware that through all these years she had tried to make Evelyn pay for what her own mother had done to her, that she had turned her relations with Evelyn into a medium for coming to grips with her own unresolved conflicts and seemingly unendurable frustrations, as these related to her own mother.

In addition to thus casting Evelyn, in important respects, in the role of her own mother (that is, parentifying Evelyn), she had also attributed to her daughter many qualities of her cousin Erna, the emulated idol of her own adolescence. Thus, Mrs. Allen brought further conflicting pressures to bear on Evelyn. She covertly encouraged Evelyn to reenact Erna's wild adolescent sprees and to thereby provide her, the mother, with vicarious thrills. At the same time, she castigated Evelyn for being wild, promiscuous and irresponsible, spicing such castigation with all the envious hatred she had felt—and still felt—for Erna.

In beginning to experience grief and sadness, the mother started to work on her reparative reconciliation, facilitating thereby her own and Evelyn's liberation from the burdens of their past. And this process had to be mutual. Evelyn, also, we noticed, began to appear sad and grief-stricken and, we can assume, had started to reappraise her mother. But why, we must ask, was the work of repair and grief punctuated by relapses into the bitter game of defiance and victimization?

These relapses, I believe, become understandable when one is cognizant of the massive guilt which began to pervade the mother's—and Evelyn's—awareness. To the extent that the mother could start to see Evelyn as a person in her own right and to undertake long overdue repairs in her relations to her daughter, she could not help becoming more conscious of what she had done to Evelyn. Hence the onrush of guilt which superimposed more pain on the pain she already felt. It was in an attempt to cope with this guilt and its pain, I believe, that the mother turned again into a ruthless victimizer. And it was, I believe further, in an attempt to assuage the mother's guilt and pain that Evelyn, by being outrageously provocative, offered herself to be victimized. We may speak of a collusion between the mother and daughter in the service of a mutual assuagement of guilt, a process which has been thoroughly described by I. Boszormenyi-Nagy (3).

I consider it one of the central tasks of family therapy to break up such collusion in the service of guilt assuagement and thereby to facilitate each family member's reparative reconciliations.

This, then, finally brings into focus the system aspect of the family interaction. This system aspect, as it relates to the issue under discussion, has already been adumbrated by Hegel in *The Phenomenology of the Spirit* (written in 1805). Herein Hegel made the relationship between master and servant (*Herr und Knecht*) the paradigm of a relationship between two unequals, of which one presents himself as the powerful victimizer and the other as the weak victim. This relationship, Hegel pointed out, tends to create a dialectic momentum through which the victimizer loses and the victim gains psychological power. The more the master has to rely on the servant for making his (the master's) life productive and meaningful, the more he becomes psychologically dependent on and governed by the latter. The victim, in other words, becomes more powerful as he lets himself be more victimized.

Translated into modern family dynamics, this means that the victimized adolescent usually becomes the most powerful family member because he is in the best position to operate the guilt lever. It means also that, in order to spare himself the painful work of separation and growth, he will tend either to provoke or hold onto his victimization. And it means, further, that the therapist, in order to break up the above-described collusion and to facilitate a reparative reconciliation in all concerned, must erode the victim's powers for inducing guilt. He must interpret the victim's masochism, that is, his enjoyment of suffering, and the sadism which is therein implied. (Such masochism presents the most difficult technical problem in the psychoanalysis of individual patients, just as it does in family therapy.)

In the case of the Allens this meant, above all, that the provocative and, yet, underhandedly masochistic and controlling elements in Evelyn's behavior had to become analyzed before the parents could make substantial progress in their own task of reparative reconciliation. We recognize here one of the paradoxes with which family therapy constantly confronts us: in order to help Evelyn in her separation *from,* and self-determination *against,* her parents, the therapists seemingly had to align themselves with the parents against the hapless Evelyn. (I emphasize the word *seemingly,* because the analysis of Evelyn's wielding of power through the enjoyment of her victimization represents at best a "dialectical" sort of alignment.) In so doing, they helped to undermine the total family system wherein victimizer and victim appeared bound to each other and where, in such mutual bondage, real individual growth and separation had become impossible for all.

If we look back on our exposition of the adolescent's and his family's separation drama, we notice how our awareness of the problems and of the necessary therapeutic interventions shifted. At first the adolescent's plight, as conventionally described in the psychoanalytic and psychiatric literature, came into view. In then considering the family context we saw how the parents, on account of their own immaturities and unresolved conflicts, had given rise to this plight and tended to prolong it. Yet, when we asked how we should deal with the parents, our focus shifted again to the adolescent as the one who held the most powerful guilt leverage. From there we could support the parents in their grief work, which only then had become possible. And so, I believe, it has to go on—in a complex dialectical process of shifting foci. This process, hopefully, leads to an expanding awareness and growth—on the part of the family members *and* on the part of the family therapists—and reflects successful reconciliation on all the three levels outlined above.

References

1. Blos, P. *On adolescence: a psychoanalytic interpretation.* New York: Free Press of Glencoe, 1962.
2. ————. *The young adolescent: clinical studies.* New York: Free Press, 1970.
3. Boszormenyi-Nagy, I. Loyalty implications of the transference model in psychotherapy. *Archives of General Psychiatry* 27: 374-380, 1972.
4. Boszormenyi-Nagy, I., and Spark, G. *Invisible loyalties.* New York: Harper and Row, 1973.
5. Erikson, E. H. *Childhood and society.* New York: Norton, 1950.

6. ———. *Identity and the life cycle.* New York: International Universities Press, 1959.
7. ———. *Identity, youth and crisis.* New York: Norton, 1968.
8. Freud, A. *The ego and the mechanisms of defense.* New York: International Universities Press, 1946.
9. Hegel, G. *The phenomenology of the spirit, (1805)* 2 vols. Translated by J. B. Baillie. London: Swann Sonnenschein, 1910.
10. Singer, M. T., and Wynne, L. C. Thought disorder and family relations of schizophrenics. III. Methodology using projective techniques. *Archives of General Psychiatry* 12: 187-200, 1965.
11. ———. Thought disorder and family relations of schizophrenics. IV. Results and implications. *Archives of General Psychiatry* 12: 201-212, 1965.
12. Stierlin, H. *Conflict and reconciliation.* New York: Doubleday Anchor and Jason Aronson, 1969.
13. Sugar, M. Normal adolescent mourning. *American Journal of Psychotherapy* 22: 258-269, 1968.
14. Wynne, L. C., and Singer, M. T. Thought disorder and family relations of schizophrenics. I. A research strategy. *Archives of General Psychiatry* 9: 191-198, 1963.
15. ———. Thought disorder and family relations of schizophrenics. II. A classification of forms of thinking. *Archives of General Psychiatry* 9: 199-206, 1963.

Chapter 14

Countertransference
in Family Therapy with Adolescents

Countertransference in family thereapy refers to phenomena that
are controversial, ambiguous, and complex. To understand this
ambiguity and complexity we must first briefly trace the shifting
and widening meanings of the terms *transference* and
countertransference in psychoanalytic therapy.

TRANSFERENCE
IN THE PSYCHOANALYTIC SITUATION

Freud first mentioned *transference* in 1895, in his *Studies on Hysteria*
(10). He defined the term in 1905, when publishing the Dora case,
as a "special class of mental structures, for the most part
unconscious." These are "new editions or facsimilies of the
impulses and fantasies which are aroused and made conscious
during the progress of the analysis; but they have this peculiarity,
which is characteristic for their species, that they replace some
earlier person by the person of the physician"(p. 116).

After this initial definition, Freud and his followers widened our perspective on transference. They described its affective and perceptual components, distinguished positive, negative, and ambivalent transferences, and related these to the dynamics of introjection, projection, repression, and acting out (e.g., the view was held that memories which are repressed and cannot be remembered must be repetitively acted out as transferences). Also, they developed the concept of the transference neurosis.

Transference phenomena—like Sullivan's parataxic distortions—were seen as ubiquitous. However, they were held to have special affinity with the psychoanalytic situation. It was this situation which bred them in pure culture, as it were, and provided optimal conditions for their examination and final resolution. The patient as well as the analyst structured this situation by sticking to the terms of the analytic contract: the patient mainly by trying to comply with the basic analytic rule (to say everything that comes to his mind); the analyst chiefly by being "abstinent"—i.e., frustrating to the patient—but also stable, firm, and free from "blind spots." In his frustrating firmness, he became a bulwark which the patient's transference processes could butt up against and thus reveal their intensity and inappropriateness; in remaining free from the blind spots of unconscious biases and neurotic anxieties, he could examine the patient's transference distortions objectively as well as empathically.

Inevitably, the above meaning of transference changed with the changing psychoanalytic situation. Analysts began to analyze patients whom they had previously considered unanalyzable—such as schizophrenics, whom Freud had viewed as incapable of developing transference. The notion of the therapist as an abstinent, detached observer now became problematical, and new aspects of transference came into focus. I have traced some of these in my book *Conflict and Reconciliation* (23), which deals with the special therapeutic situation required for schizophrenic patients.

COUNTERTRANSFERENCE
IN THE PSYCHOANALYTIC SITUATION

Countertransference can be viewed as the mirror concept of transference. But since Freud introduced it in 1910 in his paper on the future prospects of psychoanalytic therapy, the concept of countertransference, even more than that of transference, has remained ambiguous and controversial.

Essentially, two major meanings emerged: first, countertransference was viewed simply as the analyst's reaction to the patient's transference; and, second, it was defined as the analyst's transference to the patient for other reasons. These differing meanings then created different vantage points for further observations and conceptualizations. Within the first definition, countertransference primarily provided information about the patient. The therapist used his own feelings and reactions as major data about the patient. Within the second definition, the therapist tended to emerge as a stumbling block to his patient's progress. The focus there was on his blind spots, neurotic or character problems, rigidities, etc., which interfered with his patient's unfolding transference, therapeutic progress, and growth.

Often these two aspects—the information-providing aspect and the stumbling-block aspect—are interwoven, as when a usually mild stumbling block in the therapist also facilitates pertinent information about a certain patient. (M. B. Cohen (5) has well illustrated such clinical situations.) Since this is the case, I shall not here make a deliberate choice between them.

As happened with transference phenomena, processes of countertransference became more difficult to assess as the classic dyadic analytic situation with a well-motivated, neurotic patient became less prevalent. The contributions of H. Searles (21), F. Fromm-Reichmann (13), D. W. Winnicott (29), and others on countertransference in the treatment of schizophrenics are here illuminating. Searles used his countertransference reactions chiefly as primary data sources on the complex dynamics of his schizophrenic patients. For example, he described *his* (therapist's) vengefulness, primitive wishes for fusion, feared loss of boundaries, etc. as signals alerting him to corresponding or complementary experiences in his patients. F. Fromm-Reichmann and D. W. Winnicott, in contrast, focused on those personality aspects or "blind spots" in the therapists of schizophrenics—such as an excessive conventionality, or use of intellectualization as a defense—which could seriously limit their therapeutic effectiveness.

TRANSFERENCE AND COUNTERTRANSFERENCE IN GROUPS

Groups introduce new therapeutic and conceptual paradigms and added complexities. The terms *transference* and *countertransference* become even more problematical here than in dyadic relations. Although a group consists of individual patients with individual problems, we must now focus on the multi-person unit, and, where applicable, conceive of the group as *the* patient. Freud (12), Bion (2), Ezriel (6), and many others have described typical group dynamics.

Transference and countertransference phenomena (or their analogues) in groups, like those occurring in individual therapy, are shaped by the patients' and therapist's contributions to the therapeutic situation. The special quality of the patients' contributions derives mainly from the fact that they constitute an "ad hoc" group, i.e., an aggregate of people who lack a common history, real-life bonds, or commitments to each other beyond those resulting from their transient group experience. Within such an ad hoc group, typical group processes and group fantasies can unfold. The group therapist or leader who follows a psychoanalytic model and remains abstinent influences these group processes and fantasies.

Bion (2), Turquet (26, 27), Argelander (1), and others have described the leader's contributions, chiefly to those group fantasies which unfold in small groups, also called Bion groups. The leader of such groups must be abstinent to an unusual degree, thereby structuring and maintaining an asymmetry between himself and the group. By avoiding all acting out with the group and by giving interpretations on the group level only, he insures that the group stews in its own anxiety, as it were. In this way, the group members are forced to rely on their own resources, largely seeking their own answers to emerging problems.

In addition to reflecting the differing contributions of patients and therapists, the concepts of transference and countertransference have come to reveal the differing theoretical leanings (e.g., more Freudian or Kleinian) of group therapists. Grotjahn (14), for example, standing mainly in the classical psychoanalytic tradition, has distinguished three major transference dynamics in groups: first, the transference relation to the therapist or central figure, presumably developing out of a transference neurosis, as patterned in psychoanalysis; second, the transference relations among the members of the group; and, third, a transference developed to the group as a pre-oedipal mother.

My own view on transference and countertransference in groups builds essentially on the ideas of Bion and the Tavistock group as represented, among others, by Turquet (26, 27), Rice (19), Shapiro and Zinner (22), and Rioch (20).

Group transference and countertransference processes, according to this view, interlock with the vicissitudes of certain typical group fantasies. These group fantasies mirror, as well as shape, certain types of recurrent group behavior. At the same time, they give evidence of characteristic "basic assumptions" shared by the whole group. Essentially, these are the basic assumptions of "dependence," "fight-flight," and "pairing," as originally described by Bion. They derive from a group climate which exerts a strong regressive pull. The members' feeling of group omnipotence that lacks a sense of responsibility and a sense for temporal sequences and realistic constraints is here the most striking feature. It colors all fantasies that evolve, often giving them a volatile, primary process quality.

These group fantasies, or basic assumptions, in turn structure the group's perceptions and expectations of the leader. Such group attitudes we may then call the "group transference." The leader may be approached and perceived as an all-giving and all-knowing father (or mother), able—though often not willing—to satisfy the exorbitant, regressive dependency needs of the group. He may be perceived as an intrusive enemy whom the group must either fight or flee. Or he may be perceived as a partner for, or enabler of, pairing activities. Countertransference within such a group, by the same token, denotes a leader's acting out *with* the group, i.e., a deviation from his asymmetric, abstinent role. Typically, such "countertransference" occurs in three major ways: first, the group therapist lets himself be forced into the role of the all-giving and all-knowing father/mother, i.e., he tries to satisfy the group's excessive and regressive dependency needs; second, he confirms through his actual behavior the group's perception of him as a controlling, authoritarian intruder who must be fought or fled; or, third, he allows or covertly encourages excessive pairing relations within the group. All three countertransference patterns lead to characteristic impasses in group therapy (as group therapists well know) unless they are quickly recognized and checked.

"TRANSFERENCE" AND "COUNTERTRANSFERENCE" IN FAMILY GROUPS

Families are groups and as such appear not to be exempt from the above considerations and principles. However, as groups they are unique and require an almost entirely new script. And this applies, above all, to the meanings of transference and counter-transference in family therapy.

Two features of families are crucial here.

First, families are the opposite of transient, ad hoc groups, who lack a common history and a mutual involvement beyond that which their group relationship generates. Rather, families share such history, and their members have been and will be fatefully enmeshed with one another.

Second, families do not primarily reveal the same kind of transferences and countertransferences found in either dyadic relations or groups. For transactional phenomena in families, whatever their specific content and source, reflect chiefly one fact—*that transferences originate within families. It is family transactions which give rise to those relational patterns which later, inappropriately and repetitively, are transferred to non-family contexts.*[1]

These two facts—that family members are fatefully enmeshed with one another and that transferences originate within their sphere—account for the importance of one phenomenon that is central to the theory and practice of family therapy and especially for our conceptualization of transference and countertransference processes in families: the existence of family myths.

Family myths, as here intended, have been extensively described and illustrated by Ferreira (8), who emphasized their homeostatic function. He maintained that "the family myth is to the relationship what the defense is to the individual." I myself have recently outlined the varying functions and structures of family myths (see Chapter 9).

Here it must suffice to say that family myths fulfill the major function of providing a shared formulation which makes some sense out of the family members' involvement with, and their rights and obligations toward, one another. Thus, myths serve cognitive needs (they give a more or less coherent picture of "where the family is at"), relational needs (they anchor the members in mutual relatedness), as well as needs for interpersonal justice (they assign blame or grant exculpation to certain members). In brief, they provide cognitive, relational, and ethical meaning and are therefore affectively charged. To make this clearer, let us recall one particular family myth mentioned which

centered on the "badness" of an alcoholic father (who happened to
be no longer in the picture).

This father, so the myth went, had malevolently deserted his
faithful wife and loving children. Therefore, all members agreed
that he needed to be shunned and castigated, and they all shared in
the belief that this bad, deserting, alcoholic father was innately
corrupt, irresponsible—in brief, the scum of the earth. This
father's "desertion" occurred approximately ten years before the
family entered therapy. Meanwhile, the mother had remarried.
Her new husband, the children's stepfather, had also come to
believe that the family's current difficulties—such as the mother's
depression, the oldest girl's promiscuity, the boy's school difficulties—were essentially due to this father's desertion. Thus, this
myth tried to make sense of the family's relatedness, history, and
plight, as it assigned blame to one member (the father) while
exculpating all others.

Gradually, though, this myth was punctured as it became
known that the father's "desertion" was in part engineered by the
mother, who then had a love affair with her boss. More and more
this father came to be seen not so much as an irresponsible
runaway, but as a pathetic evictee who again and again clamored
to re-enter the family yet each time was rebuffed. As a result of
the exploratory family therapy, a more complex view of the
family's history emerged, and each member's merits and demerits
appeared more evenly balanced.

When we focus on specific transference-countertransference
dynamics in families, we find, thus, that myths have characteristic
effects on them. First, they distort as well as disguise these
dynamics—to the family members, as well as to outsiders. In the
above case, for example, the myth almost totally ignored or
obfuscated the nature of those formative, primary relationships in
this family which later gave rise to compulsive, repetitive
transference patterns in individual members. For while the myth
directed everybody's attention to the father's desertion, it left

unrecognized and unexplored the mother's intrusive and controlling relationship with her daughter (which later became a central focus in the family therapy). At the same time, the myth painted a distorted picture of the members' involvement with one another: while it scapegoated the absent father, it whitewashed all other members.

Second, to the extent that this myth could be "sold" to outsiders, including family therapists, it invited from them a typical "countertransference" response—one that condemned the father and exculpated the other family members. Had such "countertransference" response actually occurred, it would not have been a reaction to the family's transference (be this from individual members or the family as a whole), but rather an unwitting reaction to, as well as acceptance of, the family's collaborative and distorted script of the family drama. As such, it would have proven a stumbling block to family therapy, attributable chiefly to a blind spot in the family therapist's perceptiveness and objectivity.

In short, transferences in families are not quick to develop. As relational patterns, they appear locked up within the family system and pressed into the distorting straitjacket of myths, which prevent them from being pried loose and experienced and recognized as transferences. This contrasts with the easily mobilized transferences found in many neurotic patients, described by Ferenczi (7) and many others, and in the earlier-mentioned ad hoc groups. Consequently, also, the term countertransference must take on a new meaning in family therapy.

COUNTERTRANSFERENCE AS A DEVIATION
FROM "INVOLVED IMPARTIALITY"

To grasp this new meaning, we must keep in mind that for the family therapist the primary issue is not so much one of reacting inappropriately to the family members' transference as it is of dealing with their defenses—particularly myths—which hide and

distort, to the family members and to the therapist, these
members' deeper, formative, and transference-generating relations.

This implies that the family therapist must move into the family
system, but not with a hammer, as it were. Rather, he should do
this in ways which are consonant with an increasing build-up of
trust with *all* family members. He must involve himself
meaningfully and empathically with each one of them, yet in so
doing he must remain fair to all. This does not mean he must be
obsessed with whether he gives each member exactly the same
amount of attention, but that he, in the long run, makes each
member feel understood and appreciated.

I. Boszormenyi-Nagy (3) spoke of the family therapist's multidirectional partiality—a partiality afforded individual members,
yet one that goes out in all directions. I would like to speak of the
therapist's *involved impartiality*, thereby emphasizing the therapist's
basic fairness, maintained under conditions of increasing involvement with each member. While he tries to gain each member's
trust, the therapist explores and thereby punctures the family
myths. This allows him and the members to reassess basic family
dynamics and to evaluate ever more fairly each member's rights,
obligations, and accountability. In this process, the family
therapist must be active, as Wynne (30), Boszormenyi-Nagy and
Spark (4), and others have pointed out; but his activity is less a
matter of his style (silent therapists can sometimes be more
effectively active than many talkative ones) than of his concern
and dynamic involvement. Yet, while active, he must always let
himself be guided by what the family presents as its problem; that
is, he must not be ahead of the family and must not let his
interventions or interpretations be dictated by what *he* thinks the
family's problem is.

To the extent that trust develops, transferences are pried loose
from within the family and the therapist becomes their likely
recipient. Once this happens, classical views and formulations as
to the development of transference-countertransference reac-

tions become more applicable. We observe how parents increasingly relate to the therapist as they related to their own parents, while their children bring to bear on him those relational patterns which originated in *their* parent relationships. As he turns increasingly into a target for individual transferences, the therapist tries to provide each member with a corrective emotional experience, even though he might often not be able to deal exhaustively with the transference reactions he elicits. At the same time, it becomes often more difficult, but also more important, that he maintain his overall attitude of involved impartiality.

Boszormenyi-Nagy (3) has described how the therapist is often "parentified" by parents who, until then, tended to parentify their children. By letting himself become parentified in their stead—i.e., by offering himself as an object for those longings, repair needs, retaliatory impulses, etc., which originated in regard to the parents' own parents but until now had been displaced onto their adolescent children—the therapist often has a striking, immediate liberating impact on the latter: they stop being "problem" adolescents, get more easily and constructively involved with peers, and in the family sessions become more helpful, thoughtful, and communicative.

Thus, I define countertransference in families operationally as any deviation from a therapeutic position of involved impartiality, as outlined above.

PHASES IN THE DEVELOPMENT OF FAMILY
TRANSFERENCE AND COUNTERTRANSFERENCE

Such deviation reflects always the phase of the therapeutic process, and derives its specific meaning chiefly from what transpires in *two phases:* a first phase during which the therapist, by building and using trust, penetrates the distorting straitjacket of family myths, thereby shaking up the family homeostasis and prying loose the members' transferences (mainly parent-derived

and parentifying); and a second phase during which he increasingly becomes a target for such "unhooked" transferences, to which
he then reacts.

These two phases represent ideal types rather than lawfully
unfolding phenomena. Certain families—mainly those which are
amorphous and fragmented—appear highly transference-prone
from the beginning, whereas other families seem so tightly locked
up within themselves that they resist to the end any meaningful
"unhooking" of individual transferences. Ordinarily, though, the
two phases can be clearly observed.

During each phase, the therapist's "countertransference" might
be a response to taxing treatment challenges and then serve
primarily as a source of information about the family or some
member, or it might primarily reflect certain defenses, personality
traits, growth lacunae, or blind spots in himself which interfere
with his therapeutic task and require corrective action.

"Overactive" or "passive" therapists, for example, may reveal
different "countertransference" problems during the two phases.
Thus, an overactive therapist during the first phase might become
a manipulative interventionist who "shakes up" the family, but
fails to build trust; whereas the more passive—frequently
psychoanalytically trained—therapist may miss his chance to
move dynamically into the family.

During the second phase, the overactive and passive therapists
may fail in different ways to serve as receptive targets for
unhooked individual transference reactions—the overactive
therapist by dispensing cheap consolation or advice, the passive
therapist by remaining detached and remote.

SPECIFIC "COUNTERTRANSFERENCE" PROBLEMS IN THE TREATMENT OF FAMILIES WITH ADOLESCENTS

Adolescents, with their specific strengths, weaknesses, and
problems, introduce a further complexity into an already complex

treatment situation. Most important from the vantage point here adopted is the centrifugal momentum of adolescence—the tendency of adolescents to move out of the family field and thereby upset the family homeostasis. This implies, among other things, multileveled conflicts of missions and loyalties which I have described elsewhere (24, and, with Ravenscroft, 25). It is, above all, conflicts of loyalties which tend to elicit characteristic "countertransference" responses from family therapists—that is, tempt them to deviate from a position of "involved impartiality." Instead of maintaining such a position, they side with one party against the other—with parent against child, child against parent, or one generation against the other—thereby deepening the members' loyalty conflicts and problems.

Let us, then, consider more closely how such countertransference, revealed in a taking of sides by the therapist, might show up in the family therapy with adolescents.

THE THERAPIST SIDING WITH THE "SICK" VICTIMIZED ADOLESCENT

Such siding seems often irresistible when a perceptive family therapist realizes how certain parents "dump" their own "sickness" and disturbance on their adolescent offspring via projective identification. In so doing, these parents define the latter to himself as sick, depressed, anxious, etc., whereas they consider themselves healthy and reasonable. This process I have elsewhere defined as delegating in the service of the parents' self-observation and conscience (with Ravenscroft, 25). When such a family comes to see a psychiatrist, a showdown situation has usually developed. At this juncture in the family's life, an adolescent offspring is expected to deliver the living proof of being *the* sick family member by acquiescing to patient status or even to hospitalization. Particularly, certain mothers of schizophrenic patients, as described by L. Hill (15), T. Lidz et al. (18), and others, have gained a reputation as devastating victimizers of their adolescent children. Hence the concept, highly charged and problematical, of the "schizophrenogenic mother" who disowns and projects onto her captive child her own anxiety, depression, confusion, or badness.

Instead of overtly or covertly taking sides with the victim against his parental victimizer—this constituting a countertransference reaction according to the above operational definition—the therapist must now maintain his involved impartiality in ways which also do justice to the victimizing parent. To do so, he needs to realize the immense power the willing "victim" frequently wields over his parent. Boszormenyi-Nagy (3), and, with Spark (4), has well described this process. He pointed out that this willing victim is in a strategic position to operate the guilt lever over his parents by delivering himself to them as the living proof of their failure or badness as parents. The therapist who consciously or unconsciously sides with this victim against his parents stirs their guilt ever more deeply, for he now supports with his medical authority the patient's masochistic power ploy. A parent can usually discharge this increased guilt only by assuming an even harsher punitive and blaming—that is, victimizing—stance vis-à-vis the adolescent who, his own unconscious guilt rising, will be driven further to live up to his parents' victimization of him, thereby locking him and them ever more tightly in a "spiral of negative mutuality" (23, and see Chapter 8).

Such siding with the adolescent victim may derive from an unrecognized and unworked-through separation problem of the therapist. Unwittingly, he might need to make the patient's parents feel bad for things which his (the therapist's) own parents did to him. Also, he might—again unconsciously—revel in the role of rescuer of mistreated victims, and in this role discharge righteous (though misplaced) indignation against the victim's oppressors. Such combination of rescue drive and righteous indignation may for a while "vitalize" his overall therapeutic work, but in the end it will bring about its ruin.

THE THERAPIST SIDING WITH THE "REBELLIOUS" ADOLESCENT

Overtly, this rebellious adolescent—i.e., one who curses his parents, does not follow orders, stays out late, dresses and acts like a bum, etc.—may seem to wage a battle for independence in which he asks his therapist's support. Covertly, though, he usually hangs on to immature forms of dependence and conforms to his parents' (conflictual and ambiguous) expectations. Not infrequently he enacts—again via projective identification—his parent's disowned rebellious impulses as their loyal delegate (see Johnson and Szurek, 16, and Stierlin, 24). Whatever the major motivational dynamics, the therapist is usually ill advised to serve as spokesman for this "rebellion." This becomes more evident when such "rebellion" is acted out in sexual promiscuity, dangerous motorcycling, or drug use. A therapist, in secret alliance with an adolescent "rebel," may empathically share his exposure to contradictory messages and loss of needed identity support structures, but usually is unable to help him—unless he dissolves the alliance and returns to an involved impartiality.

The motivational dynamics in the therapist can vary here; yet usually they point to his own unresolved problems of adolescent individuation and separation. In particular, this seems to hold true for certain young therapists who appear still close to, if not stuck in, their own late adolescence. Through their dress and manner of speech they manifest their identification with the protesting younger generation. Having not yet achieved a more mature dependence (or independence, if you wish) in relation to their own parents, they recruit their patients to unwittingly and vicariously continue their own "rebellious" struggle.

THE THERAPIST SIDING WITH THE VICTIMIZED PARENT

Siding with the victimized parent differs from empathic appreciation of the plight of the victimized victimizer, described

above, and represents a "countertransference pattern." The siding
therapist overidentifies—again without being aware of it—with
the "poor, well-meaning, decent" parent whom the "spoiled,
obstreperous" adolescent has pushed into a corner. He unwittingly shares sentiments, articulated and exploited by conservative
spokesmen, of toughness and "law and order" in dealing with the
"Spock-marked" generation. In siding with the victimized parent,
he may encourage the latter to punish drastically or reject the
adolescent, rationalizing such a stance as "firmness" or "setting of
limits." But rather than helping the parents to stand firm, he only
supports the rejecting, hostile side in their ambivalence, thereby
courting disaster; for the more the parents reject and punish, the
more they also alienate their adolescent. Consuming themselves
with guilt, the parents often waver between strictness and
permissiveness. At the same time, they make themselves more
vulnerable to their adolescent victim's masochistic power ploys, as
earlier described. And again the result is a "negative mutuality,"
which blocks the process of individuation-separation for parents
and adolescent offspring.

Therapists who unwittingly side with parents tend in my
experience to be older than therapists who side with adolescents.
Often they have adolescent children with whom they unsuccess-
fully struggle. At closer inspection, they, too, appear burdened
with problems that often date back to their own adolescence. As a
rule, this adolescence seems to have been difficult and deprived.
We may discover that their own parents treated them then in the
same manner in which they, as parents, now treat *their* adolescent
children. They cannot help taking their children—as well as their
adolescent patients—to task for what *their* parents once did to
them.

UNWITTING COMPETITIVE DISPLACEMENT OF PARENTS

Here the therapist installs himself unwittingly as a more
effective parent than the adolescent's actual parents. Typically, he

is unaware of how this affects the displaced parent. A recent study of a group at the Family Studies Section of the Adult Psychiatry Branch, National Institute of Mental Health with which I was associated illuminated this problem (see Levi, Stierlin, and Savard, 17). In follow-up interviews of previously treated families, we found that a number of fathers, during and after family therapy, appeared to have become more depressed and less effective as parents. These fathers, we came to realize, had for some time been suffering from chronic, insidious depression, deriving largely from their unresolved mid-life crises. Wrapped up in their depression, they had subjected themselves to incessant harsh self-assessment which found them wanting as fathers, professionals, and providers. When this happened, they withdrew emotionally from their adolescent sons. Instead of engaging them in a "loving fight," urgently needed for the delineation of the sons' budding male identities, they left them stranded in a relational vacuum. From this vacuum the sons would then turn to their mother's emotional orbit, frequently becoming spoiled and infantilized in the process. Without the counteracting force of a father *against* whom they could bump and *with* whom they could identify, their oedipal problems intensified.

These fathers could not help comparing themselves to their younger, more energetic, and more effective male therapists. But rather than identifying with these therapists and learning their parenting skills and effectiveness, they experienced further proof of their own failure and unworthiness.

In reappraising this outcome, we realized that the therapists had here also deviated from a position of involved impartiality and thus had engaged in characteristic "countertransference." This time, however, it was less a matter of taking sides with some family member (or members) against another member than of not sufficiently and tactfully appreciating the side of one member— the father. In brief, the therapists were insufficiently tuned to the emotional dynamics and plights of these middle-aged fathers.[2]

Closer inspection points also here to recurrent unresolved

"adolescent" problems of therapists. These therapists tend to displace parents, while unwittingly they reenact an earlier competitive and/or oedipal struggle. Typically, they need to take charge in a sometimes unreflective and even controlling way. While activity by family therapists is crucial, as indicated earlier, such taking charge is often detrimental to the parent and the progress of therapy, because it amounts to a humiliating oedipal dethronement of a parent by a younger, more successful rival.

The family background of one young family therapist seemed here illuminating. The oldest of several children and his mother's favorite son, he had from an early age taken over much of his father's role in controlling the younger children and supervising the large household. Professionally he had become more successful than his father, who had held lowly positions throughout his life. Thus, this very gifted and hard-driving therapist won a striking oedipal triumph over his father. However, this triumph remained shallow in at least some respects. As a family therapist, he could not help—albeit compulsively and unwittingly—competing with, and winning out over, any new father who came into sight. This "countertransference" problem, which also affected his non-therapeutic relationships, made a later personal analysis advisable.

Analogous to the above is the compulsive need of certain female therapists to be a more effective (more nurturant, giving and loving) mother than is the adolescent's actual mother. Competition with this mother may here also reinforce the wish to rescue the victimized adolescent—an endeavor likely to fail for the reasons already given.

SOME CONCLUSIONS

I have tried to show that the therapist's countertransference in families takes on a meaning different from that it has in individual analysis and group therapy. Above everything, the family therapist must be able to practice an "involved impartiality," and countertransference in families can be defined operationally as a deviation from such therapeutic position. When we look more closely at the dynamics of such deviation, we often find, as we do in other countertransference contexts, that information-providing and stumbling-block aspects interweave. Where the latter dominate, we are alerted to "growth lacunae" and "blind spots" in the therapist. These often reflect difficulties the therapist had or still has in growing up and separating from his own family, and frequently date back to his own adolescence.

Freud recommended the didactic (or training) analysis of the psychoanalyst as the best—and perhaps only—method to eliminate his blind spots. From the vantage point adopted in this chapter, a similar didactic (and therapeutic) family therapy would be indicated for the therapist of families. Such "training family therapy" is now, at least in some quarters, being recommended for the younger generation of family therapists, while other family therapists still consider it impractical or outright impossible.

I believe an individual therapeutic or training analysis can substitute for such desirable family therapy—at least to some extent. (After all, an individual psychoanalysis brings us into touch with our formative family relations—albeit now shaped by the nature and vicissitudes of the psychoanalytic transference.) Apart from such individual analysis for the family therapist, co-therapy with, and observation by, colleagues can help us to increase our awareness of our growth lacunae, blind spots, and resulting countertransference reactions. And there is, finally, our experience with our own families—our family of origin as well as our family of procreation—which may provide us with vital insights and opportunities for growth that eventually serve to counteract, if not eliminate, undesirable countertransference processes.

Notes

[1] Closer inspection reveals that transferences originate in different, though related, families. For example, the presenting parents had their formative, transference-generating relationships as children to their parents; and now their children, whose relational patterns the presenting parents fatefully shaped (and still shape), will in turn have an impact on their own children, etc. Given such a multigenerational perspective, so-called "parentifications" can be viewed as transferences within families or as *trans-generational transferences:* parents "transfer" to their children those expectations, unfulfilled longings, needs for nutriment, wishes for revenge, etc., which derived form their own child-parent interactions.

[2] This raises the question of how well any family therapist not yet middle-aged can empathize with such middle-aged parents. Martin Buber, during his last stay in Washington, is said to have stated: "No one under the age of 45 should be a therapist" (Weigert, 28). This might be even more true for family therapists.

References

1. Argelander, H. Gruppenprozesse/Wege zur Anwendung der Psychoanalyse. In *Behandlung, Lehre und Forschung.* Reinbeck: Rowohlt, 1972.

2. Bion, W. *Experiences in groups.* London: Tavistock, 1961.

3. Boszormenyi-Nagy, I. Loyalty implications of the transference model in psychotherapy. *Archives of General Psychiatry* 27: 374-380, 1972.

4. Boszormenyi-Nagy, I., and Spark, G. *Invisible loyalties.* New York: Hoeber & Harper, 1973.

5. Cohen, M. B. Countertransference and anxiety. *Psychiatry* 15: 231-243, 1952.

6. Ezriel, H. A psycho-analytic approach to group treatment. *British Journal of Medical Psychology* 23: 59-74, 1950.

7. Ferenczi, S. Introjection and transference (1909). In *Sex in psychoanalysis.* Boston: Gorham Press, 1916.

8. Ferreira, A. Family myths and homeostasis. *Achives of General Psychiatry* 9:457-463, 1963.

9. Freud, S. The future prospects of psycho-analytic therapy (1910). *SE* XI, 139-151. London: Hogarth Press, 1957.

10. ———. Studies on Hysteria (1895). *SE* II, 43-365. London: Hogarth Press, 1955.

11. ———. Fragment of an analysis of a case of hysteria (1905). *SE* VII, 3-122. London: Hogarth Press, 1953.
12. ———. Group psychology and the analysis of the ego (1921). *SE* XVIII, 67-143. London: Hogarth Press, 1955.
13. Fromm-Reichmann, F. *Principles of intensive psychotherapy.* Chicago: University of Chicago Press, 1950.
14. Grotjahn, M. Special aspects of countertransference in analytic group psychotherapy. *International Journal of Group Psychotherapy* 3: 407-416, 1953.
15. Hill, L. *Psychotherapeutic intervention in schizophrenia.* Chicago: University of Chicago Press, 1955.
16. Johnson, A., and Szurek, S. A. The genesis of antisocial acting out in children and adults. *Psychoanalytic Quarterly* 21: 323-343, 1952.
17. Levi, L. D., Stierlin, H., and Savard, R. J. Fathers and sons: the interlocking crises of integrity and identity. *Psychiatry* 35: 48-56, 1972.
18. Lidz, T., Cornelison, A. R., Singer, M. T., Schafer, S., and Fleck, S. The mothers of schizophrenic patients. In *Schizophrenia and the family,* ed. T. Lidz, S. Fleck, and A. R. Cornelison. New York: International Universities Press, 1965.
19. Rice, A. K. Individual, group and intergroup processes. *Human Relations* 22: 565-584, 1969.
20. Rioch, M. "All we like sheep—" (Isaiah 53:6): followers and leaders. *Psychiatry* 34: 258-273, 1971.
21. Searles, H. *Collected papers on schizophrenia and related subjects.* New York: International Universities Press, 1959.
22. Shapiro, R., and Zinner, J. Family organization and adolescent development. In *Task and organization,* ed. E. Miller. London: Tavistock Publications, 1970.
23. Stierlin, H. *Conflict and reconciliation.* New York: Doubleday Anchor and Jason Aronson, 1969.
24. ———. Family dynamics and separation patterns of potential schizophrenics. In *Proceedings of the Fourth International Symposium on Psychotherapy of Schizophrenia,* ed. Y. Alanen and D. Rubinstein. Amsterdam: Excerpta Medica, 1972, pp. 156-166.
25. Stierlin, H., and Ravenscroft, K. Varieties of adolescent "separation conflicts." *British Journal of Medical Psychology* 45: 299-313, 1972.

26. Turquet, P. Bion's theory of small groups. Lectures presented at the National Institute of Mental Health, Bethesda, Maryland, June 8, 9, 1965.
27. ———. Four lectures: The Bion hypothesis: the work group and the basic assumption group. Presented at the National Institute of Mental Health, Bethesda, Maryland, May 26, 28, June 2, 6, 1971.
28. Weigert, E. Personal communication. 1973.
29. Winnicott, D. W. Hate in the countertransference (1949). *Collected Papers*. New York: Basic Books, 1958.
30. Wynne, L. C. Some indications and contraindications for exploratory family therapy. In *Intensive family therapy: theoretical and practical aspects*, ed. I. Boszormenyi-Nagy and J. L. Framo. New York: Hoeber, 1965.

Chapter 15

Toward a Multigenerational Therapy

We find in family therapy a new paradigm insofar as the locus for therapeutic intervention is the supra-individual system rather than the individual patient. Yet from its inception, modern family therapy was hard pressed to reconcile a systems approach with one that would do justice to individual members. There were, and still are, family therapists who decry those others—some of them psychoanalysts—who "merely treat individuals in a family context," rather than being strictly systems oriented. But, in the actual practice of family therapy, it was difficult, if not impossible, to disregard individual members who had their own wishes and needs, who had benefited or suffered from the actions of other members, who blamed or absorbed blame, who felt guilty or made others feel guilty, and whose interests clashed or agreed.

The family model, as here presented, introduces a systems perspective, but also takes account of (past and present) individual actions, obligations, rights, and needs. Therefore, it demands from the therapist an attitude of, in the words of I. Boszormenyi-Nagy, *"multidirectional partiality"* (1, 2) or, as I called it earlier, "involved impartiality". Both terms denote that the family therapist must be involved with the family system, while, at the same time, remain fair and attentive to all members. All my following considerations of treatment reflect this dual orientation.

THERAPY AS UNBINDING

The family model, as here presented, suggests differing therapeutic approaches depending on whether we deal primarily with binding, delegating, or expelling families. For brevity's sake, I shall here distinguish between, on the one side, binding and delegating and, on the other, expelling ones. Only the former types of families fit (more or less) a homeostasis model.

So far, most treatment efforts have been geared to these families because, in general, it is easier to recruit, treat, and study families which are homeostatically enmeshed than those which are broken or adrift. In line with our greater experience with homeostatic families, I shall, in the following, chiefly consider their treatment and only touch on the treatment of undercohesive and fragmented families.

Essentially, in treating homeostatic families, we aim at unbinding them—i.e., we try to promote each member's (and thereby the whole family's) individuation, differentiation, and relative autonomy. At the same time, we try to explore each member's rights and obligations, as well as his "ledger of merits" (2) in the family system.

Unbinding, in the meaning here intended, implies *demystification, belated mourning, balancing of accounts,* and *reconciliation across generations.* Let us consider each of these aspects in turn.

Demystification. Mystification, we saw in Chapter 10, involves attribution (of negative traits which denote either "weakness" or "badness"), invalidation, and induction. Demystification, accordingly, implies that the therapist must counter such attributions, invalidations, and inductions. To counter damaging attributions (calling a person weak or sick) the therapist must make sure that each member learns to speak for his own feelings, needs, and interests. For example, a mother who constantly says, "Louise [her adolescent daughter] is always so depressed," "Louise is afraid of boy friends," "Louise hates her teachers," etc., must learn that Louise can be spokesman for her own feelings, experiences, and interests. At the same time, this mother must learn to be a spokesman for herself and hence must learn to communicate: "I feel depressed," "I need to be alone," "I am annoyed when Louise wears dirty blue jeans," or even, "I need Louise as a buffer between me and my husband." V. Satir (7), above others, has described such demystification.

To counter invalidations, the therapist often has to validate— i.e., explore and possibly support and declare legitimate—statements of a child or patient which a parent or doctor (the possessor of the "stronger reality") invalidated.

To counter inductions, the therapist has to explore the inductee's compliance with the stronger person's definition of his (the inductee's) psychological reality. Here the therapist must focus on how the "willing victim" actively contributes to mystification and homeostasis. To this end the therapist must understand the power the victim derives from his "weakness, badness, or suffering." I. Boszormenyi-Nagy has well described this situation. In letting himself be mystified, and in living up to his parent's negative attributions, the victim delivers himself as the living proof for his parents' badness and failure as parents—even though he wrecks his life in the process. Thus, he is strategically placed to operate the guilt lever. If his parents, for a change, make demands that could promote his autonomy but also cause him anxiety (e.g., ask him to move out of the house), he can make "inoperative" these parental expectations by presenting himself as too sick, inept, anxious, nervous, etc., to comply with them. Many schizophrenic patients are adept at this ploy, which reinforces the homeostasis. To counter this, the therapist must empathize with the victimized (binding or delegating) victimizers no less than with the bound or delegated victim, and must interpret how this victim uses his "sickness" to devastate his parents.

Belated mourning. Demystification alone usually does not suffice to unbind a tight family homeostasis. Unbinding, then, must include a belated mourning process. Since Freud's seminal paper on "Mourning and Melancholia" (4), we know that losses of all kinds—e.g., losses of beloved persons, of ambitions, of ideals, of skills and physical assets—need to be mourned in order that growth and psychological separation (from the lost person or object) can ensue. Yet a person can deny the loss and thwart the mourning process by, for example, becoming overly busy, by developing somatic symptoms, or by getting stuck in a pathological depression. Then we speak of aborted or pathological mourning. A family homeostasis reflects, as well as sustains, such aborted or pathological mourning, as all family members, glued to each other in "intersubjective fusion," prevent those separating moves which would cause them to truly experience and grieve their losses. Hence, the therapist's task is to facilitate belated mourning in families. N. Paul (6), above others, has spelled out this task. Referring to their "operant mourning," he showed families gripped by painful but liberating grief after years of collusive denial. After such grief experience, family members related to each other more warmly and affectionately, but also more forcefully than seemed possible before. Mourning, clearly, allowed the members to differentiate themselves from one another, to become more autonomous, and hence to loosen the homeostasis.

However, such mourning often becomes difficult in actual family practice due to certain features of the binding and delegating modes. For parents who bind and delegate their children ordinarily manage to avoid the very mourning process which they, the parents, should have experienced while they related to, and tried to separate from, *their* parents. For example, one father, a lowly and frustrated government employee, had delegated his son to become the successful scientist he himself had failed to become. The son, overtaxed and despairing, floundered as such a delegate and dropped out of school. Yet even in his failure— or because of it—he allowed his father to abort and delay overdue mourning processes. For while this father remained preoccupied with his good-for-nothing, dropout son, he continued to hold an idealized, unblemished image of his own father as a humanitarian and educator. Never throughout his life had he doubted this idealized image, which began to collapse only during family therapy. When this happened, his seemingly superachieving father turned out to have been, among other things, a cheating and, on the whole, mediocre student. This loss of his idealized father image caused the father deep grief, making him look pained and haggard. Yet, while this happened, he also began to relate differently—more warmly and empathically—to his son and realized how he had exploited the latter in order to remain faithful to his idealized father. Only after he had thus accepted and worked through this loss could he begin to understand his son in his own right. And the son, less needed as his father's delegate and more appreciated as a person with his own needs and interests, could now, on his part, empathize more freely with this father and his plight. Thus, "unbinding" of the homeostasis triggered, as well as reflected, a "positive (i.e., liberating) mutuality" of two generations.

Balancing of accounts. Mourning, in the above example, could become an unbinding force only after some "accounts" had been set straight. Initially, the father here held his son accountable for what *his* father had (or had not) done to him—for the failure to serve as a father and model whom he (now a parent himself) could respect and love without distorting idealization. In order to redress such displaced and hence exploitative accounting, we must explore what I. Boszormenyi-Nagy (1, 2) has called the "balance of accounts," or "ledger of merits," in families. Such "ledger of merits," according to this author, is regularly, though often invisibly, kept. Each member of a family, this means, keeps a ledger of what the others have and have not done to him, and vice versa. For example, a daughter might never forget that her mother betrayed her at a crucial juncture in her life by disavowing, in the presence of the father, her complicity in this daughter's clandestine affair that led to a pregnancy. The daughter might never mention this fact and might even repress it; it will nonetheless become a potent motivational force throughout her life.

However, invisible loyalties may also disrupt the very book-keeping process which, on another level, they foster. A grown-up child who remains loyalty-bound to his parents may therefore hold his spouse accountable for his parents' unfair and neglectful treatment of him. While he avoids blaming his idealized parents, he castigates his spouse relentlessly and hypercritically. Thus, his accounting becomes skewed. A parent may also—in a similarly skewed manner—hold his child accountable for what *his* parents did or did not do to him, as the earlier example showed. In trying to set such accounts straight, a family therapist must therefore adopt a trans-generational perspective.

Reconciliation. To set the account straight, we saw, requires at least three generations. This, then, raises the question whether these three generations should or could participate in joint family therapy, as this was originally proposed by Mendell and Fisher (5). My answer is "yes." Naturally, many living parents of parents cannot attend such family meetings. They may be too feeble, live too far away, or appear too set in their ways to stomach a charged encounter with their children and grandchildren. However, thanks mainly to my contacts with I. Boszormenyi-Nagy, I have increasingly come to practice and advocate a three-generational approach. For, contrary to what common sense or compassion with the elderly may tell us, many of these parents' parents, frequently feeling burdened and alienated from their children, and approaching death, welcome the opportunity to set the account straight.

Often, though, one's parents' parents are no longer alive or are unavailable for joint meetings. In these cases, such parents' parents must come alive through the memories of the living—not as targets for blame and hate but as persons who, whatever their shortcomings or destructive actions, need to be understood and, hopefully, forgiven. What this involves has been well described by I. Boszormenyi-Nagy and G. Spark (2).

BINDING THOSE WHO ARE
WITHOUT BONDS

So far I have talked about the unbinding of (more or less) homeostatically deadlocked families. These, however, we found to be not the only families who have serious difficulties. There are also many families where the expelling mode prevails—i.e., where children, rather than being excessively bound and/or delegated, are neglected, abandoned, and pushed into premature autonomy. And these children, as well as their parents, appear no less in need of help than those subjected primarily to the binding or delegating modes. Elsewhere (8) I have described these children as "wayward" which, according to Webster's Dictionary, derives from the word "awayward," meaning "turned away," and suggests expulsion as well as escape. The person turned away becomes self-willed, wanton, and prone to follow his or her own caprices. Many such wayward persons are labeled sociopaths. Unburdened by loyalties and seemingly immune to shame and guilt, they appear able to manipulate, cheat, rob, and maybe even kill without qualms. Recently the anthropologist Colin Turnbull described a society of seemingly wayward people called the Ik (9). Several years ago the Ik roamed the borders of Uganda, Kenya, and the Sudan as hunters, yet when a large game preserve was created, they were resettled and forced to give up their hunting and nomadic ways. Uprooted, their social organization shattered, their skills made useless, and threatened by starvation, they turned (to all appearances) wayward: *Homo* became *homini lupus*. Family bonds seemed to dissolve, and only the expelling mode appeared to prevail. Turnbull compares the Ik to the inhabitants of modern shanty towns and ghettos who lost their family and social cohesion. But, if my experience and books such as U. Bronfenbrenner's *Two Worlds of Childhood* (3) are any guide, wayward youths emerge increasingly also from the "wastelands" of America's middle-class suburbia.

How should we treat these wayward children and their parents? Clearly, before we can unbind them, we must bind them—i.e., instill in them that sense of belonging and being loved which should be every child's birthright. Yet such primary binding seems even more difficult a therapeutic task than unbinding.

APPLICATION OF THEORY: "THE SUTTONS"

To illuminate the above theoretical model, I shall now describe a family whom I shall call the Suttons. The Suttons were a homeostatically enmeshed family in which the binding and delegating modes were strong. Hence, the family therapy had to aim at unbinding. Rather than trying to be comprehensive, I shall focus on a few of those aspects in the Suttons' family relations which cast into relief the concepts described above.

The Suttons consisted of Mr. and Mrs. Sutton, both in their forties, and their sons Dennis and Walter, aged 24 and 20, respectively.

My contact with this family began when Mrs. Sutton called me one evening to tell me she had been referred to me by another psychiatrist. This psychiatrist, I learned, had treated her older son

Dennis for approximately one year in a nearby psychiatric hospital. Now Dennis was about to be discharged. His psychiatrist had recommended couple or family therapy. She asked therefore whether I could see her together with her husband, and I arranged for a joint interview a few days later.

Mrs. Sutton turned out to be a dark-haired beauty, lively, expressive, and wearing a sweater at least one size too small. Her husband, a vice-president of a small local bank, was personable, yet apprehensive and depressed. When I asked them to tell me about their problems and family situation, they immediately began to argue and shout. As the fight got underway, I realized I was witnessing a scene which, with minor variations, must have occurred innumerable times. Mr. Sutton accused his wife of spoiling Dennis. Just over the last weekend, he explained, when Dennis visited from the hospital, she had given him an expensive stereo set. And, he went on to complain, while she showered Dennis with presents, she neglected and deprived him, her husband. That was her pattern. Mrs. Sutton, in turn, called her husband a demanding, dependent, never-satisfied child. She said that he had no friends, only business associates, and that all his emotional supplies had to come from her. She added that her husband, in his clinging petulance, was poisoning her relationship with Dennis and that she could not stand this any longer.

The above interchange, here greatly condensed, suggested that Mr. and Mrs. Sutton were deadlocked in a homeostatic configuration of pseudo-hostility. While intensely boundup with one another, they seemed capable of expressing only angry, hostile, and sadistic feelings. I learned later that, despite repeated efforts, they had never been able to break the homeostatic deadlock. For example, a number of years ago (I was told) Mr. Sutton had suddenly exploded in frustration, packed his bags, and taken off to a midwestern metropolis. He had then told his wife that this was the end of their relationship, that he would make a new professional start, and that he would search for and find more rewarding female company than hers. However, after ten days of dismal loneliness—spent in bars and movie theaters, without professional initiative or female company—he was back home and back in the old pseudo-hostile rut.

To a large extent, the Suttons' marital arguments centered on Dennis, and, to understand better their and the whole family's plight, we must now turn briefly to him.

Dennis, a lanky, handsome youth, had always been shy. As an adolescent, he had preferred to ensconce himself in his room with his piano and records rather than become "one of the crowd." By the crowd he meant his peers, who found him increasingly difficult to deal with—too sensitive, too easily hurt, aloof, and perhaps grandiose in his ambitions. Yet while he had managed to maintain at least marginal contacts with male friends, he had shunned girls almost totally. He used to admire them from a distance as exotic and exciting but also dangerous creatures who wielded enormous power over men, particularly men who made inept sexual advances. Not surprisingly, he fell in love only with one or two movie heroines, whose celluloid images haunted him while he, ashamed, masturbated in his bed.

Yet while his world of real peers and girl friends had become ephemeral, his relationship to his mother had remained intense. Throughout his childhood and adolescence his mother had hovered over him. When he, as an early adolescent, played the piano, she would sneak in some orange juice and cookies just to let him know she was there and listening, and, in the evenings, while holding his hands, she would tell him she saw him developing into a famous concert pianist, with the world at his feet, and her, his mother, sitting in the front row.

Subsequent events, though, made such maternal dreams seem hollow. For as he grew into late adolescence, Dennis neglected his piano practice and appeared torn by conflicting emotions and wishes. He would suddenly shout at his mother, slam the door, smash a present she had given him, and then embrace her frantically. Such outbursts became more and more frequent until he finally (approximately a year before my contact with the Suttons) attempted suicide and was hospitalized.

The above background information, albeit limited, reveals a lack of differentiation (and hence violation of boundaries) between Mrs. Sutton and Dennis. In important respects, Mrs. Sutton related to Dennis as if he were her adult confidant and partner. The intimacy between mother and son, charged with erotic undercurrents, contrasted with Dennis's and Mrs. Sutton's otherwise barren sex lives. (Intercourse between the spouses had come to a stop during the last five years—except in rare situations where, exhausted from fights and loosened up by one or two drinks, they engaged in sex "like animals.")

If we look now at the workings of transactional modes, we notice that Dennis was bound up with his mother on three major levels. He was "id-bound" in the sense that his mother subjected him to constant regressive gratification, of which cookies, orange juice, and expensive gifts formed only a small part. He was "ego-bound" in the sense that he was mystified by her. For she attributed to him an extreme sensitivity and nervous fragility and weakness which caused him to develop the (largely negative) self-image of a vulnerable artist-patient. At the same time she invalidated Dennis's angry outbursts by labeling them signs of nervous imbalance and, finally, in collusion with a psychiatrist, evidence of mental illness. And she induced Dennis to become a willing, self-sacrificing victim, but one—as we shall see shortly—who gained the power to inflict on her severe guilt and pain. This implies, lastly, massive binding on the loyalty level. Dennis sensed here that his mother could not psychologically survive without him, which burdened him with deep breakaway guilt.

Dennis was thus bound, yet he was also delegated. As her delegate, he was to become a world-renowned pianist and thereby realize her own unfulfilled ego-ideal. Yet while she delegated him, she also interfered with the implementation of his mission, which

would have required him to move out of the maternal orbit, train
with good teachers, compete with other pianists, struggle in the
world—i.e., do the very things which her binding stratagems
prevented him from doing.

In sum, mother and son, no less than father and mother, were
caught in a homeostatic deadlock. Whatever Mrs. Sutton and
Dennis tried in order to get away from each other, they seemed to
end more bound up than before. For example, when Dennis moved
tentatively to meet a girl, his anxiety rose; but so did that of his
mother. He feared rebuff and humiliation from the girl; she,
abandonment by Dennis. Thus, centripetal forces between them
quickly won out over centrifugal ones, and Dennis once more
returned to his mother's orbit. Yet while in her orbit he could not
help torturing her in overt and covert ways—he cut her down, was
rude, or annoyed her by just sitting and doing nothing. Thus he
delivered himself as the living proof of her failure and badness as a
parent, increasing *her* despair and guilt. She, in turn, to relieve
such despair and guilt, would further blame him, pressure him,
intrude on him—in brief, would further victimize him by acting as
his binder and delegator. And so the negative homeostatic
mutuality worsened.

Liberating moves. As the Suttons' therapist, my task was to counter
mystification and victimization in the family. However, merely
telling Mrs. Sutton to stop mystifying and victimizing Dennis
would not have been enough. In fact, at this juncture it would
probably have been counterproductive. Consumed by guilt and
self-doubt, she perceived me then as accuser and judge, and
whatever I could have said most likely would have increased her
guilt. Accustomed to discharge such guilt by projection, she would
then have turned into an even fiercer—albeit perhaps more underhanded—victimizer of Dennis. Therefore, I focused on Dennis. I
suggested to him that in being stubbornly passive or crazy he had
the power to make his mother anxious and guilty, for he could

thereby deliver himself as the living proof of her failure or badness as a parent. This might have looked as if I was further accusing and victimizing Dennis, already a victimized patient. In reality, I believe I reassured him—I let him know I was aware of his potential destructiveness and thereby lessened *his* anxiety and guilt over it. For a sense of destructiveness could mushroom in his imagination as long as it remained unacknowledged, uninvestigated, and hence unchecked. (From my individual therapy with schizophrenic patients, I have come to view the handling of a patient's real and imagined aggression and destructiveness as the most difficult, yet also most important, therapeutic task.) At the same time, I allowed him to see and possibly accept a share of the responsibility for the family's plight. Yet also, while focusing on his masochistic power ploys, I lessened his mother's guilt: I avoided singling her out for an attention which she, under the circumstances, would have perceived as blame. This, in turn, lessened her need compulsively to blame and victimize Dennis. As a result, she could then begin to reflect on the nature and sources of her own behavior toward Dennis and to own up to and thus "own" some of the pain and conflicts she had so far disowned by binding and/or delegating Dennis. Such "owning" became central to this whole family's unbinding. It implied a family-wide demystification and made Mr. and Mrs. Sutton into more assertive and effective parents. In order to trace important moves here, we return once more to Mrs. Sutton.

Mrs. Sutton: overt giver and covert demander. The subsequent therapy sessions showed that Mrs. Sutton's binding and delegating of Dennis fitted into a basic role which permeated her dealings with all family members and even outsiders. That was the role of the overt giver and covert demander.

Her overt role as generous giver was visible to all and shaped her conscious image of herself. In accordance with it, she showered— or tried to shower—people (most of all Dennis) with gifts, unending attention, and interest. Also, it was consonant with this role that her husband viewed and courted her as an inexhaustible source of nurturant warmth, emotional support, and sexual gratification. And in appearing able—though possibly unwilling—to give all these things, she appeared strong. She therefore seemed destined to keep the unsteady family boat afloat while everybody else faltered (i.e., became sick, agitated, or clingingly dependent).

However, as the therapy progressed, her role as the strong giver showed flaws. For it became evident that she, in giving, shunned reciprocity. She could not tolerate being given to; if others were giving her gifts or doing her favors, she always had to outgive or outdo them. Similarly, she could be strong only by keeping others dependent and weak. Thus, she helped to cement a homeostasis of rigidly fixed but complementary family roles, as earlier described.

In being the strong and seemingly inexhaustible giver, she also acted as covert demander. And Dennis, the target of her most lavish and devoted giving, inevitably became also that of her strongest (though covert) demands. For example, she demanded: that he fill the emotional—and even erotic—void left by her husband; that he, as her loyal delegate, realize her unrealized ego-ideal and become a renowned pianist; that he embody (and thus keep at a safe working distance from her ego) the frailty and helpless dependence she had to disown; and that he (contrary to what even the above mission would have required) jeopardize his growth and separation and remain forever captive to, and bound up with, her. In living up to these demands, Dennis turned victim; but in this very process, we saw, he gained the leverage to devastate his mother.

Mrs. Sutton's belated mourning and repair work. How had Mrs. Sutton developed into overt giver and covert demander? The answer to this question—which puzzled me, as well as, increasingly, Mrs. Sutton—pointed to Mrs. Sutton's mother. This mother, Dennis's grandmother, was still alive when the family therapy began. As the therapy progressed, her name came up more frequently, and I began to ponder how she might possibly join our meetings. However, unforeseen events brought such plans to naught. One evening Mrs. Sutton's mother was attacked on the street and thrown to the ground. (She lived in an area with a rather high crime rate and had steadfastly rejected all proposals to move into a safer part of the city.) She suffered multiple fractures which required hospital treatment in an intensive care unit and, after several agonizing weeks, led to her death. But although her injury and death precluded a three-generational therapy with her present, they proved pivotal in reorienting the lives of Mrs. Sutton and the family as a whole.

To grasp what was here involved, we have to realize that Mrs. Sutton's mother, up to the time of the assault and injury, had always seemed undaunted. Also, she had never been ill enough to elicit or warrant nursing care from the others, particularly her children. Therefore, like Mrs. Sutton, she was cast into the role of a powerfully independent lady, and, again like Mrs. Sutton, she was seen as a generous giver. Almost from the first family session on, I heard tales of how she, "this extraordinarily strong and loving person," would never forget to send a birthday gift, and how she, out of deep concern for her children's welfare, solicited their daily telephone reports, dutifully executed by the latter throughout their adult lives. But here also, as in the case of Mrs. Sutton, overt strength and generous giving hid demandingness and the creation of dependency. Through her giving and constant show of strength, she made her daughter (Mrs. Sutton) indebted to her and never gave her a chance to pay back her debts. Accordingly, Mrs. Sutton's mother could no less help binding and delegating her daughter than the latter could help binding and delegating Dennis. There existed an intergenerational chain of binding and delegating involvements.

It was the dramatic and tragic events of the attack on Mrs. Sutton's mother which, more than anything else, cracked this chain. For these events caused the grandmother to become bed-

ridden and helplessly dependent, thereby providing Mrs. Sutton a
final chance to repay her debts. And she eagerly embraced this
chance when, from early morning until night, she tried to make
her mother's last weeks as comfortable as possible. When her
mother finally died, she was desolate over not having been a more
effective comforter and nurse, the more so as her mother's mostly
comatose and unresponsive condition left her in doubt as to how
much she had really helped. Still, for the first time in her life she
had been the giver and her mother the recipient.

Therefore, with her mother's death, she mourned not only the
loss of her as a person but also the loss of further opportunities for
paying off her excessive debts—debts which, she now began to
realize, *faute de mieux* she had tried to pay off to Dennis. For, in
having been prevented from giving to her mother, she "gave,"
inordinately and lavishly, to Dennis—only to bind him tragically,
just as her own mother had bound her.

As the family therapy went on, it aimed at more unbinding
across generations. Thus, it fostered, among other things, a shift
in Mrs. Sutton's major relational focus away from Dennis and
toward her mother. While she mourned and revived and
reappraised her relationship with her mother, Dennis, almost to
his surprise, found himself (relatively) neglected—i.e., less bound
and hence more apt to go his own way. But this, Dennis now
realized, was a mixed blessing. For just as his mother, in
psychologically separating from her parent, had now to "own"
(accept and work through) *her* disowned dependency and
avoidance of age-appropriate challenges, so had he. He now had to
face the fact that he often, too easily and readily, retreated into his
mother's protective orbit rather than face peer competition, the
uncertainties of the job market, or the hazards of heterosexual
relationships. As it turned out, to unbind, and keep unbound,
mother and son was no easy task. Whenever Dennis felt lonely or
discouraged about his progress with peers, girlfriends, or difficult
academic subjects, he tended to alarm his mother with his

floundering or apparent re-emerging craziness, thereby unleash-
ing—or hoping to unleash—the binding maternal juggernaut. And
she, in turn, would anxiously scan Dennis for just such signals
whenever she felt overtaxed by the task of "owning" her so far
disowned feelings, needs, and problems. The family therapy, no
less than an individual therapy or analysis, had to plow the same
ground again and again in order to break up entrenched
homeostatic patterns.

Balancing of accounts. We learned from the above how Mrs. Sutton,
in binding and delegating Dennis, held him accountable for what
her parents, and particularly her mother, had done to her. In order
that accounts could now be balanced, it was necessary that Mrs.
Sutton's mother—in one way or another—become an active factor
in the system of treatment. As it turned out, this came about in a
tragic, unexpected turn of events, which nonetheless helped to
unbind this family. For these events, while triggering appropriate
and belated mourning in Mrs. Sutton, cast into relief some of the
skewed accounting this family had practiced and suffered. And to
the extent that accounts were thus reappraised—and, hopefully,
balanced—Mrs. Sutton, along with her experience of guilt, could
begin to experience some of the hate and frustration toward her
exploitative mother she had disowned, just as Dennis, on his part,
could now more openly experience and "own" such hate of his
mother, rather than channel it into often masochistic power ploys.

Reconciliation. But to feel and express hate and frustration toward
one's binding and delegating parents is not enough. Such feelings
are but elements in the process of unbinding. Finally, reconciliation is needed. And this requires, above all, that bound and
delegated children (grown-ups remain here children to their
parents) try to understand and, out of such understanding, try to
forgive their parents. Thus, Mrs. Sutton had to understand her
mother's exploitative binding of her in the light of the mother's

experience with her own parents (here omitted), just as Dennis
had to understand—and, hopefully, forgive—his mother's exploitation of himself in the light of Mrs. Sutton's experiences with *her*
mother. Thus, reconciliation involves, in the words of I.
Boszormenyi-Nagy (2), "a reconstructive dialogue across the
generations."

CONCLUDING NOTE

For the sake of brevity, I have omitted many aspects of this
family's treatment. For example, how the father's relationship
with his wife and with Dennis, as well as with his other son,
formed part of the binding and delegating modes that accounted
for this family's plight. Also, I have not described how the father's
relationship to his own parents, and particularly to his mother,
contributed to the prevailing homeostasis. However, I would like
at least to mention that this mother entered treatment, thereby
making it, after all, a three-generational venture.

SUMMARY

Family theory represents a new paradigm in which the unit of
treatment is no longer the person but a set of relationships. Many
family disturbances suggest a homeostatic deadlock marked by
restrictive, impoverished, stereotyped, and nearly unbreakable
family ties. Pseudo-mutuality and pseudo-hostility are two
varieties of such deadlock. Disturbed families lack essential
differentiations also, as when boundaries between the generations and genders are insufficiently drawn and members fail to
articulate their needs, wishes, and roles *vis-à-vis* one another.
Mystification reflects and causes such lack of differentiation. The
mystifying person (usually a parent) attributes to another (usually
a child) negative feelings or qualities, invalidates this other's view
of himself, and induces him to comply with the mystifier.

We can define family disturbances as transactional mode disturbances. Transactional modes operate as the covert organizing background to the more overt and specific child-parent interactions. When age-appropriate transactional modes are too intense, out of phase, or inappropriately blended with other modes, the negotiation of a mutual individuation and separation between parent and child is impeded. We can distinguish between the modes of binding, delegating, and expelling. Where the binding mode operates, families are homeostatically deadlocked. This can occur on a dependency level, a cognitive level, or an archaic loyalty level. Where the delegating mode predominates, binding and expelling elements blend. Held on the long leash of loyalty, the delegate carries out parental missions, as when he fulfills his parents' unrealized ego-ideal or enacts their disowned delinquent impulses. Psychological exploitation and guilt are further dynamic forces in families. To deal with them therapeutically, a multi-generational perspective is needed. The process of "unbinding" homeostatically deadlocked families includes demystification, belated mourning, balancing of accounts, and reconciliation across generations.

References

1. Boszormenyi-Nagy, I. Loyalty implications of the transference model in psychotherapy. *Archives of General Psychiatry* 27: 374-380, 1972.
2. Boszormenyi-Nagy, I., and Spark, G. *Invisible loyalties.* New York: Hoeber & Harper, 1973.
3. Bronfenbrenner, U. *Two worlds of childhood: U.S. and U.S.S.R.* New York: Russell Sage Foundation, 1970.
4. Freud, S. Mourning and Melancholia (1917). *SE* XIV, 237-258. London: Hogarth Press, 1957.
5. Mendell, D., and Fisher, S. An approach to neurotic behavior in terms of a three generation family model. *Journal of Nervous and Mental Disorders* 123: 171-180, 1956. Also: D. Mendell and S. Fisher.

PSYCHOANALYSIS AND FAMILY THERAPY

A multi-generation approach to treatment of psychopathology. *Journal of Nervous and Mental Disorders* 126: 523-529, 1958.

6. Paul, N., and Grosser, G. Operational mourning and its role in conjoint family therapy. *Community Mental Health Journal* 1: 339-345, 1965.

7. Satir, V. *Conjoint family therapy: a guide to theory and technique.* Palo Alto: Science and Behavior Books, 1964.

8. *Stierlin, H. Separating parents and adolescents.* New York: Quadrangle, 1974.

9. Turnbull, C. *The mountain people.* New York: Simon & Schuster, 1972.

INDEX

Balint, M., 144, 194, 195, 196-199, 207
Balint groups, fantasies in, 196-199
Basamania, B., 117
Bateson, G., 68, 155, 171, 184, 213, 216, 268, 269
Baudelaire, Charles, 165
Beethoven, Ludwig van, 83, 98
Bettelheim, B., 164, 172
Beissner, F., 98, 106
Benedek, T., 64
Benjamin, W., 83
Bertaux, P., 103
binding, in multigenerational therapy, 329-330
See also unbinding
Binswanger, L., 20, 25-26, 32
Bion, W., 171, 193, 194, 195, 199, 200, 205, 206, 207, 225, 304, 305
Bleuler, E., 39, 51-61, 98
concept of schizophrenia, 51-61
Blos, P., 173, 285
bonds. *See* binding; unbinding
Boss, M., 20, 25, 26, 27, 35, 36
Boszormenyi-Nagy, I., 132, 155, 188, 203, 206, 221, 226, 228, 251, 257, 282, 293, 294, 310, 314, 323, 325, 328, 329, 340
Bowen, M., 41, 155
Brecht, B., 83, 95-96
Brenner, C., 143, 224, 225
Bridgman, P., 38
Bronfenbrenner, U., 242, 330
Bruch, H., 113, 166, 213

Bumke, O., 58
Buytendijk, F., 29

Camus, Albert, 18, 19
Celan, P., 83
Chekhov, Anton, 42
child-parent interaction. *See* parent-child interaction
children, separating, parental perceptions of, 171-189
expectations to induce or inhibit separation, 183-185
fixed vs. changeable parental perceptions and expectations, 185-186
how parents anticipate being affected by, 181-183
implications for family therapy, 186-189
parental perceptions affecting separation, 172-175
perceptions as molding forces, 171-172
varieties of parental perceptions and expectations affecting adolescent's separation, 175-181
Christian, P., 29
Cohen, M. B., 32, 303
competition, therapist's, with parents, 316-318
conflict
vs. deficiency dispute in family model context, 222-229
dialectic of intrapsychic and

Gruhle, H., 58
guilt and shame in family relations,
    233-257
  differing phenomenologies and
    dynamics, 233-236
  in groups, 239-241
  intergenerational cycles, 248-
    255
  in involvement with others, 237-
    239
  marital shame-guilt cycles, 243-
    248
  and shame-guilt cycles, 236-237
  therapeutic implications, 256-
    257
Guntrip, H., 143

Haley, J., 213, 269
Hamlet, 219
harmony, family, myths of, 202
Hartmann, H., 133, 134, 140, 143
Hegel, G. W. F., 83, 93, 162, 251,
    294-295
Heidegger, M., 18, 19, 20, 21, 22-
    25, 26, 27, 28, 29, 30, 31, 33,
    34, 35, 36, 38, 42, 83, 233
Heston, L., 87
Hill, L. B., 66, 73, 74, 313
Himmler, Heinrich, 240-241
Hitler, Adolf, 202
Hoche, A., 58
Holderlin, Friedrich, schizo-
    phrenic psychosis in fate of,
    and lyrical creativity, 83-
    107
Holzman, P., 233
Husserl, Edmund, 28

"inner objects," functions of, 131-
    146
  disturbances of, 134-138
  and ego functions, 133-134
  and classical psychoanalytic
    theory, 139-142
  and object concepts of Klein and
    Fairbairn, 142-146
involved impartiality, counter-
    transference as a deviation
    from, in family therapy with
    adolescents, 309-311
involvement, with others, shame
    and guilt in, 237-239
interaction, parent-child. See
    parent-child interaction
interpersonal dialectic, and mis-
    sion and role compared in
    family theory, 280-281
interpersonal survival, See survival,
    interpersonal

Jackson, D. D., 242, 264
Jacobson, E., 134, 140, 141, 142
Jaspers, K., 18, 20-21, 57, 83, 85,
    86, 233
Johnson, A. M., 172, 173, 315
Joyce, James, 98
Jung, C. G., 53, 59

Kafka, J. S., 184
Kahlbaum, K., 53
Kallmann, F., 71
Katan, A., 175
Kaufmann, I., 241

DATE DUE